TIME

ANNUAL

1995

TIME ANNUAL 1995

EDITOR
Edward L. Jamieson

MANAGING EDITOR
Kelly Knauer

ART DIRECTOR
Gigi Fava

RESEARCH DIRECTOR
Leah Gordon

PICTURE EDITOR
Rose Quinn Keyser

EDITORIAL PRODUCTION
Michael Skinner

ASSOCIATE ART DIRECTOR
Tony Limauco

RESEARCH ASSOCIATES
Anne Hopkins, Valerie J. Marchant

COPY DESK
Bob Braine, Doug Bradley,
Bruce Christopher Carr

TIME INC.
NEW BUSINESS
DEVELOPMENT

DIRECTOR
David Gitow

ASSOCIATE DIRECTOR
Stuart Hotchkiss

ASSISTANT DIRECTOR
Pete Shapiro

FULFILLMENT DIRECTOR
Mary Warner McGrade

DEVELOPMENT MANAGERS
John Sandklev, Robert Fox

OPERATIONS MANAGER
John Calvano

PRODUCTION MANAGER
Donna Miano-Ferrara

ASSOCIATE DEVELOPMENT MANAGER
Mike Holohan

ASSISTANT DEVELOPMENT MANAGERS
Allison Weiss, Dawn Weland

MARKETING ASSISTANT
Charlotte Siddiqui

THE WORK OF
THE FOLLOWING TIME
STAFFERS AND CONTRIBUTORS
IS INCLUDED IN
THIS VOLUME:

Ginia Bellafante, Jeffrey H. Birnbaum,
James Carney, Howard Chua-Eoan,
George J. Church, Richard Corliss, Martha Duffy,
Michael Duffy, Philip Elmer-DeWitt,
Christopher John Farley, Kevin Fedarko,
Nancy Gibbs, Elizabeth Glieck,
Christine Gorman, Paul Gray, John Greenwald,
Bruce Handy, Robert Hughes, Leon Jaroff,
Richard Lacayo, Brad Leithauser,
Michael Lemonick, Belinda Luscombe,
J.F.O. McAllister, Lance Morrow,
J. Madeleine Nash, Bruce W. Nelan, Eric Pooley,
Richard N. Ostling, Joshua Quittner,
Suneel Ratan, Richard Schickel,
Michael S. Serrill, Jill Smolowe, John F. Stacks,
Karen Tumulty, David Van Biema, Claudia Wallis,
James Walsh, Steve Wulf, Richard Zoglin

AND SPECIAL THANKS TO:

Gerard Abrahamsen, Ames Adamson, Louella Armstrong,
Ken Baierlein, Robin Bierstedt, Susan L. Blair, Andrew Blau,
Jay Colton, Anne Considine, Richard Duncan, Osmar Escalona,
Linda Freeman, MaryAnne Golon, Dan Goodgame,
Matthew Herman, Arthur Hochstein, Raphael Joa, Nora Jupiter,
Kevin Kelly, Maureen Kelly, Nancy Krauter, Morgan Krug,
Jason Lee, Joe Lertola, Robyn Matthews, Peter Meirs, Gail Music,
Amy Musher, Peter Niceberg, Rudy Papiri, Ron Plyman,
Hillary Raskin, Sue Raffety, Edel Rodriguez, Anthony Ross,
Lamarr Tsufura, Barrett Seaman, Michael Sheehan,
Kenneth B. Smith, Michele Stephenson, Cornelus Velwaal,
Janet Waegel, Miriam Winocur, Beth Zarcone, Carrie A. Zimmerman.
Additional thanks to the TIME Imaging staff.

TIME

ANNUAL

1995

The Year in Review

By the Editors of TIME

TIME ANNUAL

40 NATION

58 WORLD

SOCIETY **107**

THE YEAR IN REVIEW

128 SCIENCE

154 ARTS&MEDIA

174 MILESTONES

EDITOR-IN-CHIEF: Norman Pearlstine
EDITORIAL DIRECTOR: Henry Muller
CORPORATE EDITOR: James R. Gaines
EDITOR OF NEW MEDIA: Paul Sagan

TIME INC.
CHAIRMAN: Reginald K. Brack Jr.
PRESIDENT, CEO: Don Logan

TIME

Founders: Briton Hadden 1898-1929 Henry R. Luce 1898-1967

MANAGING EDITOR: Walter Isaacson
DEPUTY MANAGING EDITOR: James Kelly
EXECUTIVE EDITORS: José M. Ferrer III, John F. Stacks
ASSISTANT MANAGING EDITORS: Joëlle Attinger, Stephen Koepp, Christopher Porterfield
EDITOR AT LARGE: Karsten Prager
DIRECTOR OF OPERATIONS: Andrew Blau
REGIONAL EDITORS: Charles P. Alexander (Deputy, International), Donald Morrison (Asia), Christopher Redman (Europe), Ken Edwards (South Pacific)
SENIOR EDITORS: Lee Aitken, Howard Chua-Eoan, James Collins, Marta Fitzgerald Dorion (Research), Philip Elmer-DeWitt, Nancy Gibbs, Bruce Handy, Priscilla Painton, John Cooper Ramo, George Russell, John Saar
ART DIRECTOR: Arthur Hochstein **PICTURE EDITOR:** Michele Stephenson
ADMINISTRATIVE EDITOR: Suzanne Davis **COPY CHIEF:** Susan L. Blair **PRODUCTION MANAGER:** Gail Music
SENIOR WRITERS: Margaret Carlson, George J. Church, Richard Corliss, Martha Duffy, Elizabeth Gleick, Paul Gray, John Greenwald, Robert Hughes, Richard Lacayo, Erik Larson, Michael D. Lemonick, Lance Morrow, Bruce W. Nelan, Eric Pooley, Michael S. Serrill, Jill Smolowe, Richard Stengel, David Van Biema, James Walsh, Steve Wulf, Richard Zoglin
STAFF WRITERS: Ginia Bellafante, Christopher John Farley, Kevin Fedarko, Christine Gorman, Belinda Luscombe, Thomas McCarroll, Emily Mitchell, Joshua Quittner, Barbara Rudolph, Anastasia Toufexis
CONTRIBUTORS: Bonnie Angelo, Robert Ball, Bill Barol, Laurence I. Barrett, Jesse Birnbaum, Nina Burleigh, Jay Cocks, Barbara Ehrenreich, John Elson, Pico Iyer, Edward L. Jamieson (Consulting Editor), Leon Jaroff, Gregory Jaynes, Michael Kinsley, Charles Krauthammer, Brad Leithauser, Eugene Linden, Christopher Ogden, Frederick Painton, John Rothchild, Betty Satterwhite Sutter (Letters Editor), Richard Schickel, Walter Shapiro, R.Z. Sheppard, John Skow, Anthony Spaeth, Mark Alan Stamaty, George M. Taber, Andrew Tobias, Lisa H. Towle, Calvin Trillin, Rod Usher, Michael Walsh, Robert Wright
ASSISTANT EDITORS: Ursula Nadasdy de Gallo, Andrea Dorfman, Tam Martinides Gray, Brigid O'Hara-Forster, Ariadna Victoria Rainert, William Tynan, Sidney Urquhart, Jane Van Tassel (Department Heads); Bernard Baumohl, David Bjerklie, Val Castronovo, Oscar Chiang, Mary McC. Fernandez, Lois Gilman, Georgia Harbison, Ratu Kamlani, Valerie Johanna Marchant, Adrianne Jucius Navon, Sue Raffety, Susan M. Reed, Elizabeth Rudulph, Susanne Washburn, Linda Young
REPORTERS: Elizabeth L. Bland, Hannah Bloch, Barbara Burke, Tom Curry, Julie K.L. Dam, Leslie Dickstein, Tamala M. Edwards, Kathryn Jackson Fallon, Janice M. Horowitz, Jeanette Isaac, Nadya Labi, Sinting Lai, Daniel S. Levy, Lina Lofaro, Barbara Maddux, Lisa McLaughlin, Lawrence Mondi, Alice Park, Aixa Pascual, Stacy Perman, Michael Quinn, Jeffery C. Rubin, Megan Rutherford, Andrea Sachs, Alain L. Sanders, Sribala Subramanian, David E. Thigpen
COPY DESK: Barbara Dudley Davis, Judith Anne Paul, Shirley Barden Zimmerman (Deputies); Dora Fairchild, Evelyn Hannon, Jill Ward (Copy Coordinators); Minda Bikman, Doug Bradley, Robert Braine, Bruce Christopher Carr, Barbara Collier, Bland Crowder, Julia Van Buren Dickey, Irene Gashurov, Judith Kales, Sharon Kapnick, Claire Knopf, Jeannine Laverty, Ellin Martens, Peter J. McGullam, M.M. Merwin, Maria A. Paul, Jane Rigney, Elyse Segelken, Terry Stoller, Amelia Weiss (Copy Editors)
CORRESPONDENTS: Joëlle Attinger (Chief); Richard Hornik (Deputy, Foreign); Janice C. Simpson (Deputy, Domestic) **Chief Political Correspondent:** Michael Kramer **Washington Contributing Editor:** Hugh Sidey **National Political Correspondent:** Michael Duffy **Senior Foreign Correspondent:** Johanna McGeary **Senior Correspondents:** Jonathan Beaty, Jeffrey H. Birnbaum, J. Madeleine Nash, Richard N. Ostling, Michael Riley **National Correspondents:** Margot Hornblower, Jack E. White **Diplomatic Correspondent:** Dean Fischer **Washington:** Dan Goodgame, Ann Blackman, James Carney, John F. Dickerson, J.F.O. McAllister, Viveca Novak, Elaine Shannon, Ann M. Simmons, Mark Thompson, Karen Tumulty, Douglas Waller, Adam Zagorin, Melissa August **New York:** John Moody, Edward Barnes, William Dowell, Sharon E. Epperson, Marguerite Michaels, Elaine Rivera, Jenifer Mattos **Boston:** Sam Allis **Chicago:** James L. Graff, Wendy Cole, Elizabeth Taylor **Detroit:** William A. McWhirter **Atlanta:** Adam Cohen **Austin:** S.C. Gwynne **Miami:** Cathy Booth, Tammerlin Drummond **Los Angeles:** Jordan Bonfante, Patrick E. Cole, Elaine Lafferty, Jeanne McDowell, Sylvester Monroe, Jeffrey Ressner, James Willwerth **San Francisco:** David S. Jackson **Denver:** Richard Woodbury **Europe:** James O. Jackson **London:** Barry Hillenbrand **Paris:** Thomas Sancton **Brussels:** Jay Branegan, Larry Gurwin **Bonn:** Bruce van Voorst **Central Europe:** Massimo Calabresi **Moscow:** John Kohan, Sally B. Donnelly **Rome:** Greg Burke **Istanbul:** James Wilde **Middle East:** Lara Marlowe (Beirut), Lisa Beyer (Jerusalem), Scott MacLeod (Paris) **Nairobi:** Andrew Purvis **South Africa:** Peter Hawthorne **New Delhi:** Dick Thompson **Beijing:** Jaime A. FlorCruz **Hanoi:** Frank Gibney Jr. **Hong Kong:** Sandra Burton, John Colmey **Tokyo:** Edward W. Desmond **Ottawa:** Gavin Scott **Latin America:** Laura López **Bureau Administration:** Susan Lynd, Susanna Schrobsdorff, Sheila Charney, Donald N. Collins, Corliss M. Duncan, Ann V. King, Anne D. Moffett, Sharon Roberts, Judith R. Stoler **News Desks:** Pamela H. Thompson, Brian Doyle, Anderson Fils-Aime, Eileen Harkin, Alexander Smith, Diana Tollerson, Mary Wormley
ART: Deputies: Sharon Okamoto (U.S.), Jane Frey (International); Linda Louise Freeman (Covers); Steve Conley, Jamie Elsis, Susan Langholz, Thomas M. Miller, Janet Parker (Associate Art Directors); Joseph Aslaender, Kenneth B. Smith (Assistant Art Directors); Victoria Nightingale, Ron Plyman, Leah M. Purcell, Edel Rodriguez (Designers) **Maps and Charts:** Joe Lertola (Associate Graphics Director); Paul J. Pugliese (Chief of Cartography); Kathleen Adams, Steven D. Hart, Deborah L. Wells
PHOTOGRAPHY: Richard L. Boeth, MaryAnne Golon, Hillary Raskin (Deputy Picture Editors); Julia Richer, Robert B. Stevens, Eleanor Taylor, Karen Zakrison (Associate Picture Editors); Bronwen Latimer, Gary Roberts, Cristina T. Scalet, Nancy Smith-Alam, Marie Tobias (Assistant Editors) **Traffic:** Ames Adamson, Jon Abbey, Christina Holovach **Bureaus:** Martha Bardach, Paul Durrant, Leny Heinen, Stanley Kayne, Barbara Nagelsmith, Anni Rubinger, Mark Rykoff, Mary Thompson, Simonetta Toraldo **Photographers:** Forrest Anderson, Terry Ashe, P.F. Bentley, William Campbell, Greg Davis, Dirck Halstead, Barry Iverson, Kenneth Jarecke, Cynthia Johnson, Shelly Katz, Steve Liss, Peter Magubane, Christopher Morris, Robin Moyer, Carl Mydans, James Nachtwey, Robert Nickelsberg, David Rubinger, Anthony Suau, Ted Thai, Diana Walker

EDITOR, CREATIVE DEVELOPMENT: Lee Eisenberg
SPECIAL PROJECTS EDITOR: Barrett Seaman **DESIGN DIRECTOR:** Janet Waegel
TIME ONLINE: Janice Castro (Senior Editor), Robertson Barrett (Deputy Editor); Peter Meyer (News Editor); Morris Barrett, Mark Coatney, Chris Hart-Nibbrig (Writers); Jay Colton (Picture Editor); Sara Golding (Assistant Art Director); Waits L. May III (Manager)

TIME FOR KIDS: Claudia Wallis (Managing Editor); Jason Lee (Art Director); Martha Pickerill (Senior Editor); Nelida Gonzalez Cutler (Chief of Research); Deborah Parks (Education Editor); Lucinda Rector (Writer/Reporter); Sarah Tuff (Editorial Assistant); Kimberlee Acquaro (Photo Editor); Lisa Quiroz (General Manager)

MAKEUP: Robyn M. Mathews (Chief); Alison E. Ruffley (International Makeup Editor); Kris Basciano, Chris Caratzas (Managers); Annmarie Baldelli, Peter Farrell, Jackie Fernandez, Betsy Hill, Colm O'Malley, Adam Redfield, Loretta Rogers, Lynn Ross, Caroline Schaefer
EDITORIAL OPERATIONS: Peter Meirs (Deputy Production Manager); Anne Considine (Asst. Manager); Peter K. Niceberg (Applications); Gerard Abrahamsen, Trang Ba Chuong, Raphael Joa, Theresa Kelliher, Louella Rufino-Armstrong (Supervisors); Steven Cadicamo, Charlotte Coco, Silvia Castañeda Contreras, Michael Dohne, John Dragonetti, Osmar Escalona, Paul Gettinger, Garry Hearne, Therese Hurter, Carl Leidig, Sandra Maupin, Linda Parker, Mark P. Polomski, Lois Rubenstein, Richard Shaffer, Michael Skinner, David Spatz, Lorri Stenton, Paul White
PRODUCTION: Stephen R. Best (International Operations Director); Joe Eugenio, Tracy Kelliher (Managers); Jackie Daniels, Sherry Gamlin, Patrick Hickey, Angie Licausi, Meghan Milkowski, Lauren Planit, Patty Stevens, Craig Stinehour, Juanita Weems
TECHNOLOGY: Maureen Kelly (Director); Ken Baierlein (Associate); David Richardson (Manager); Andrew Dyer, David C. Forte, Nora Jupiter, Kevin Kelly, George Mendel, Michael M. Sheehan, Lamarr Tsufura
HEADQUARTERS ADMINISTRATION: Alan J. Abrams, Denise Brown, Breena Clarke, Elena Falaro, Helga Halaki, Grace Hunter, Marilyn V.S. McClenahan, Barbara Milberg, Rudi Papiri, Elliot Ravetz, Teresa D. Sedlak, Marianne Sussman, Raymond Violini, Miriam Winocour, Carrie A. Zimmerman
EDITORIAL FINANCE: Nancy Krauter (Manager); Carl Harmon, Morgan Krug (Domestic); Camille Sanabria (News Service); Linda D. Vartoogian, Wayne Chun (Pictures) **Production:** Nadine Candemeres (Manager), Bill Holtmeyer, Chris Marcantonio

TIME INC. EDITORIAL SERVICES: Sheldon Czapnik (Director); Claude Boral (General Manager); Thomas E. Hubbard (Photo Lab); Lany Walden McDonald (Library); Beth Bencini Zarcone (Picture Collection); Thomas Smith (Technology); Maryann Kornely (Syndication) **TIME INC. EDITORIAL TECHNOLOGY:** Paul Zazzera (Vice President); Dennis Chesnel

PRESIDENT: E. Bruce Hallett
PUBLISHER: Jack Haire
GENERAL MANAGER: Karen Magee
VICE PRESIDENT: Kenneth Godshall
ASSOCIATE PUBLISHER: Richard A. Raskopf
PUBLIC AFFAIRS DIRECTOR: Robert Pondiscio
CONSUMER MARKETING: William Furlong Jr., Paul Masse, Lisa Quiroz, Nancy Rachman, Timothy D. Twerdahl (Directors); Ellen Hodo, Wendy Metzger, Christine Shappell, Herta Siegrist, Greg A. Sutter, Nanette Zabala (Managers); Naida Chilcott, Roseanne Edie, Kristy Lo Russo, Holley Vantrease, Andrew Winston
ADVERTISING SALES: Headquarters: John Heyd (Manager) **Atlanta:** John Helmer (Manager) **Boston:** Don Jones (Manager), John Shaughnessy **Chicago:** Kathy Kayse (Manager); Randy Holloway, Tim Schlax, Amy Weber **Dallas:** Lisa Bentley (Manager) **Detroit:** Brett Wilson (Manager); Michael Clark, William Fay, David Howe **Los Angeles:** Matt Turck (Manager); Mike Purcell, Patti Roderick, Mark Updegrove **New York:** Peter Krieger, Maureen McAllister (Managers); Peter Britton, Mike Callahan, Richard Caprio, Chris Carter, Joan Carter, Carrie Howard, Charles R. Kammerer, Tom Kealy, Bruce Kostic **San Francisco:** Fred Gruber (Manager); Jay Howard **Washington:** Hal Bonawitz (Manager)
ADMINISTRATION: Headquarters: Ellen Harvey, Delia Leahy, Margie McNulty, Karen Ziegler **Atlanta:** Lori McElhaney **Boston:** Bonnie Walter **Chicago:** Barbara Henkel, Nicole Wood **Dallas:** Beth Singer **Detroit:** Monica Delise, Jan Eggly **Los Angeles:** Monica Mallen Benson, Sabrina Vargas **New York:** Addie Boemio, Jane Cole, Susan Considine, Marie DiFiore, Renee Geathers, Tanya Tarek **San Francisco:** Sheila Phillips **Washington:** Charlotte Gay
MARKETING: David Becker, Alison Collins, Katherine Douvres, Susan Federspiel, Liza Greene, Nini Gussenhoven, Jennie Hunnewell, Matt Sterling (Managers); Betty Barth, Teresa Belmonte, Scott Einhorn, Jill Goldring, Joe Johnson, Mikel Magee, Wendy Olesen, Paton Roth, Trish Ryan-Sacks, Cynthia Shauck, Mary Shaw, Susan Sklar, Tom Tagariello, Andrea Wagner, Marlene Zeddies
BUSINESS OFFICE: Karen Maikisch-Markle, Gail Portier, Marilynda Kelly Vianna (Managers); Patti Brasfield, Anita Cordani, Jane Hayes, Ruth Hazen, Nancy Mangieri, Aston Wright
PUBLIC AFFAIRS: Kelly Keane, Nancy Kearney
LETTERS: Amy Musher (Chief); Gloria J. Hammond (Deputy); Robert Cushing, Sonia Figueroa, Winston Hunter, Marian Powers, Edith Rosa, Patrick Smith, Alex Tresniowski
LEGAL: Robin Bierstedt, Robin Rabie
HUMAN RESOURCES: Joan Dauria, Peter Reichman

Copyright 1996 by Time Inc. Home Entertainment

Published by TIME Books • Time Inc. 1271 Avenue of the Americas, New York, NY 10020

All rights reserved. No part of this book may be reproduced in any form by any electric or mechanical means, including information storage and retrieval systems, without permission in writing from the publisher, except by a reviewer who may quote brief passages in review. TIME and the Red Border Design are protected through trademark registration in the United States and in the foreign countries where TIME Magazine circulates.

Printed in the United States of America • First edition

Some years have predictable elements—like 1996, with a presidential election and summer Olympic games. Other years, like 1995, are an assembly of astonishments: news arrives as shards of information, as random shocks, as blows to the heart. A federal building in Oklahoma—bombed. Yitzhak Rabin—murdered. O.J. Simpson—not guilty. But in these pages the events of 1995 begin to form a pattern, for time has transformed them. Once they were news—now they are history. ■

THE YEAR IN REVIEW

'95

IMAGES '95

NOT FORGOTTEN

Amateur photographer Charles
H. Porter IV snapped the image
of fire fighter Chris Fields
holding one-year-old Baylee
Almon—already dead—after the
explosion at Oklahoma City's
federal building drew Porter
from his job at a nearby bank.
"Fate and the Lord put me in
that place," he says. Eight
months later, he still has
nightmares. The photo at right
was taken by Steve Liss
at a memorial service in
Stillwater, Oklahoma, for the
169 who died.

READY FOR
HISTORY'S
CLOSE-UP

In September, White House photographer Barbara Kinney caught Israeli Prime Minister Yitzhak Rabin, Egyptian President Hosni Mubarak, King Hussein of Jordan, Bill Clinton and the P.L.O.'s Yasser Arafat as they were about to enter the East Room for the signing of an accord to expand Palestinian self-rule on the West Bank. Reports Kinney: "An aide said, 'Oh, Mr. Clinton, your tie's a little crooked. You might want to fix that.' He did, and out of the corner of my eye, I realized they were all doing it, out of instinct." Five weeks later, Rabin was assassinated at a peace rally, his blood soaking the page, above, bearing lyrics e the So of Peace

IMAGES '95

ONE IN A MILLION

Taiwanese-born photographer Chien-Chi Chang didn't appreciate the irony in this image of a lone boy at the Million Man March until after the film was processed and a friend explained the backdrop—a Civil War memorial. Says Chang: "I just saw him standing there. There was a sense of visual completeness. It was beautiful, actually." The photo of the march's almost a million men was taken by P.F. Bentley from the balcony of Newt

IMAGES '95

ON THE RICHTER SCALE

Patrick Robert took the photograph at right from a rooftop in Kobe, Japan, shortly after the city was devastated by an earthquake on Jan. 17. Robert got around town on a child's bicycle he found in front of a flattened house. Kaku Kurita was able to get the aerial view of the tortured city's burning skyline, above.

IMAGES '95

IF THE GLOVE FITS ...

It was perhaps the single most dramatic moment in the trial of O.J. Simpson. Impulsively—and against his superior's orders—assistant prosecuting attorney Christopher Darden had asked the football legend to try on the famous "bloody gloves" that the prosecution claimed Simpson had worn as he murdered his ex-wife Nicole and Ron Goldman. Prepped by his defense team for such an eventuality, Simpson appeared to struggle to don the gloves, then held his hands aloft and declared, "They're too small!" Lead defense attorney Johnnie Cochran jumped on the prosecution gaffe in his summation to the jury: "If it doesn't fit, you must acquit." Above, crowds gather to watch the verdict on October 3 in New York City.

IMAGES '95

UNDER FIRE

Russian troops and Chechen rebels were still battling in the capital city of Grozny when Anthony Suau took the photograph at left (which makes quite clear the effectiveness of Russian artillery). "It was really suicidal for [the old man] to be walking down the street that way," says Suau. "I believe he wasn't shot because he was old and walking slowly with a cane. Had I walked out there, I'm sure it would've been different." The photo above, taken by Christopher Morris, shows a Chechen soldier running from the Presidential Palace shortly before it was captured by the Russians.

IMAGES '95

PILLARS OF CREATION

Once written off as a near total loss because of an inaccurately ground mirror, the repaired Hubble Space Telescope has since redeemed itself spectacularly. In 1995 it offered close-up pictures of distant galaxies that are 10 times as sharp as those produced by earthbound telescopes. At left, immense clouds of interstellar gas and dust are slowly boiled away by the intense ultraviolet light of nearby stars, gradually exposing the densest clumps of matter, visible as wispy tendrils that are especially clear at the top of the leftmost pillar. These projections cradle newborn stars. Above, the Cartwheel Galaxy, 500 million light-years away in the constellation Sculptor.

HILLARY CLINTON
•••

*In the dragon's den, she brought fire to
the women's conference in Beijing*

BOB DOLE
•••

*Arghh! Movie moguls were scared plenty
by his attacks on sex and violence*

HUGH GRANT
•••

*To err is Hugh, man.
To forgive, Divine*

ROBERT S. MCNAMARA
•••

*The year's most public confession failed
to quiet bad memories of Vietnam*

BILL CLINTON
•••

*Bosnian badlands beware! The marshal's
deputies aim to keep the peace*

OMAR ABDEL RAHMAN
•••

*The sheik who aimed to shake up the
States was found guilty of conspiracy*

RICHARD HOLBROOKE
•••

*The year's talkiest diplomat rattled
sabers, promised peace—and delivered*

LOUIS FARRAKHAN
•••

*America loved the Million Man March
but rejected its messenger*

SHOKO ASAHARA
•••

*The guru of gas invented the
do-it-yourself apocalypse*

MARK FUHRMAN
· · ·
Marcia Clark says I'm her man—
Got my lingo from a garbage can!

JANET RENO
· · ·
Still defending her decision, she
became the last hostage of Waco

BORIS YELTSIN
· · ·
He promised to end the war in
Chechnya, and it promised to end him

COLIN POWELL
· · ·
The Great Black Hope turned out
to be not ready for Rushmore

MICHAEL JORDAN
· · ·
Glory, Glory, Hallelujah! His return to
the court set off heavenly vibes

LANCE ITO
· · ·
As much ringmaster as judge, he grew
fond of the robes of celebrity

SLOBODAN MILOSEVIC
· · ·
"The Butcher of the Balkans" applied
for a new job as patron of peace

BRIAN "KATO" KAELIN
· · ·
Longing for movie immortality, this
live-in became so much trivia fodder

JOHN MAJOR
· · ·
Progress in Northern Ireland netted a
moment's glory for the fading Tory

"You are going to keep me locked up in Dayton, Ohio? I'm not a priest."

—*Serbian President Slobodan Milosevic, joking about the location of talks to end the war in Bosnia*

"Do you have cows in your home?"

—*Unidentified Bangladeshi woman to Hillary Clinton on her Southeast Asian tour*

IN ORDER TO GET OUR MESSAGE BEFORE THE PUBLIC WITH SOME CHANCE OF MAKING A LASTING IMPRESSION, WE'VE HAD TO KILL PEOPLE.

—*The Unabomber*

"Keanu Reeves remembered his lines . . . and he does look great in tights."

—*Review of Hamlet in the Toronto Globe and Mail*

"LOOK, HALF THE TIME WHEN I SEE THE EVENING NEWS, I WOULDN'T BE FOR ME, EITHER."

—*Bill Clinton*

GIVE & TAKE

"Barney Fag."

—*Republican House leader Dick Armey, mispronouncing the name of Rep. Barney Frank, D-Mass., an avowed homosexual*

"There are a lot of ways to mispronounce my name. That is the least common."

—*Frank, in rebuttal*

"We not only played the race card, we dealt it from the bottom of the deck."

—*Simpson defense attorney Robert Shapiro*

"We chose to call it the credibility card."

—*Fellow Simpson defense attorney Johnnie Cochran*

"We were wrong, terribly wrong. We owe it to future generations to explain why."

—*Robert S. McNamara, former Defense Secretary, on Vietnam*

"It would have been helpful, in May of 1967, when I volunteered for Vietnam, if he had said then that the war was unwinnable."

—*Max Cleland, former V.A. director, who lost both legs in Vietnam, on McNamara's comments*

"If we had God booked and O.J. was available, we'd move God."

—*Interviewer Larry King*

"SOMETIMES I READ STORIES AND HEAR THINGS ABOUT ME, AND I GO 'UGH. I WOULDN'T LIKE HER EITHER.'"

—*Hillary Rodham Clinton*

MODESTY!

"I have lied in good faith."

—*French politician and business man Bernard Tapie, caught perjuring himself in a sports-fixing scandal*

"How's the wound?"

—*Former President George Bush, after hitting a spectator with a golf shot at a charity tournament*

"I never thought I'd work for a guy named Mickey."

—*ABC's Good Morning America anchor Charles Gibson, after the Walt Disney Co. bought ABC*

SUCH

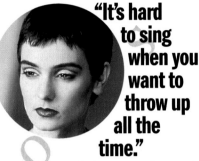

"It's hard to sing when you want to throw up all the time."

—*Sinead O'Connor, on leaving the Lollapalooza tour because of pregnancy*

"We are one, we are human!"

—*Russian cosmonaut Aleksandr Viktorenko, after a U.S. shuttle linked with a Russian space station*

"There were three of us in this marriage, so it was a bit crowded."

—*Diana, Princess of Wales*

"This is Basher-52. I'm alive and I need help."

—*Captain Scott F. O'Grady, before his rescue in Bosnia*

W O M E N

"Females have biological problems staying in a ditch for 30 days because they get infections . . . men are biologically driven to hunt giraffes."

—*House Speaker Newt Gingrich, on genders in the armed forces*

"At least she's president of something, which is more than I can say."

—*Senator Robert Dole on his wife Elizabeth, head of the American Red Cross*

"I'd rather have more sex at home and keep my clothes on at work. I'm maturing."

—*Actress Sharon Stone*

"Do we have sex? Yes, yes, yes."

—*Michael Jackson's wife Lisa Marie Presley, to Diane Sawyer*

"I didn't mind looking like I have three breasts, but the problem is I could never find a man who has three hands."

—*Socialite Nan Kempner on altering a Christian Lacroix dress*

"My behavior was disloyal and shabby and goatish."

—*Hugh Grant to Larry King*

"The only thing less popular than a poor person these days is a poor person with a lawyer."

—*Jonathan D. Asher, director of the Legal Aid Society of Denver*

"She's a bitch."

—*Kathleen Gingrich on her son Newt's opinion of Hillary Clinton, to CBS's Connie Chung*

"This is it! No one will come out alive! We're all doomed!"

—*Talk-show host and panicky flyer Tom Snyder, reacting to light turbulence on an airplane flight*

"It's the dawning of a new era. If you're losing money in this business, you're an idiot."

—*Damian Clayton, a computer programmer who switched from selling stocks*

WINNERS & LOSERS

Who sizzled and who fizzled in 1995

Jay Leno

COMEBACK OF THE YEAR:
Jay Leno. Runner-up: Philippine Congresswoman Imelda Marcos. Third place: John Travolta.

SECOND ACT OF THE YEAR:
Court star Michael Jordan. Runner up: court star Monica Seles. Third place: court star F. Lee Bailey.

SENTIMENT OF THE YEAR: Nostalgia. Jane Austen, the Beatles, *Nixon, Apollo 13* ... the Nick-at-Niteing of U.S. culture. Runner-up: self-righteousness. Paging Bill Bennett, Ralph Reed & Co.

FAVORITE TEAM OF THE YEAR: Northwestern's Cinderella football Wildcats—too bad about the Rose Bowl. Runner-up: Hollywood's heavily hyped "dream team": Spielberg, Geffen, and Katzenberg.

Martha Stewart

SHOW-OFF OF THE YEAR:
Martha Stewart. She likes those rustic bushel baskets—as long as they don't cover her light.

STREET OF THE YEAR: Wall Street, where the bulls ran every day. Runner-up: the White House's traffic-free Pennsylvania Avenue.

CALCULATING MACHINE OF THE YEAR: Writer Richard Paul Evans, whose treacly little book *The Christmas Box* was a heat-seeking missile aimed at the Christmas market—and scored a direct hit.

SURPRISE VICTORY OF THE YEAR: Police departments everywhere reported unexpected success in the war on crime. Runner-up: In Krajina, the Croats smashed the Serbs, bullies of the Balkans.

CITY OF THE YEAR: With its Rock Hall of Fame and the resurgent Indians playing in a great new ballpark, Cleveland came back strong. Too bad Browns owner Art Modell had to spoil the party.

FADE-OUT OF THE YEAR: Lech Walesa, electrician turned ex–Polish President. Runner-up: Pete Wilson, Governor who hoped to turn Prez.

Lech Walesa

ROOKIE OF THE YEAR: Jacques Chirac, who bombed in the South Pacific, then got fouled up in France by tangling with the unions.

ASSORTED NUTS OF THE YEAR: U.S. "militias." Runner-up: Israeli settlers. Third place: the Newt-niks in the House G.O.P. freshman class. Why save the government when it's more fun to destroy it?

SKELETON-LADEN CLOSET OF THE YEAR:
Belongs to ex-President Carlos Salinas de Gortari of Mexico. Runner-up: His brother Raul—who's living the high life while Mexico sinks deeper into debt.

BLACK EYE OF THE YEAR: Larry Tisch may have made millions by selling CBS, but he left the once-dazzling Tiffany network in tatters.

SCAPEGOAT OF THE YEAR:
Gangsta rap. Runner-up: Tabloid talk-show hosts. Third place: Immigrants, whether they were legal or not.

Laurence Tisch

MEDIA MERGER WALLFLOWER OF THE YEAR:
Barry Diller. 1994—he tries for Tiffany Network. 1995—he gets Home Shopping Network. Runner-up: Rupert Murdoch. It's getting lonely at the top!

SHAFTEE OF THE YEAR: Connie Chung, weighing anchor fast from CBS News. Runner-up: Kit Gingrich, Newt's mom, caught in mid-bitch by Connie Chung.

FADING POP IDOL OF THE YEAR:
Michael Jackson, falling flat onstage—as well as with his much touted CD, *HIStory*, which quickly became just that.

Michael Jackson

REVOLUTION
in the
A·I·R

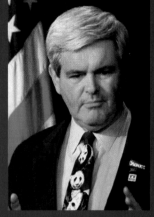

Washington in 1995 was a capital in upheaval, where a troika of powerful politicians fought to control a tide of revolution inspired by the smashing Republican victory in the 1994 elections. In the House, new Speaker Newt Gingrich was the Robespierre of the G.O.P. onslaught: the firebrand threatened by the very forces he had unleashed. In the Oval Office, though, President Bill Clinton found in opposition the stature he had lost in pursuing his own agenda. And in the Senate, veteran Republican leader Bob Dole kept an arm's length from Gingrich's rebels as he eyed his last chance for a bid at the White House in the 1996 election. ■

NEWT'S

How a new Speaker shook up the House, changed the

✫ MAN *of the* YEAR ✫

L̲EADERS MAKE THINGS POSSIBLE.
Exceptional leaders make them inevitable. Newt Gingrich belongs with the exceptional. All through 1995—ruthlessly, brilliantly, obnoxiously—he worked at hammering together inevitabilities: a balanced federal budget, for one. Not so long before, a balanced budget was a marginal, we'll-get-to-it-someday priority. Other urgent work needed doing: the Clintons' health-care program, for example, which would have installed elaborate new bureaucratic machinery. Because of Newt Gingrich, the question as 1995 ended was not whether a balanced-budget plan would come to pass but when.

Gingrich changed the center of gravity. From Franklin Roosevelt onward, Americans had come to accept the Federal Government as the solution to problems, a vast parental presence. Ronald Reagan

WORLD

way Washington thinks, took on the budget—and had a great fall

preached that government was the problem, but his Administration focused mostly on the Evil Empire; it did not overturn the grand centralizing legacy of the New Deal and the Great Society. Newt Gingrich wanted to reverse the physics and make American government truly centrifugal, with power flowing out of Washington, devolving to the states.

A sometimes unlovely blur of headlong energy and pinwheeling, roughhouse creativity, the Speaker transformed both the House of Representatives and the speakership into unprecedented instruments of personal and political power. It was an amazing performance and, for all its scattershot quality, a display of discipline that was either impressive or scary, depending on one's sympathies.

Having organized an insurrectionist crew in the House, Gingrich seized the initiative from a temporarily passive President and steered the country onto a heading that the Speaker accurately proclaimed to be revolutionary. His venture was in a stormy midpassage at year's end. It might ultimately be forced back or even sunk. Yet Gingrich did the work—crude, forceful, effective—that compelled the voyage in the first place. It is for that reason that he was TIME's Man of the Year.

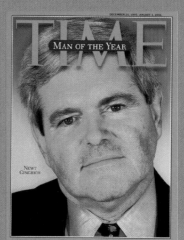

Gingrich envisions a promised land—an America that may lie just over the horizon, in his cherished Third Wave Information Age, where traditional values connect to the future. He hopes to get to a place beyond poverty and violence and moral decay by leaving behind the welfare state and the deadening, blockheaded bureaucratic mind of Washington: a renewed civilization, says Newt—Norman Rockwell in the 21st century, a wholesome Utopia. Newt's destination has the refulgence of a never-never land—that is, an ideal. But in America ideals have always been a necessary and efficient form of national energy. Which came first—Newt's vision of the future? Or his fierce personal ambition? Which drives the other? The nearest answer may be found in W.B. Yeats' line (in language prettier than Gingrich might use): "How can we know the dancer from the dance?" Gingrich decided not to run for President in 1996. That may be just as well: the polls say more than half the American people disapprove of him. His negatives reached critical mass just before Christmas, 1995, whereupon Democrats began to rouse themselves amid the wreckage left from '94 and tend small campfires of hope again.

They worked on the idea of running in 1996 against one man, Newt Gingrich, a vividly inviting target who virtually poses for cartoons of himself. Enemies picture Newt as the Simon Legree of school lunches and Medicare, the golfing partner of capital gains, the Churchill from K Mart, the nerd *pistolero* of the punitive right, the all-purpose villain.

If Gingrich were to run for President, of course, he might be applying for a job inferior to the one he has created for himself as Speaker of the House. Whatever his fortunes in the polls and at the hands of a special counsel to the House ethics committee, Gingrich has the American genius for reinventing himself. The Gingrich Republicans, however, may be in danger of exercising their party's perverse talent for throwing away its advantages with both hands. Clinton is a superb campaigner, himself a gambler with a gift for new lives. And Republicans underestimate him.

Americans in 1995 kept a wary, ambivalent eye on both Clinton and Gingrich, the famous fraternal twins of American power, yin and yang of the baby boom, polar extremes of Pennsylvania Avenue. A generation or two ago, leaders were father figures. For better and for worse, Clinton and Gingrich—powerful yet indefinably immature—gave off a bright, undisciplined energy, a vibration of adolescent recklessness.

Justice Holmes judged that Franklin Roosevelt had a "second-class intelligence but a first-class temperament." Newt Gingrich has a first-class intelligence that fires through a strangely refracted temperament—not exactly second-class, but agitated and sometimes grandiose enough to make Americans nervous. He proved himself an impresario of leverage in using Congress to change America, a sort of hothouse genius. Americans might discover in 1996 whether Gingrich could evolve outward—as a truly popular leader in the open air. ∎

REBEL WITH A CAUSE

NEWT GINGRICH HAD A FAVORITE GAME WHEN HE WAS GROWING UP IN HUMMELS-town, Pennsylvania. His pal Dennis Yantz would pretend to beat him up and leave him crumpled on the curb. "When a car would pull up to see what was wrong," Yantz recalls, "Newt would jump up and scream, 'SURPRISE!' We would do this over and over again." For some reason, Yantz says, Newt always wanted to be the one who played dead.

By the end of 1995, Newt Gingrich had every reason to want to play dead again. He was in deep trouble, much of it of his own making. In his year of triumph, the Speaker of the House was nonetheless plagued by ethics charges and his own tantrums, to the point where Gingrich had become the single greatest liability to the revolution he had launched. Even

TRIUMPHANT

★★★★★★★★★★

With, from left, his stepfather, wife and mother, Gingrich attends church before becoming Speaker

while that revolution was transforming Washington, Gingrich was suffering not only for what he had done but also for how he did it. Without so much as a decent burial, he had killed the old order of American politics. No U.S. President, Democrat or Republican, is likely to propose for at least a generation spending more than the government earns or expanding what it tries to do.

Gingrich had spent not just his adult life but his entire life since grade school believing that such a lofty role was his destiny. To explain why an unlikable man could carry out such an unlikely ambition, it helps to understand some skills and obsessions that were planted very early. They had had a long time to ripen.

According to his mother Kit, Gingrich's first taste of politics came when his estranged father Newt McPherson made a deal: if he no longer had to pay child support for young Newt, he would waive his parental rights and let the boy's stepfather, Bob Gingrich, adopt him. Newt's legal parentage was thus the product of a budget deal.

Bob Gingrich was a combat-hardened Army lieutenant colonel whose soldiers called him "Stoneface." He spoke three languages and served as an intelligence officer, but was twice passed over for full colonel because he did not hide his contempt for incompetent superiors. As stern as he was, Bob came to embrace a wounded mother and her young son. Kit had been 16 when she fell for a tall, strapping 18-year-old named Newt McPherson, whom she married on Sept. 12, 1942. One day shortly thereafter, he struck her after he had stayed out drinking the night before. She left immediately; the couple broke up within days. But Kit was already pregnant. On June 17, 1943, her baby was born, and she named him Newton after her estranged husband.

BOB GINGRICH MARRIED KIT WHEN NEWT WAS THREE and spent the next 16 years trying to tame his adopted son. Newt spent those years trying to get his stepfather's attention. Bob was a Democrat; Newt, almost from childhood, a Republican. Bob was a disciplinarian, Newt a rebel. Kit was the gentle buddy who sometimes let her kids stay home from school just to be with Mom (Newt eventually had three half-sisters) but would hide them in the closet at lunchtime when Bob came home so he wouldn't get angry. Until he was nine, Newt shared a room with a free-spirited grandmother, who taught him to read and write before he started school. With an IQ of 124 by third grade, he did well only in the subjects that interested him.

Early on, Newt perfected the Gingrich paradigm: civic progress on a tight budget. One day when he was 10, the animal-loving boy told Kit he was going to the library but instead took a bus to Harrisburg, Pennsylvania, to lobby city and state officials about building a zoo. Newt pressed his cause for the next two years. "Don't you know an African

much care—as long as they would read about him one day.

When he was 14, Gingrich traveled with his stepfather to the World War I battlefield of Verdun, France—a journey he claims changed his life. As he tells it, they wandered the fields, the scene of ghastly sacrifice, and then slipped into the ossuary. There were private stairs leading down to a basement, walled off by windows that had been painted black to hide what was inside. The paint had peeled, so they took a peek. What they saw was horrifying: rib cages, skulls, long bones, all piled high in a huge mound. The two walked silently back up the steps. "That was where he really got his

Gingrich's nickname in Congress was Newtron; he made it plain he

lion costs only $250? And it's easily gotten!" argued the budget-minded boy crusader. "We wouldn't even have to start out with the more expensive animals." The zoo never got built, but Newt had made the newspapers and decided he was "hooked forever on public life."

From the age of 10 on, Gingrich lived the wandering life of an Army brat. Other children, no surprise, found him rather strange, and he quickly stopped trying to prove otherwise. He found books more reliable than friends, particularly tales of men who brought old empires crashing down and built new ones in their place. Everyone from Ataturk to the Duke of Wellington to Abraham Lincoln figured in his pantheon. If people didn't like him, if they mocked his aspirations or despised his principles, he didn't

political aspiration," says Bob. "He vowed to do everything he could to see that this never happened again."

When Bob Gingrich rotated back to Fort Benning, Georgia, Newt attended Baker High School in nearby Columbus, where he was voted "Most Intellectual" in his senior class. A crushing break with his stepfather came when he was a sophomore at Emory University. Gingrich announced to his stunned family that he wanted to get married—to his high school math teacher, Jacqueline Battley, who was seven years older. Bob was adamantly opposed: he had never become a doctor because he had had to work long hours as a bartender to support his family while going to college. He didn't want Newt stalled with such burdens.

Newt and Jackie got married anyway. Bob refused to go

ON THE RISE

★ ★ ★ ★ ★ ★ ★ ★ ★ ★

Clockwise from left: Gingrich was already a father of two as a grad student at Tulane in 1969; with both daughters attending, he marries Marianne Ginther in 1981; as an animal lover at age eight; first wife Jackie stands by him through his first electoral defeat in 1974.

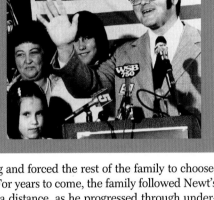

less, "This book is the truth! It's the best book I ever read!"

He was by all accounts the kind of popular, high-energy teacher who could get kids to come to a 7 a.m. class. Gingrich's effort to build such a large student following had a pragmatic side to it—a number of his students eventually became the ground troops in his campaigns for Congress.

Gingrich saw his big opening in 1974, when he challenged Sixth District Congressman Jack Flynt, a silver-haired patrician, very much part of the Democratic establishment. Flynt was no raving segregationist but, unlike Gingrich, he declined to talk racial justice, the environment and other populist themes. In this situation, Gingrich, with his bushy black hair, sideburns and citrus-colored double knits, came off to most people as the more liberal of the pair.

The fact that he lost that race did not stop him from thinking about what he would do once he won. In December 1975 Gingrich went to Milwaukee, Wisconsin, to attend Paul Weyrich's class on how to run a winning campaign. Weyrich, a guru of the New Right, would become Gingrich's political godfather. Though Weyrich was in charge, Newt quickly took over the meeting. Voice chiming, arms waving, Gingrich "began to lecture me about how we should run as a team," Weyrich recalls, "and how all of the people that were there, if they all ran with the same theme, they would be far better off than if they ran singly, and that it was my responsibility to put together a theme for all of these candidates." Almost 20 years later, that strategy produced the Contract with America, the Gingrich agenda for revolution.

GINGRICH LOST AGAIN TO FLYNT IN 1976, BUT THEN Gentleman Jack retired, and in 1978 Gingrich faced state senator Virginia Shapard. It was that race, locals say, that first marked the hard shift to the right and the acid attacks that would distinguish Gingrich for years to come. The former moderate comdemned Shapard for planning to split up her family by commuting to Washington, leaving her husband and children behind with a nanny. Gingrich's slogan: "When elected, Newt will keep his family together."

It was a campaign promise quickly broken. A year and a half into his first term, Newt demanded a divorce from Jackie. By now the story has become a part of the Gingrich legend that he would just as soon erase. She was in the

to the wedding and forced the rest of the family to choose: no one went. For years to come, the family followed Newt's career only at a distance, as he progressed through undergraduate and graduate school and then a teaching post at West Georgia College. Newt had no real academic ambitions. When Pierre-Henri Laurent, who supervised Gingrich's dissertation at Tulane (on education in the Belgian Congo) offered to help him get a good first teaching job, Gingrich told him not to bother. "He said, 'Don't worry; I'm close to getting something at West Georgia College.' 'West Georgia College?' I said. 'What is this?'" Gingrich proceeded

wanted to clear out the Congress and leave only the building standing

to offer a detailed analysis of Georgia's Sixth Congressional District and why he had a good shot at getting elected there.

These were, as he himself might say, fluid years for Gingrich. As a student and later professor, he was no conservative firebrand; at Tulane, he admits, he smoked pot, protested the administration's decision to censor a photo of a nude sculpture in the school newspaper and generally maintained a high profile as a Rockefeller Republican. At West Georgia he started an environmental-studies program, an outpost on the lefty fringes of academia. His fellow professors nicknamed him Mr. Truth. Whenever Gingrich had finished reading a new book, a colleague recalls, he would come flying into the history department, brandishing the volume in question and declaring, more or

hospital, the day after surgery for uterine cancer, when he appeared at her bedside and proceeded to spell out the terms of separation. Six months after the divorce, Gingrich married Marianne Ginther, whom he had met at a political fund raiser in Ohio. She would become his confidant, sounding board and reality check.

Newt Gingrich arrived in Washington without a hint of backbencher's humility. His nickname in Congress was Newtron; he made it plain that he wanted to clear out the Congress and leave only the building standing. He quickly joined forces with fellow apostates to form the Conservative Opportunity Society, a group of Republican lawmakers who sought an antidote to the "liberal welfare state." In the view of colleagues from both parties, the COS was a noisy,

BREATHER
★★★★★★★★★
Newt and Marianne escaped to La Jolla, California, and hit the beach during his book promotion tour

funding the troops who would later become his Republican Guard. In 1986 he took over as general chairman of GOPAC, the fund-raising machinery created in 1979 to help get Republicans into state and local office. Gingrich made himself available to G.O.P. candidates in weekly conference calls, mailed them his audiotapes and appeared in their districts. His acolytes all across the country struck the same themes, with the same language.

buffoonish fraternity of outcasts and troublemakers. Senior Republicans took newly elected ones aside and counseled them that if they wanted to have any future in the House, they would do well to avoid the COS crowd.

Time and again, Newt was told by his elders to sit down, shut up, quit making a fool of himself and the institution. But on he went. While they had few sympathizers in the House, Gingrich and the COS were developing an audience outside it. The happiest coincidence of Gingrich's political career is the fact that he and the TV cameras arrived in the House the same year. While most members avoided the floor for all but votes, Gingrich and the COS crowd seemed to live there. After official business was done, they would rail on for hours, with only the weary doorkeepers there to hear them. Thanks to rules that kept the cameras fixed on the talker, millions of viewers had no idea that the orators were addressing empty leather seats.

Finally an exasperated Speaker Tip O'Neill decided to call their bluff and order the cameras to pan the chamber. It amounted to a declaration of war, ultimately leading to an infamous 1984 showdown. O'Neill referred to one of Gingrich's antics as "the lowest thing I've seen in my 32 years in Congress." Whereupon Gingrich succeeded in having O'Neill formally disciplined for having made a personal criticism of a House member, Gingrich, on the floor.

Gingrich next took on Democratic Speaker Jim Wright, launching a yearlong ethics probe that ultimately brought Wright down. Gingrich needed to destroy Wright because Wright had begun to take the very steps that Gingrich planned to take when he himself became Speaker: reining in his committee chairmen and forcing discipline on his unruly troops. By the time Wright resigned, House Republicans had elected Gingrich to their No. 2 post of minority whip by a two-vote margin.

Even as he was learning to be statesmanlike, to buckle down and count votes and hold his tongue when the circumstances required, Gingrich was recruiting, training and

Democrats were to be described with such adjectives as sick, corrupt and bizarre. Divisive issues such as abortion were avoided; the focus was on strategy, not philosophy.

Within a year of becoming minority whip, Gingrich was already obsessed by the next job, which became clear when President Bush and congressional leaders met to hash out a deal to reduce the deficit by $500 billion by raising taxes. A normal whip would have energetically supported the deal. But Gingrich, never normal, declared war on his own party's President. In a stunning vote, 105 House Republicans sided with Gingrich to defeat the plan; only 71 voted with Bush. "I was astonished that they didn't understand we were the party of no taxes," Gingrich says. In a single skirmish he had cast himself as a populist and antitax revolutionary, vanquishing both the Democrats and the moderate Republicans who had stood in his way.

His rebellion very nearly brought him down. In 1990 Gingrich held on to his seat by fewer than 1,000 votes, after his opponent charged that he was more interested in playing God in Washington than in seeing to the needs of his constituents. But the narrow winner went on to become the architect of the G.O.P.'s ascent to power in 1994.

ON DECEMBER 5, 1994, WHEN THE WHOLE BREATH-taking strategy paid off and the Republicans nominated him to become the first G.O.P. Speaker in more than four decades, Gingrich dialed a number in Dauphin, a quaint Pennsylvania Dutch village just north of Harrisburg, where he reached Bob Gingrich. "I want to thank you for being an influence in my life," the new Speaker told his stepfather, his voice choking. "You had a great deal to do with me being where I am today." Bob Gingrich listened, stunned. In 48 years Newt had never talked to him like that. "We had a very distant relationship," Newt says. "It's the first time I'd ever talked to him emotionally." The unbending soldier and the hell-bent rebel had made their peace at last. ∎

MASTER OF THE
HOUSE

THE QUALITIES THAT BROUGHT NEWT GINGRICH FROM AN OBSCURE GEORGIA COLLEGE to the Speakership of the House of Representatives were also the ones that conspired to get him in trouble by the end of 1995: militance, arrogance and a lot of nerve. The year showed Gingrich at his very best and his very worst. His discipline in pursuing his grand design revealed a level of political talent that few people outside his inner circle ever imagined he had. To wield that kind of power from the House required that he transform a weak, discredited institution into a humming legislative engine that could tow the Senate and White House behind it. He did it with such focus and shrewdness that even his opponents were perversely grateful. America's House had been broken, and someone finally fixed it.

But sometimes Gingrich forgot who he had become. Under pressure, he reverted to the pompous thug lobbing grenades on C-SPAN about sick Democrats who were enemies of normal Americans. He did not realize that his every remark would now be measured for maturity, not ferocity. He did not understand that once a battle is won, it's time

THE BOSS
★★★★★★★★★★★★
Gingrich takes on his free-spirited G.O.P. freshmen

to move graciously to the peace table. "I have consistently, all year, said things that made no sense for the Speaker of the House," he told TIME at year's end. The voters seemed to agree. During 1995, his unfavorable rating had shot up from 29% to 56%. Americans had learned how far he was willing to go to achieve his larger goals: shut the government down to make a point with the President; invite lobbyists not just to lobby, but to draft the laws themselves; and give a huge tax break to his party's allies at the expense of services for the poor, with the explanation that this is what it takes to keep his Republican coalition together.

In the areas of his greatest success, it was Newt the professor at work, a careful student of power who recognized that, if he hoped to change the world, he would need to change the Congress first. His problem was that the House was never intended to be very powerful. The Founding Fathers designed a legislative body that could boil over with parochial passions, only to be cooled by the sober Senate. Senators can filibuster; Presidents can veto. All the Speaker can do is create the appearance of momentum so that the rest of the government will get out of the way.

W HEN GINGRICH ARRIVED IN THE HOUSE IN 1979, he refused to accept the status quo that deemed Republicans an eternal minority. Instead, he spent 10 full years methodically recruiting and training his own private army. And when the time was right, he gave them the banner that brought them victory, the brilliantly conceived Contract with America. His 10-point plan captured the smoldering anger of a nation suffering from stagnant wages, chronic federal overspending, failure in the schools, the decline of public decency and an immovable underclass. The Contract bundled up these anxieties and set them ablaze. The result was the stunning G.O.P. sweep of November 1994 that enshrined Newt's recruits as the majority in the House—and made him its master. Now that he was Speaker, his zealous troops supported all the House restructuring he proposed, not least because it gave them a more central role than any generation of congressional arrivistes in modern history.

Gingrich and the newcomers saw that the gravest threat to the revolution came from the committee chairs.

100 days. By that deadline he had actually rammed everything through the House, with the single exception of term limits. On the few occasions when the freshmen rebelled— as when they pressed for campaign-finance reform—he shut them down with a promise to do it next year.

This tactic was only one of the handy lessons Gingrich had learned in 1995. Another was the value of setting the bar high, in the belief that it's sometimes easier to do the impossible than the merely improbable. He insisted on balancing the budget in seven years, for instance, when conventional wisdom held that no politician had the stomach to balance it at all. Gingrich also learned the value of sleeping with the enemy. The strategy worked best with the Republican plan to restrain the growth of Medicare. In end-

"I am too intense and I am too unsteady. I have consistently

Even with Republicans in control, Gingrich's agenda could easily have been buried by chairmen who were intent on exercising the power they had finally won. So he scrapped the seniority system, and installed as chairmen those who had proved their fealty. Then, to make sure the chairmen behaved, he packed the key committees with his acolytes. He even required all members of the Appropriations Committee to sign an oath of loyalty to the Contract with America as a condition of serving. He abolished three committees and 25 subcommittees and sliced staffs by a third, making it harder for rivals to create their own mini-empires.

At first the system he installed worked wondrously. To much ridicule and skepticism, Gingrich had promised to bring to a vote the 10 items in the Contract during the first

less meetings, Gingrich graciously met with the lobbyists representing for-profit hospitals, solicited their ideas, and even accepted some of them. But he also made it clear that a bill was inevitable, that the numbers would be huge, and that they stood to suffer far more by opposing it and being frozen out than by playing along. They went along because they had been included from the start—and other health groups held their fire as well.

Gingrich also marshaled his forces in a completely new way: by offering his colleagues glory instead of goodies. It was near midnight on the night of August 3 when he faced the prospect of watching his revolution stall before his eyes. The measure he was pushing through the House was a crucial 1996 spending bill designed to slice everything

WILD MAN
★★★★★★★★★

Ouch! Meeting his
match for a change,
Gingrich plays host
to a touring bearcat

from summer-jobs programs to home-heating assistance. But in the byzantine way Congress packages its legislation, the bill had become laden with several measures involving abortion, the rare issue where principle promised to trump politics. With precious time ticking away, Gingrich still needed at least 10 votes.

At such a moment as this, a traditional Speaker might have reached into his pocket and pulled out a water project here, an Air Force base there, to secure the last votes he needed. But Gingrich had little in common with his predecessors; he had never even chaired a committee in Congress, where he might have learned the brokerage business. The conservatives held a prayer meeting, then came around. Now he needed the moderates to cede ground. "This is a time when the American people are looking at what we are doing," he told them. Did they want to go home (for the August recess) as losers? What's more, he said, several vulnerable freshmen who opposed the bill had privately offered to switch their votes if it were necessary. Did these moderates, most of whom enjoyed relatively safe seats, want to put the freshmen's survival on the line ? The bill passed, 219 to 208.

Gingrich called the moment "mystical, magical." That night he erased decades of habit in the House: the givens that members are more loyal to their supporters than to their Speaker, that the real work of Congress amounted to horse trading small favors in the committee room, that freshmen in Congress are about as powerful as the doorkeepers, that the House is where bold schemes come to die.

Conviction and charisma helped Gingrich transform the House and press his agenda, but ego and hubris produced his major miscalculations. Once he became Speaker, his adversaries began holding him to the same ethical

documents filed by the Federal Election Commission charged that the lobby spent more than $250,000 in "Newt support" to help Gingrich hang onto his seat. Democrats had long claimed that Gingrich used GOPAC as his political piggy bank; the FEC charged that GOPAC paid his American Express fees, lent him consultants for his campaign "to help Newt think" and urged its big donors to direct their money to the re-election effort.

Moreover, though he had often railed against vested interests, in Gingrich's House the most powerful interests acted as honorary members. With his party now in power, lobbyists who contributed to G.O.P. coffers were given awe-inspiring access to the legislative process, including the right to write the bills themselves, like the one passed in February that imposed a 13-month moratorium on federal regulations. During floor debate, the Gucci set stood close by, typing out on their laptop computers the talking points that Republican leaders would use on the floor.

G INGRICH'S AUTUMN WAS FULL OF FUMBLES. FOR the first time, he had to close a deal, to bargain with someone whose interests were at odds with his own. The Democrats rose from the dead with the lethal charge that the Republican push to reform Medicare was actually just a way to give a tax break to the rich by robbing from the old. Gingrich, who had carefully drilled his troops to take the high ground, failed the test. "The tax cut is the glue that holds together the coalition that balances the budget," he said.

The greatest blunder, the ultimate example of Gingrich making a personal moment out of an impersonal one, came with the first government shutdown in November. He could have stuck to his argument that the ordeal was necessary because what he was trying to do was so bold, so historic that the country should come to a halt and reflect on the choices before it. Instead, he said that he was peeved about his treatment aboard Air Force One, when he had flown with the President to the Rabin funeral in Israel. He had been forced to use a rear exit, he whined, and the President had failed to use their proximity on the flight to discuss the budget wrangle. Chastised everywhere for his outburst, the smarting Speaker vowed to speak a bit less in the future.

said things that made no sense for the Speaker of the House."

standards he had so righteously enforced as the House proctor. During his first months in the job, the Democrats hounded him for his lavish $4.5 million book deal with Rupert Murdoch, to the point that he settled for a $1 advance, plus royalties. As early as the spring there were no fewer than five ethics charges pending against him, and by year's end the ethics committee had recommended bringing in outside counsel to investigate Gingrich's dealings with GOPAC, the Republican political action committee.

As the head of GOPAC from 1986 until May of 1994, Gingrich studied the ways and means of campaign cash flow. Some of the charges that haunted him at the end of 1995 stemmed from that experience. GOPAC was permitted by law to help only candidates for state and local offices, but

Gingrich's opponents savored the irony of his decline; the man whose career had been built on making demons of others could not control his own unruly spirits. But whatever his standing in the polls, his troubles over GOPAC, and his struggles to control himself, few could argue with his assessment of his achievement. Asked by TIME's editors to sum up his year as Speaker, he said: "We have changed the whole debate in American politics. There is now a universal agreement you've got to balance the budget. The argument is over exactly how much, exactly when." Whatever happens to Gingrich himself, it will take years to undo what he had done in months: ground down the Congress into a precision instrument of his personal power. And he had only begun. He wants a multivolume biography. ■

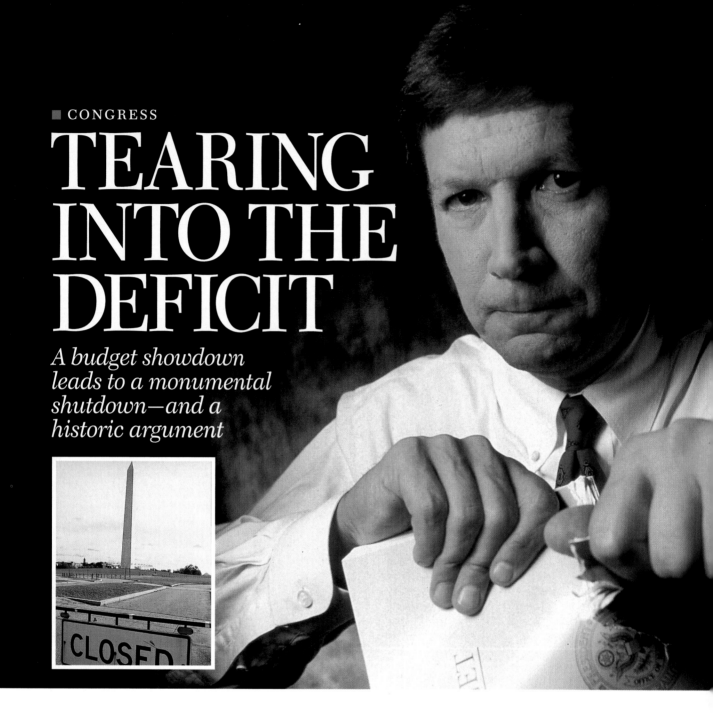

TEARING INTO THE DEFICIT

A budget showdown leads to a monumental shutdown—and a historic argument

By JAY CARNEY FOR THE TIME ANNUAL

GIDDY FROM THEIR NOVEMBER 1994 ELECTION sweep, the new Republican majorities on Capitol Hill seemed invincible early in 1995. They would have to be to achieve their primary goal: to tame once and for all the runaway fiscal prodigality that had created a $4.8 trillion national debt. But to their surprise, Bill Clinton, who had seemed irrelevant early in the year, stood up to them in the fall. The resulting budget stalemate led to the shutdown of large portions of the government, not once but twice. 1995 ended with Washington in a state akin to siege, with federal services hobbled, tourists turned away from the National Gallery—and the public swinging to the President's side.

As the House took up the G.O.P.'s Contract with America in January, there were early signs of the budget battle to come. During debate on welfare reform, Democrats excoriated House Republicans as cruel to children for wanting to cut the federal school-lunch program and turn it over to the states. The attack exposed the G.O.P.'s Achilles' heel: the lingering perception that the party served the interests of the rich and powerful and not those of the average American. Indeed, the Contract called for deep cuts in social spending not only to balance the budget, but also to pay for G.O.P.-promised tax cuts of more than $330 billion, with many of the benefits skewed in favor of wealthier Americans.

In March the Republicans met with a failure that could have derailed their budget-cutting locomotive. Earlier on, the House had voted overwhelmingly—and bipartisanly—in favor of a constitutional amendment requiring a balanced federal budget by 2002. But in the Senate the measure fell one vote short of victory. Instead of giving up, G.O.P. leaders turned their defeat into a motivator. More than ever, bal-

JOHN KASICH The G.O.P.'s chief budget-cutter boasted, "The thing I love about our plans is that everybody is feeling the ouch"

ancing the budget became their primary goal. Speaker Gingrich predicted a showdown between Congress and the White House by year's end over G.O.P. bills to cut social programs like Medicare while lowering taxes. If the President vetoed the bills, Gingrich warned, his troops would not compromise, and the government, deprived of operating funds, would shut down.

Clinton did not back down. Instead, he exercised his veto several times. But first, in mid-June he put forward his own kinder, gentler plan to eliminate the deficit. Clinton said he would achieve balance in 10 years, not seven, and would do it by cutting spending but without gutting social, educational and environmental programs. As the October 1 end of the fiscal year approached, with 13 government-funding bills still being worked on, congressional leaders and the White House worked out a funding extension until mid-November. But the inevitable test of wills was only postponed.

Acrimony increased as the second deadline approached; the two sides were far apart. Finally, at midnight on November 13, many federal government services closed down, with only military and other "essential" personnel going to work the next day. As the shutdown became the longest in history, public opinion began to turn against the G.O.P. and Gingrich.

The six-day shutdown ended on November 20, after Clinton and Congress agreed to another short-term extension of government spending. But this time the President had to commit himself to the G.O.P.'s goal of balancing the budget by 2002. In exchange, Republicans pledged to "protect" Medicare, Medicaid, education and environmental programs. A real compromise—and the first balanced budget since 1969—seemed within reach. But the talks failed again, and in the week before Christmas, a second, smaller shutdown idled some government agencies.

Facing growing anger from furloughed federal workers, tourists shut out of national parks and frustrated citizens, Clinton and congressional leaders kept meeting to try to end the debacle. But 1996 dawned with the government crippled. In the first week of the new year, Senate majority leader Bob Dole would lead a revolt against Gingrich's rabid House freshmen, resulting in a compromise that restored federal services until January 26.

The lasting image of the budget stalemate of '95 was the line of angry tourists who were shut out of the historic Vermeer exhibit at the National Gallery. That was fitting, for the Republicans' campaign to redefine the relationship between the U.S. government and its people had been waged purposefully, passionately—and artlessly. ∎

The Medicare Scare

WHY DID 1995'S BUDGET BATTLE COME DOWN to an argument over Medicare and Medicaid? And why did it cause such a fuss? Two of the government's most expensive programs—Social Security and the defense budget—were considered untouchable by politicians from both parties. If the budget was to be balanced, that left only two reservoirs of government cash big enough to be raided: Medicare, the federally funded health-insurance program used by 37 million senior citizens, and Medicaid, the jointly funded, federal-state health program that served 36 million poorer Americans.

Warning that Medicare's skyrocketing costs would bankrupt the program within the decade if nothing was done, the Republicans unveiled a plan that would slice those costs by a huge $270 billion over seven years. (Left untouched, the program, which cost $176 billion in 1995, would grow to $286 billion in the year 2000 and then explode as baby boomers began to retire.) The G.O.P.'s promised saving would be achieved by sharply hiking the premiums paid by beneficiaries, limiting payments to doctors and hospitals, and encouraging seniors to follow the national trend into health-maintenance organizations or other versions of "managed care." While charging that the G.O.P. wanted to squeeze money out of Medicare only to pay for its promised $245 billion tax cut, President Clinton included $124 billion in Medicare cuts in his own balanced-budget plan.

But the prospect of major cuts in Medicare riled senior citizens—the same voters whose powerful lobby, the American Association of Retired Persons, had helped keep Social Security off the table. As for the federal- and state–funded Medicaid program, the Administration, the American Medical Association and even some Republican Governors felt that the G.O.P.'s proposals—which included transferring all responsibility for Medicaid programs to the states—would fall too harshly on the nation's neediest.

Medicaid's beneficiaries included more than just impoverished Americans. The basic coverage it provided for 26 million poor children and adults accounted for just a quarter of the program's $156 billion annual tab. The big costs came from providing long-term care for 10 million elderly and disabled Americans. All told, Medicaid covered 1 in 4 American children, paid for 1 in 3 births and financed more than half the nursing-home care in the country. In its current form, Medicaid was also an "entitlement," like Social Security and Medicare, a status it would lose if transferred to the states. As the G.O.P. learned, messing with health care touched a deep nerve in American life. ∎

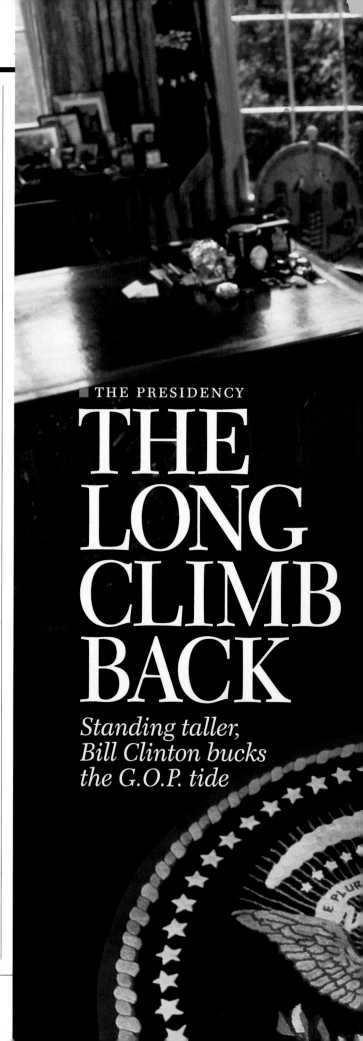

By MICHAEL DUFFY FOR THE TIME ANNUAL

A FTER TWO YEARS IN THE OVAL OFFICE, BILL Clinton was under no illusions about his parlous position. Nearly everything that could have gone wrong in 1994 seemed to have done so. His party had suffered record-breaking losses in the midterm elections. The Democratic Congress had soundly rejected the centerpiece of his presidency—his health-care reform plan—and just about everything else he had proposed. Months of scandal, poor judgment and a hapless management style conspired to drive the President to the political brink. Complaining to an adviser in January 1995, Clinton said, "If you had told me two years ago that I could have done all that I have and be this far down the tubes, nobody would have believed you."

Twelve months later, he had much less cause for complaint. Bill Clinton's third year in office would prove to be a long climb back. After some initial hesitation, he executed a major course correction, altering not only what kind of Democrat he would be but also redrawing the arc of his Presidency. With the Congress firmly in Republican control, and the public deeply skeptical of his performance, Clinton pivoted from offense to defense. He abandoned his lengthy activist agenda, began fighting much smaller battles at the margins of change and cast himself as the only thing that stood between a defenseless America and the Revolution of Newt Gingrich. The abrupt change in direction produced a remarkable reversal of fortune and served as a welcome prelude to his coming re-election campaign.

The U turn produced two other side effects, both beneficial. First, after years of posing (but not actually governing) as a new kind of Democrat, Clinton shuffled unmistakably rightward in 1995, adopting Republican-style solutions to problems for which he had long prescribed liberal antidotes. That repositioning alone won him points with independent voters as a hard-headed problem solver. More significant, Clinton in his junior year appeared to become more comfortable as Commander in Chief. Barring a couple of notorious gaffes, he was a more careful public speaker. He even relaxed more often. And if he still had weaknesses as an executive, his luster as a campaign-style pol was undimmed. Cast as the lonely opposition to a G.O.P. majority, Clinton was able to define himself not in terms of who he was and what he wanted to do, but who he wasn't and what he didn't want to do. This presented, according to White House chief of staff Leon Panetta, a tremendous advantage. "The silver lining in what happened in the election is that we now have the opportunity to define what this President is all about through the battles he fights."

But first he had to wrestle with his monumental defeat at the polls in 1994. Worried about Democratic challengers to his incumbency, Clinton tended his left flank first. He reached out to women, to minorities, to labor unions and to farmers. He removed Democratic Party chairman David Wilhelm and named two liberals—Senator Christopher Dodd and National Committeeman Don Fowler—to run the Democratic National Committee. And he began months of soul searching aimed at reconnecting with voters. He reread his oldest speeches. He held bull sessions with

■ THE PRESIDENCY

THE LONG CLIMB BACK

Standing taller, Bill Clinton bucks the G.O.P. tide

friends, advisers and pollsters. But he was unsatisfied with the conflicting chorus of advice—and his inability to gain any traction. His approval ratings declined in the first two months of the year. By April he had become so marginalized to the action in Congress that he declared in a press conference that he was, in fact, "relevant" to the political process.

But even as he propped up his left flank, he was listening to a new voice on his right. In October 1994, when the President's own advisers seemed unconcerned, Republican pollster Richard Morris warned Clinton of a 50-seat loss in the House. Morris and Clinton had deep roots: a one-time Democrat, Morris had advised Clinton in his 1982 comeback gubernatorial race in Arkansas. Their relationship had at times been stormy: Clinton once got in a shoving fight with Morris at the Governor's mansion, and the two had drifted apart over the next 15 years as Morris toiled for conservative Republicans.

Nudged by the First Lady, Clinton called on Morris frequently after the 1994 election ended in the fiasco Morris had predicted. The President kept his Republican consultant a secret from his staff at first—referring to him as "Charlie" whenever he telephoned. Even after word of Morris's influence spread, the pollster preferred to talk to his client by telephone and slipped into the Clinton's private residence instead of the West Wing on his rare visits.

Morris believed that Clinton's chief problem was that he had aligned himself too closely to the distinctly liberal Democratic leaders in Congress during 1993 and 1994. Morris advised Clinton to move closer to the Republicans on balancing the budget, reforming welfare and providing families with tax cuts—but not too close. That way, he could distinguish himself from the liberals while still keeping a safe distance from Republican excesses. Morris called his strategy "triangulation" and told Clinton that if he followed its dictates, he would gain 10 points in the polls.

In the liberal-leaning Clinton White House, Morris' ideas, as well as Morris himself, were immensely controversial. Morris had helped G.O.P. candidates defeat several Democrats in 1994 by having them run against Clinton's record, and he was a frequent adviser to Senate majority whip Trent Lott. The unconventional arrangement with the President infuriated congressional Democrats and disturbed many White House officials. At times Clinton appeared to slalom back and forth between Morris' influence and that of his more liberal staff.

Alone among Clinton's core advisers, Morris pushed for a balanced budget. The others—Panetta, senior adviser George Stephanopoulos, deputy chief of staff Harold Ickes and Hillary Rodham Clinton—argued that it would be a betrayal of Democratic Party principles. But Clinton ultimately sided with his newest adviser. It was to be the most pivotal shift of his presidency: in mid-June, less than six months after he had proposed a budget plan that envisioned deficits of $200 billion for a decade, Clinton switched gears and proposed balancing the budget by the year 2005. In his speech to the nation on June 13, Clinton could have been speaking of his presidency when he said of his new proposal, "This can be a turning point for us."

Clinton acknowledged, in essence, that Americans had more faith in the broad outlines of the Republican agenda

In Golf We Trust

BILL CLINTON, THE MOST GOLF-CRAZY PRESIdent since Dwight Eisenhower, uses his time on the links to relax and work through tough issues. Or so claims adviser George Stephanopoulos, who says, "It's a think pad. There are no phones, and he can use the game to distract part of his mind and let the other part do its work." In June the President was thrilled at the renovation of Ike's old putting green on the White House's South Lawn. Designed by the renowned course architect Robert Trent Jones Jr, the green is a putter's paradise: 1,500 sq. ft. of Southshore Creeping Bentgrass. In the months before he headed for his golf-saturated August vacation in Jackson Hole, Wyoming (above), Clinton could be found on the green almost daily. Sometimes he forgot that others didn't share his passion. Winding up a critical phone call on Bosnia to French President Jacques Chirac, who was in Morocco, Clinton said: "Give my regards to the King. Tell him I'm using those golf clubs he gave me, and I'm hittin' 'em real sweet!" The President's small talk bewildered the starchy Gaul. ∎

the government rather than allow Republicans to cut his cherished programs. The various tactics had a transforming effect on someone who had once been regarded as unable to make up his mind. By year's end, Clinton was miraculously seen by a majority of voters not only as a President with principles, but as a leader who was willing to fight for them.

But if the comeback was ultimately successful, it was not always smooth. Clinton was still susceptible to costly attacks of thinking out loud. Returning from a long campaign swing around the country in September, he pronounced the country in a "funk." Like Jimmy Carter, who diagnosed a national "malaise" 15 years earlier, Clinton had to scramble to explain himself. In October he told two groups of Democratic Party donors that the Democrats had "forced" him to raise taxes in 1993—a misreading of history. And in November, he angered liberals again when he mused that his own welfare-reform bill, which had been mild by any standard, had not been tough enough.

DESPITE THESE SLIPS, SOMETHING NEW WAS creeping into the Clinton vernacular: the ability to pick a theme and stick with it. First among these was "values," a favorite Clinton word that didn't mean anything specific but was simply reassuring for voters to hear. In 1995 Clinton sowed the word into his speeches, sometimes as often as once a minute. Another leitmotif was "common ground." The President told Americans time and again that the two parties must find "common ground" between (Democratic) "deadlock" and (Republican) "extremism." He was finally beginning to speak in a clear and consistent voice.

In his recovery, Clinton had some additional help from two sources. His wife Hillary carefully withdrew from the limelight, realizing that she was hindering her husband's efforts. And Newt Gingrich indirectly assisted just by being himself. The House Speaker loved the spotlight and rarely minced his words. By the time he threw a childish fit over his supposedly second-class treatment aboard Air Force One, Gingrich was in a free fall in the polls. Americans reported that the Speaker actually "scared" them. The President, by comparison, appeared steady and sound.

Clinton, meanwhile, looked for opportunities overseas to enhance his stature as both Commander in Chief and peacemaker. He continued to press the parties in the Middle East to "take risks for peace" and hosted the signing of the Israeli-Palestinian blueprint for reconciliation at the White House in September. His decision to grant a visa to Sein Fein leader Gerry Adams infuriated Downing Street, but helped spark an eventual breakthrough in bogged-down negotiations between Britain and Ireland. Clinton capped his quiet efforts on Northern Ireland in November, when his visit to Dublin and Belfast galvanized Irish public opinion and led British and Irish leaders to agree to talks leading to a formal peace conference in 1996.

But Clinton's biggest diplomatic triumph came on Bosnia, where he lobbied for a stepped-up NATO air campaign against the Serbs, ultimately helping to bring the warring factions to a U.S.-set bargaining table at Wright-Patterson Air Force Base in Dayton, Ohio. When those talks produced a peace agreement, Clinton kept a three-

than in his own. But he saw in the looming battle over the budget a way to win back many of the voters who had abandoned his party. Chief among these were senior citizens, women and young people. To court these segments of the electorate, Clinton keyed in on four targets in the Republican budget: Medicare, Medicaid, education and the environment, vowing at nearly every opportunity to resist cuts in those programs. Thus, even as he moved toward the Republicans on goals, he focused the debate on the means of getting there, and used the Republicans' specific proposed cuts in popular programs as a foil to enhance his stature.

What's more, Clinton matched that rhetoric with a powerful tool he had never used in his previous two years: the presidential veto. He vetoed several pieces of legislation in 1995 and threatened to use the device on many others. Defying predictions that he would cave in, he even shut down

year-old promise and dispatched American troops to the region to help to enforce the peace. It was a high-risk strategy: though it raised the real likelihood of casualties in an election year, it also showcased Clinton's taking a position and sticking with it for better or worse. Before long, Americans were giving Clinton better marks for his foreign policy than for his handling of domestic affairs.

By year's end, Clinton was back at the top of his game, or at least his polls. In nearly every category, he and his party were riding high: 55% of the public approved of his handling of his job. And the field of challengers to his re-election was far less formidable than it might have been. No member of his own party was seriously considering challenging the sitting President for the nomination—a first in 32 years. As for the Republicans, the two contenders he most feared had withdrawn, California Governor Pete Wilson in September and Colin Powell only two months later. As the election year opened, Senate Majority Leader Bob Dole was the clear G.O.P. front runner—and White House officials relished the idea of running against the dour septuagenarian. This bordered on overconfidence; smarter Administration officials knew that Clinton faced an uphill re-election fight, especially if Dole could compel a reluctant General Colin Powell to join the ticket. "That combination," said one wiser head, "is a silver bullet."

If a dark cloud loomed anywhere for Clinton, its name was Whitewater. The controversy over the failed Ozarks land deal entered a new phase in late 1995 when the White House refused to turn over to Congress notes of a 1993 meeting on the subject between Administration officials and the Clintons' personal lawyers. G.O.P. investigators, led by a close Dole ally, Senator Al D'Amato of New York, wanted to know if Clinton aides had intervened in independent federal probes into the matter. If D'Amato was right, obstruction-of-justice charges against some top aides might follow. The White House initially contended the notes were protected both under attorney-client and Executive privileges, but surrendered them just before Christmas. In addition, independent counsel Kenneth Starr's separate investigation of Whitewater loomed in the election year.

It was a measure of their plight that Republicans returned to Whitewater as the re-election campaign began. Whatever their regard for him as a President, they had learned to underestimate Bill Clinton at their peril. One evening during his first year in office, Clinton invited Gingrich to the White House, where the two men sat a while and talked. Gingrich later recalled that the chat came after a particularly bruising week, and the then minority whip had asked the new President how he was coping. Clinton, Gingrich recalled, was circumspect. He had known setbacks in his life, and in his career and campaigns. They were, he said, the source of his resilience. "I'm a lot like Baby Huey," he told Gingrich. "I'm fat. I'm ugly. But if you push me down, I keep coming back." And so he had. ∎

ROAD TRIP! Hillary and Chelsea tour India

Where's Hillary?

HARRY HOUDINI MIGHT HAVE ENVIED 1995'S most effective vanishing act. Hillary Rodham Clinton, who had played such a prominent and controversial role during the first two years of her husband's presidency, largely disappeared from public view in 1995. When she did surface, she was often to be seen overseas as a goodwill envoy or on TV talk shows chatting about parenting in the 1990's. She rarely appeared in public without her daughter Chelsea, who was blossoming into a poised young woman of 15. The new-model Hillary was a much more reassuring image for a country that had grown deeply suspicious of her unaccountable clout. Yet her self-imposed withdrawal from the arena was an echo of the past: after her husband's defeat in 1980 in his first re-election campaign as Arkansas Governor, Hillary Rodham had changed her name to Hillary Clinton to please Arkansas voters. This First Mate knew when it was time to trim the sails. ∎

A FEBRUARY DAY IN 1995 IN DOVER, NEW HAMPSHIRE, and Bob Dole is in a mood to marvel. "You believe this?" he marvels. "You ever seen anything like this?" Dole's incredulity is due in equal measure to the huge size of the crowd and the rapt, respectful attention he is receiving. "The rest of the country may think it's early," Dole said. "Up here they know better. This deal's gonna be over in a year."

Dole was not yet the Republican Party's nominee, but he had the timing right. The schedule of primaries had never been so compressed as it would be in early 1996. In just 44 days between Iowa's caucus on February 12 and California's primary on March 26, about 70% of the Republican delegates would be chosen. Like it or not, that meant the real primary season was beginning as Dole spoke, 20 months before the presidential election on November 5, 1996.

The Republicans who aimed to derail Dole included congressional stalwarts, right-wing ideologues, family-values mavens—and a few potential spoilers waiting in the wings. But Bob Dole, the wounded war veteran who became Senate majority leader following the Republican congressional sweep of 1994, was the clear front runner. After his two previous tries for the prize—in 1980 and 1988—Republicans across the country said Dole was leading because voters saw him as having earned "his turn." But in the Age of Newt, Dole—who, if elected, would be 73 years old on taking office in January 1997—seemed a distinct part of the old order. His challengers would not let voters forget Speaker Gingrich's old slam at him as "the tax collector for the welfare state."

Chasing Dole were Patrick Buchanan, a former speechwriter for Richard Nixon, and Senator Phil Gramm of Texas. Lamar Alexander, the former Secretary of Education under George Bush, was a notch behind. Dark horses included Senators Richard Lugar of Indiana and Arlen Specter of Pennsylvania; California Representative Bob Dornan; the wealthy magazine man Steve Forbes; and a radio-talk show host, Alan Keyes. At times during the year, General Colin Powell and Newt Gingrich seemed ready to join the race, and a strong Powell boom emerged. But by year's end, both had declared they would not seek the nomination.

Perhaps the most surprising candidate of 1995 was the bellicose Pat Buchanan, remembered for his divisive speech at the Republican Convention in 1992. Three years later, his song remained the same: strong on family values,

■ **POLITICS**

OFF AND

Sensing Clinton's vulnerability, the

down on immigrants, welfare recipients, homosexuals and "corporate chieftains" who get richer while workers' paychecks dwindle. By October, after a long period of hand-to-mouth electioneering, Buchanan was running second in the polls, just behind Dole. He also claimed second place in the money race, surpassing the third-quarter fund raising of formidable money-magnet Phil Gramm. Even more

Powell Outage

G ENERAL COLIN POWELL, FORmer head of the Joint Chiefs of Staff and hero of the Gulf War, was the most plausible former soldier to bid for the presidency since Dwight Eisenhower. Powell was a bundle of contraries: a military man with a social conscience; an African-American New Yorker who attracted white Southern voters; a geology major who became, in the words of Gerald Ford, "the best public speaker in America"; a relative political unknown who inspired trust; a black man on a white horse.

Urged on by an unofficial organization of Washington insiders, in 1995 Powell tested the waters for a presidential candidacy through a na-tionwide tour promoting his much awaited autobiography, *My American Journey*. Cautious by instinct and training, Powell refused to state he was a candidate and would not even declare a party affiliation.

As the Powell boomlet gained momentum, polls showed him to be overwhelmingly popular. The movement gathered speed in the fall: fund raisers drew up financial timetables,

RUNNING

G.O.P. pack heads right for the prize

his war chest, had more endorsements from congressional colleagues and had won six consecutive Republican Party straw polls. But his campaign never seemed to ignite, hampered by Gramm's contentious manner, deep Southern drawl and uninspired speechifying. The moralizing Senator was further hurt in June, when it was revealed that he had invested in a soft-core pornographic film in 1974.

Meanwhile, a former insider, ex–Cabinet member Alexander, donned a flannel shirt and positioned himself as the lone "outsider" in the race. He waged a Ross Perot–inspired crusade to dismantle large chunks of the Federal Government, which he described as "the arrogant empire." But he lagged in polls, and would need early success in 1996 to be a factor in the race. A true outsider—and a true dark horse—was a late entry, multimillionaire magazine heir Forbes, whose lavish spending on advertising quickly won him recognition in key primary states.

Afflicted with money problems, the rest of the field toiled on, far behind the front runners. Lugar, a plain-spoken, cheerful man who was widely respected for his expertise in international issues, seemed lost in the din. Specter positioned himself as a centrist, but the party was in no mood for the middle of the road, and he withdrew in November. Representative Dornan's far-right views held slim chance of attracting a mainstream vote, and the family-values message of Alan Keyes was potent but underfunded. California's ambitious Governor, Pete Wilson, intended a run at the nomination, but he withdrew only months after announcing, the victim of health problems and staff strife.

By the end of 1995—10 months after that exuberant rally in New Hampshire—Bob Dole remained firmly in the lead in the race. But over the course of the year, in his determination not to be outflanked on the right wing, the generally moderate Dole had followed the guidance of his campaign advisers and portrayed himself as more conservative than he really was. As a result, he appeared craven, a panderer to the right. His support was wide, but it was also shallow and unenthusiastic. Dole's November decision to support President Bill Clinton's commitment of U.S. troops to police the Bosnia accord was more characteristic of the man: gutsy and honorable. But it provided a wedge issue that could sink his candidacy if the peace mission faltered. "The road ahead," Dole was now saying, "won't be any picnic." His marveling days were over. ∎

PHIL GRAMM had a surplus of funds but ran a deficit in the polls

PAT BUCHANAN had good reason to chortle: his star was rising fast

BOB DOLE led the field from the start but breathed easier when Powell and Gingrich didn't jump in

important was the emerging sense that Buchanan was setting the pace in the race: the man with the most resonant message, the most passionate following. The entire field, including Dole, moved rightward in his wake.

Buchanan's ascendance came at the expense of Senator Gramm. The Texan had been expected to be a formidable competitor: as 1995 began, he led the field in the size of

and Congressmen, Governors, even some sitting Democratic lawmakers, pushed Powell to jump into the race

Only after the book tour did Powell address his difficult decision. Deadlines to enter primaries dictated that he must make up his mind by Thanksgiving. Powell vacillated daily, but on Nov. 8, at a press conference, he announced he would not run. The reason he gave was that he lacked the

necessary desire for the presidency—the old "fire in the belly." Many believed his wife Alma's notable lack of enthusiasm for public life may have helped sway him. The General also declared himself a Republican, saying that he hoped to work to move the party toward the center. The measured dignity with which Powell declined to run left many wishing he had entered the race.

∎ **Powell, with wife Alma, just said no**

A BLOW TO

Hundreds die when a massive bomb levels a federal building in Oklahoma—and two Americans are charged with the brutal deed

FOLKS IN OKLAHOMA GROW UP learning to live with twisters, those ugly storms that come swirling across the prairie to tear towns apart, tossing houses in their wake. To live on the Oklahoma plains means understanding that nature is not evil, only whimsical. Human nature, on the other hand, proved incomprehensible on the morning of Wednesday, April 19, 1995.

The disaster occurred at 9:02, the very height of the morning rush hour at the Alfred P. Murrah Federal Building in the center of the state capital, Oklahoma City. Suddenly, while some 550 federal employees worked inside, a huge blast rent the air and a red-orange fireball rose into the sky. The whole north side of the nine-story building seemed to collapse. The carcass left standing looked monstrous, drooling cable and concrete onto the plaza below, huffing gas and smoke and dust into the sky above.

Glass fell like sharp rain over whole sections of the city. Parking meters were ripped from the ground; roofs collapsed; metal doors twirled around themselves. Toys were scattered everywhere, haphazardly mingled with arms and legs, the remnants of a destroyed day-care center on the second floor. It was as if some immense, wicked child had ransacked her nursery and dismembered her dolls.

The massive destruction was the result of the explosion of a huge, 5,000-lb. truck bomb composed of ammonium nitrate fertilizer and a mixture of chemicals. Officials later discovered that it had been placed in a nearby truck and detonated by a safety fuse lit by hand. It left a crater 30 ft. across and 8 ft. deep.

THE BLAST The homemade bomb weighed 5,000 lbs. Its force was felt 30 miles away.

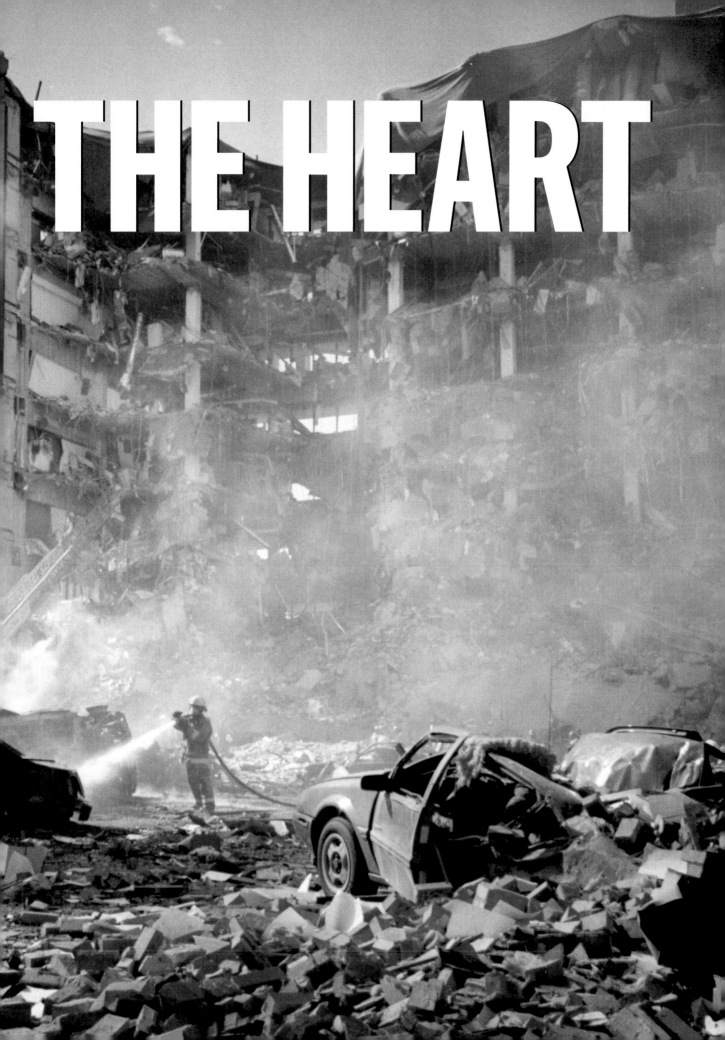

THE HEART

Out of the smoke staggered the survivors, some in their underwear, their clothes ripped along with their skin, barefoot, walking over glass, covered in blood, dust and plaster. One man tottered down the sidewalk, blood on his face, declaring that he was heading home—only he didn't know where that might be and couldn't remember his name. Others stumbled in shock, unaware that they were hurt until they felt their shoes filling up with blood. On the top floor, the explosion peeled the roof back and sliced the building in half, sparing many on one side and sending hundreds of others crashing down below. The bomb's final toll: 169 dead—including 19 children in the day-care center—and an additional 400 injured.

Sirens summoned medical students and off-duty cops, paramedics, firemen, nurses and priests, blood donors and structural engineers—anyone who could provide help or advice or comfort or expertise. Rescuers swarmed from all corners of the city and eventually surrounding states as well. So many nurses showed up so quickly, said one witness, that after half an hour there was at least one nurse for every victim. A priest wearing a purple stole and latex gloves tried to comfort the grieving and pray for the dead.

T HE SOBS FROM INSIDE THE RUBBLE TOLD rescue workers that children were still in the building, still alive. What had been the building's day-care center—a facility that usually housed 20 to 40 children each day— lay at the bottom of a crumbling layer cake stuffed with metal and concrete. Workers plunged into the debris, turning over cribs and furniture, hoping to find signs of life, catching their breath at the sight of babies burned beyond recognition. "We started moving bricks and rocks," said police sergeant John Avera, "and we found two babies." Firemen tenderly carried the infants, as paramedics wrapped them in long white gauze that looked like christening dresses. Several toddlers were found wandering around the underground parking lot, searching for parents. In turn, parents on the scene scrambled through the chaos, frantic to find their children. Nurse Shirley Moser began tagging dead children. "Their faces had been blown off," she says. "They found a child without a head."

With each passing hour the rescue forces swelled. The national-disaster plans designated by the Federal Emergency Management Agency fell into place so smoothly that the whole scene looked like a hideously realistic drill. Air Force and National Guard units and FBI counterterrorist teams and forensic specialists arrived in the early afternoon. They joined 60 fire fighters from Phoenix, Arizona, summoned for their skill in extracting bodies from rubble. A planeload of Oklahoma City's leading doctors heading for a medical retreat in Houston heard the news when they landed, got back on the next plane and came home to work.

Like an awful parade, the cranes and backhoes and heavy equipment marched in, as did the specialists with listening devices and remote-sensing equipment and dogs to help sniff out victims. The animals discovered at least 50 people, none of them alive. Outside the building, doctors and paramedics set up triage stations, including four surgi-

THE RESCUE Nearby workers rushed to help. Above, a restaurant employee aids a victim.

"SAVE THE KIDS!" Rescue workers dug frantically through the

MASSACRE: An Oklahoma County sheriff cradles a victim; 19 children from the building's day-care center died in the blast

rubble, haunted by screams and sobs from wounded children

cal units in a nearby warehouse, to assess the injuries and get help for the most grievously wounded.

As the search dragged on into the night Wednesday, floodlights made the plaza shine like noon, and the crews kept pressing deeper into the rubble. The effort proceeded an inch at a time, with people on hands and knees, working with crowbars and axes. Rescue workers were on two-hour shifts and were ordered to visit counselors to help them cope with what they were seeing. But many wanted only to get back inside the building while there was yet some hope that someone might still be alive in there.

Even as the doctors and rescuers went about their work, the rest of the city searched for ways to help. People waited in line for six hours to donate blood at the Red Cross. A sporting-goods store in Stillwater shipped every one of its kneepads to the rescuers scouring the wreckage. Nearby Tinker Air Force Base sent a truckload of helmet lights. What may have been most remarkable, in the aftermath of Oklahoma's sorrow, was that the sturdy clichés about Midwestern fortitude came to life as an entire city refused to buckle in grief. "We hate and despise the people who did it," said District Judge Fred Daugherty, who survived the blast in his courthouse office next door to the federal building. "But we're a strong and simple folk. We'll rebuild and roll with this thing."

For most Americans, the saddest aspect of the bombing was that the suspects charged with inflicting this most deadly act of terrorism ever committed on U.S. soil—the people Judge Daugherty pledged to hate and despise— were not enemies from foreign shores, but fellow citizens. Even as the rescue effort in Oklahoma City continued, a manhunt for the perpetrators of the tragedy was launched. Within days, a pair of antigovernment zealots who had served together in the U.S. Army—Timothy J. McVeigh, 27, and Terry Lynn Nichols, 40—were in custody in connection with the bombing.

Mingling with the shock that the bombers were Americans, a sense of guilty introspection swept the U.S. after the arrest of the two veterans. Immediately after the blast, some politicians and commentators had fingered Islamic terrorists as the most likely culprits, fueling anti-Muslim sentiment. When the suspects turned out to be homegrown extremists, embarrassment replaced finger pointing. Ironically too, the very governmental institutions so despised by McVeigh and Nichols—the FBI and the Bureau of Alcohol, Tobacco and Firearms—mobilized forces with astonishing efficiency after the bombing and quickly found them.

For the federal and local investigators, the manhunt was hastened by the discovery of twisted truck parts, traces of ammonium nitrate in the wreckage and forged car-rental documents. Luck played a role as well: in spite of the composite sketch resembling McVeigh that was broadcast nationally as early as Thursday afternoon, labeling the primary suspect as John Doe No. 1, McVeigh almost got away.

As in the bombing of New York City's World Trade Center in 1993, a car fragment proved crucial. The vehicle identification number of the rented Ryder truck that ultimately delivered the explosives was found near the scene of the blast. That clue gave investigators in Oklahoma the start they needed. From there it was a simple routine to

THE MANHUNT Decorated U.S. Army veteran Timothy McVeigh, in FBI custody

KANSAS: McVeigh rented the bomb truck in Junction City

ARIZONA: McVeigh lived in this trailer in Kingman during 1993

OKLAHOMA: A tow truck hauls away McVeigh's car, which had no plates—a form of protest favored by antigovernment extremists

KANSAS: Terry Nichols in handcuffs. When arraigned in mid-August, McVeigh and Nichols pleaded innocent to the bombing

trace the truck back to a Ryder outlet in Junction City, Kansas, 270 miles from the site of the attack. The feds arrived in Junction City around 8 p.m. Wednesday, got a description of the two men who had rented the truck—and the hunt for the bombers was on. By Friday, McVeigh was in federal custody. He was charged, under Title 18 of U.S. Code, Section 844, with bombing a government building.

MCVEIGH HAD CHECKED INTO THE Dreamland Motel in Junction City on Friday, April 14, signing his own name in the register and giving the Decker, Michigan, address of James Nichols, brother of Terry Nichols. During his stay, McVeigh rented a Ryder truck and parked it in the Dreamland lot far from his room, No. 25. He checked out the day before the bombing. At least three witnesses said they saw him on Wednesday morning in Oklahoma City outside the Murrah Building.

An hour and 20 minutes after the bombing, McVeigh was routinely pulled over for driving his Mercury Marquis without license plates outside Perry, Oklahoma, 60 miles north of Oklahoma City. While interrogating McVeigh, state trooper Charles Hanger discovered that he was wearing a shoulder harness bearing a Glock semiautomatic pistol, which turned out to be loaded with hollow-point "cop-killer" bullets. The trooper arrested him on charges of carrying a concealed weapon, driving without tags and driving without insurance.

For two days, local authorities kept McVeigh in jail, not connecting their quietly uncommunicative prisoner with the police sketch of John Doe No. 1. Five minutes before McVeigh was due to go before the Noble County court on Friday morning, where he might have walked away on $500 bail, district attorney John Maddox received a call from the FBI telling him to hang on to the prisoner. In response to the government's offer of a $2 million reward for information in the case, a former co-worker of McVeigh's had called in after recognizing the composite drawing on TV. He told the bureau that McVeigh was a disenchanted army vet who hated the government. A computer search produced the recent arrest record of a Tim McVeigh in Perry.

Few of the people who knew McVeigh from his hometown of Pendleton, New York, about 15 miles northeast of Niagara Falls, recognized him from the composite sketch. And some of his classmates from Starpoint High, where McVeigh graduated in 1986, would have nominated him as least likely to be the bomber. Those who had come into contact with him more recently, however, told a more disturbing tale.

McVeigh had joined the Army after high school and served as a sergeant during the Gulf War, earning the Bronze Star and several other medals. As a soldier he worked himself hard on his own time, hoping to qualify for the Army Special Forces. After he failed to make it, friends said, McVeigh, already a loner, became increasingly frustrated. His politics veered far rightward. He claimed that the Army had implanted a computer chip in his buttocks. He was distraught over the destruction of the Branch

Davidian compound in Waco, Texas, by federal agents—which occurred on April 19, 1993, two years to the day before the Oklahoma City bombing.

Federal investigators focused much of their attention on Kingman, Arizona, where McVeigh had lived in a trailer park for five months in 1994 with a pregnant girlfriend. During that period, officials said, a small bomb exploded in a residential area, damaging the windows of some houses but causing no injuries.

On Friday, April 21, Terry Nichols turned himself in for questioning in Herington, Kansas, about 25 miles south of Junction City; he had bought a house in Herington only recently. Authorities tracing McVeigh had raided Nichols' brother's farm in Michigan that morning. A search of the Herington house turned up antigovernment pamphlets, guns and explosive materials.

The federal investigators who searched James Nichols' house in Michigan found materials used to build explosives and took him into custody. At first authorities said the brothers were being held as material witnesses, not suspects, but on May 10 Terry Nichols was charged with participating in the "malicious damage and destruction" of a federal building, the same count filed against McVeigh. James Nichols was later released without being charged in the Oklahoma bombing.

The FBI had also put out an alert for a suspect it called John Doe No. 2, accompanied by a sketch of a dark-haired young man. But after an exhaustive two-month search that had the nation jittery, authorities said John Doe No. 2 was Army Private Todd Bunting, who had happened to visit the Ryder truck agency in Junction City, Kansas, near the time McVeigh did. However, several witnesses continued to state they had seen a third person in company with McVeigh and Nichols before the bombing, and the existence and identity of John Doe No. 2 remained a mystery. Although federal agents detained other individuals during their investigations, no further suspects were charged in the bombing. Timothy McVeigh and Terry Nichols were scheduled to go on trial in May 1996 in Lawton, Oklahoma, 90 miles southwest of Oklahoma City. If found guilty, they will face a death sentence.

McVeigh and Nichols joined the Army's First Infantry Division at Fort Riley, Kansas, on the same day in May 1988

and went through basic training together at Fort Benning, Georgia. According to residents of Decker, Michigan, McVeigh spent some time in the area during the winter of 1994-95 living with James Nichols in his two-story, white frame farmhouse. Neighbor Dan Stomber claimed the two brothers and McVeigh were amateur bombmakers who would invite him to watch them set off homemade bombs. It was their antigovernment convictions that led at least McVeigh, and quite possibly Terry Nichols, to search for comrades among the growing Michigan Militia, a right-wing antigovernment group founded in April 1994 that by 1995 had brigades in 66 of the state's 83 counties. The Militia moved quickly to repudiate any connection with McVeigh or the bombing, but the tragedy focused America's attention on the groups of right-wing zealots that had mushroomed around the country in the 90s.

After the blast, President Bill Clinton denounced the "loud and angry voices in America today whose sole goal seems to be to try to keep some people as paranoid as possible … They leave the impression, by their very words, that violence is acceptable." The President joined hundreds of mourners at a memorial service for the victims of the bombing in Oklahoma City on Sunday, April 23. On returning to Washington, he asked Congress for more power to fight terrorism. In addition to more money for counterterrorist activities, he asked the legislature to approve 1,000 new law-enforcement agents, to require explosive materials to carry chemical markers

THE MOURNERS Burying Chase and Colton Smith, ages three and two

making them easier to track and to permit U.S. military forces to take part in law enforcement. By year's end, a version of the bill seemed near approval.

At 9:02 a.m. on April 26, exactly one week from the time of the explosion that tore apart hundreds of lives, Oklahoma City came to another halt. Gathered at what used to be the Alfred P. Murrah Building, rescue teams stopped picking through the wreckage and stood in quiet reflection. All over the city, people bowed their heads. Outside of town, traffic stopped along Interstate 40. Beyond, in towns and cities around the country, in churches and offices and in the White House, the same pause was observed, as Americans contemplated the tragedies left in the wake of the twister of hate. For one minute, the unspeakable was commemorated by the unspoken. ∎

ZEALOTRY'S BITTER HARVEST

The Unabomber strikes again, a train is sabotaged, right-wing militias multiply—and even U.S. agents are accused of terrorism

SABOTAGE: Officials were baffled by the note left at the remote crash site

THE BOMBING OF THE FEDERAL BUILDING IN OKLA-homa City in late April was the most deadly act of terrorism ever committed on U.S. soil. The subse-quent arrest of two U.S. citizens as suspects was the first of several aftershocks that sparked fears of a heightened wave of domestic terrorism. Only five days after the Oklahoma bombing, the Unabomber, the deadly mail bomber who had killed two people and injured 22 over a period of 17 years, struck again. Later in the year, an Amtrak train in Arizona was deliberately derailed. More-over, Americans became aware of a shadowy subculture of right-wing militias whose railings against their own government, some charged, provided the fertile ground of paranoia that might encourage terrorists to strike out against their fellow citizens (*see box*). And, as if that were not enough, the U.S. government was itself charged with terrorism in two high-profile actions against U.S. citizens—the disastrous 1993 assault on the compound of religious-cult leader David Koresh in Waco, Texas, and the deadly 1992 siege of the home of white separatist Randy Weaver in Ruby Ridge, Idaho.

The Unabomber

The Unabomber struck first. On Monday, April 24, a package bomb, apparently intended for someone else, killed Gilbert Murray, 47, president of the California Forestry Association, in Sacramento. The blast was power-ful enough to knock two doors off their hinges. Soon a letter to the New York *Times* confirmed that the culprit behind the deed was the mysterious figure to whom the FBI had given the name Unabomber. "Through our bombings," said the letter, "we hope to promote social instability in industrial society ... and give encouragement to those who hate the industrial system." The bombings would end, the letter said, if a nationally prominent publication published a tract explaining the group's ideas. After months of soul searching, the New York *Times* and the Washington *Post* published the Unabomber's rambling anti-technology screed in September. But whether the bomber would keep his promise to end his campaign of terror remained to be seen.

On October 9, terrorists struck the federal train service, Amtrak. The system's *Sunset Limited* was en route from Miami to Los Angeles with 268 people aboard when it derailed in the middle of the night on a remote stretch of track in Arizona. The casualties: one crew member dead, 100 people injured. Evidence quickly led investigators to pronounce the crash sabotage. They discovered two rails deliberately uncoupled, a warning system deactivated and bolts to hold rails in place removed.

A message was found at the crash site from the so-called Sons of the Gestapo—a previously unknown group—that assailed the FBI and the Bureau of Alcohol, Tobacco and Firearms, as well as the agencies' roles in the controversial Waco and Ruby Ridge standoffs. Many immediately assumed that the crime was the work of an anti-government paramilitary group—a reasonable hypothesis, given that Arizona harbored several active militia organizations. But some authorities said the note might have been a deliberate red herring. At year's end, no arrests had been made in the *Sunset Limited* case.

Meanwhile, federal conduct in the two earlier incidents—Ruby Ridge and Waco—was probed in Washington, where congressional hearings delved into possible government culpability in the deaths of U.S. citizens. In July, House hearings into the 1993 federal assault against the Branch Davidian compound near Waco produced partisan sparks. Republicans accused federal agents of having bungled the operation. Democrats accused Republicans of having let the National Rifle Association influence key aspects of the committee investigation. Dramatic testimony also came from a teenager who described how sect leader David Koresh sexually molested her when she was 10. The government pledged to continue investigating the case.

In September a rapt Senate panel listened sympathetically to Randy Weaver's account of the deadly standoff that occurred between his family and the FBI at his remote Ruby Ridge cabin in 1992. The encounter, which began when federal agents came to arrest Weaver on firearms charges, resulted in the shooting death of Weaver's wife, his son and a federal marshal—and accusations that the FBI used excessive force to end the siege and then tried to cover it up. In their testimony, federal law-enforcement officials defended their initial decision to bring firearms charges against Weaver. The Justice Department said it would continue to investigate the controversial incident; five FBI officials involved in the siege had already been suspended.

The deadly bombings, the armed militiamen on the far right and the charges that even the government itself might have been guilty of terrorism left the uneasy sense that, in 1995, America's worst enemies were born in the U.S.A. ■

Patriots or Paranoids?

THE EXPLOSION IN OKLAHOMA CITY AND the other deadly acts of 1995 did more than just remind Americans that terrorism happens. In a nation that had entertained and appalled itself for years with overheated talk on the radio and the campaign trail, the inflamed rhetoric of the '90s became an unindicted co-conspirator in the blast. In their attempt to fathom the bombers' motives, many Americans discovered just how deep the paranoia ran among a small minority of their countrymen. And many feared that the antigovernment philosophy espoused by the generally law-abiding, self-described "patriots" of the far right may have helped plant thoughts of violence in the minds of less responsible citizens. The paramilitary organization, camouflage clothing and weekend war games favored by the increasing number of armed militia groups only added to the concern.

As many as 12 million Americans could be described as responsive to patriotic rhetoric about a sinister, out-of-control federal bureaucracy. The movement included followers of familiar elements of far-right thinking: tax protesters, Christian home-schoolers, conspiracy theorists, Second Amendment activists. A much smaller number, perhaps 100,000, were estimated to be

To arms! Wolverines in Michigan in winter training

militia members actively arming themselves against a government they saw as a kind of Great Satan—predatory, hostile and dangerous.

In a TIME/CNN poll taken a week after the Oklahoma bombing, 80% of Americans described the members of militia groups as dangerous; only 21% described them as patriots. And 68% of respondents thought the U.S. government should spy on the militias in order to monitor their activities—an act that might only feed the vigilantes' paranoia about the government. ■

The

Verdict

We, the jury in the above entitled action, find the defendant, Orenthal James Simpson, not guilty of the crime of murder

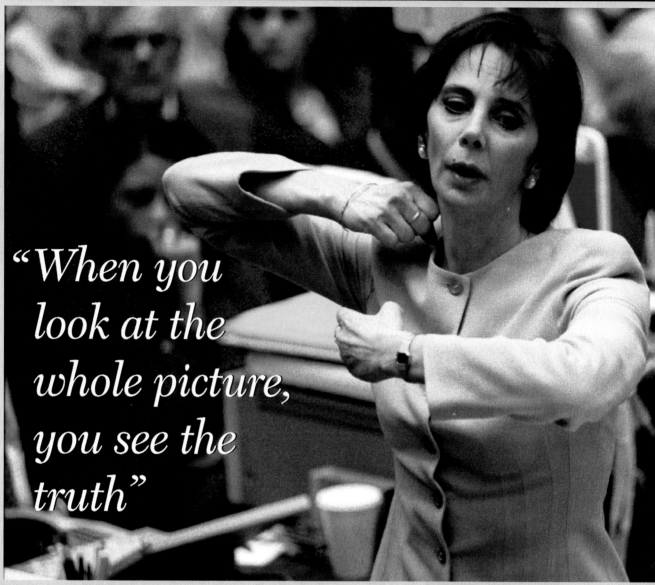

"When you look at the whole picture, you see the truth"

THE PROSECUTOR In her closing argument, Marcia Clark traced the path of the knife that slashed the victims' throats

T LEAST THERE WAS ONE MOMENT OF VISI-BLE black-and-white unity that emerged from the O.J. Simpson trial. It occurred on Tuesday, October 3, shortly after 10 a.m. Pacific time. In New York City crowds of citizens gathered together in Times Square like extras in the *War of the Worlds* movies of the 1950s, staring up at outdoor television screens, waiting for the word. In colleges and grade schools, in offices and beauty salons around the country, the scene was the same: all eyes turned to the television, to the screen that had played the double-homicide trial of the once beloved football star as a news-cum-soap opera maxiseries for the entire year. Black and white were united, briefly, in an anxious silence of the heart. As soon as the verdict was read, however, they split apart—they could watch themselves doing it on the split screens. On one side, jubilation; on the other, dismay.

"We, the jury in the above entitled action, find the defendant, Orenthal James Simpson, not guilty of the crime of murder … " intoned the clerk of the court. With those words, the end came at last, 474 days after Simpson, 48, one of America's most prominent black citizens, had been charged with the slaying of his estranged white wife, Nicole Brown Simpson, 35, and Ron Goldman, 25, a restaurant waiter. The bodies had been discovered outside Nicole Simpson's town house in the tony Los Angeles neighborhood of Brentwood, their throats brutally slashed by repeated thrusts from a knife.

Within minutes after the verdict—before the shock had even subsided—Simpson was a free man. In the sort of bizarre, made-for-television moment that had marked the case from its earliest days, he was returned to his Brentwood home in a white police vehicle that proceeded along the Los Angeles freeways, filmed from overhead by helicopter cameras. Sixteen months before, on Friday, June 17, 1994, America had watched, transfixed, as Simpson cowered in the back of his white Bronco, pointing a gun to his head, while his old football crony A.C. Cowlings drove him down

"Stop this cover-up! If you don't stop it, then who?"

THE DEFENDER Injecting racial fears into the trial, Johnnie Cochran closed by invoking past police mistreatment of blacks

those same freeways—destination unknown. Simpson and Cowlings had finally returned to Simpson's home in the Bronco, and O.J. had given himself up. He was charged with two counts of homicide. L.A. District Attorney Gil Garcetti appointed his strongest prosecutor, Marcia Clark, 41, to try the case, and Clark selected Christopher Darden, 39, a serious, bespectacled black attorney, as her assistant.

For his part, Simpson assembled a "Dream Team" of lawyers to plead his case, headed by noted defense attorney Robert Shapiro. Among the famous names sitting at O.J.'s bench were Harvard professor Alan Dershowitz and longtime celebrity advocate F. Lee Bailey. Joining the team late was the well-known black attorney from Los Angeles Johnnie Cochran Jr, 57. Renowned for his legal brilliance and for such high-profile clients as Michael Jackson, Cochran—one of the smoothest, best-connected lawyers in the city—won Simpson's trust and became the undisputed leader of the defense team, shoving Shapiro aside.

At the insistence of Gil Garcetti, the trial was held in downtown Los Angeles, rather than in the wealthy neighborhood where the crime had taken place. Garcetti wanted to avoid having Simpson tried by his neighbors from the predominantly white neighborhood. He also insisted on a multiracial jury, hoping to keep racial tensions out of the trial. Blacks had rioted only three years before in L.A. when police officers were acquitted in the beating of black traffic offender Rodney King, and racial animosities were foremost in Garcetti's mind. California Superior Court Judge Lance Ito, 44, the son of Japanese-American immigrants, was appointed to preside over the trial, and a predominantly black jury was selected.

The trial began on January 24. It hinged on four main elements: the past relationship of Simpson and his wife, with documented instances of Simpson's physical abuse of Nicole; the gloves the prosecution claimed Simpson wore during the killing; the character of Mark Fuhrman, the detective who found the gloves; and the relatively new forensic identification technology based on DNA blood samples.

HALLELUJAH! Simpson's mother Eunice and her family greeted the verdict with rejoicing and tears

BIG SHOT Famed attorney F. Lee Bailey accused Mark Fuhrman of racism

BIGOT Fuhrman denied it, but tapes caught him using the "N word" repeatedly

Ronald Goldman's Family

SHOCK Goldman's father and sister weep after the verdict

For many observers, the extensive record of Simpson's past abuse of his wife was at once the saddest and most damning revelation of the trial. There was plenty of evidence in the 85 pages of court documents, many of them sworn statements by witnesses. Here was O.J. throwing Nicole against a wall, knocking her to a sidewalk, shattering her car windshield with a baseball bat, locking her in a wine closet—the alleged episodes unfolding one after another in the courtroom. And recorded 911 calls from a frightened Nicole revealed a Simpson who was ranting, profane, out of control.

OVER STRONG DEFENSE OBJECTIONS, Judge Ito ruled that the evidence of abuse could be entered in the trial, and it became a bulwark of Marcia Clark's case. But the second pillar of her case— the testimony of Mark Fuhrman—would end in a clear victory for the defense. Fuhrman, 43, was a 19-year veteran of the police force. He had been one of the first investigators to arrive on the scene, and he had found what the the prosecution believed was its most damning evidence, the "bloody gloves"— allegedly Simpson's and allegedly covered with Nicole Simpson's blood. Fuhrman said he had found the gloves separately—one at the murder scene at Nicole's townhouse, the other at Simpson's estate. But defense attorneys suggested that Fuhrman was a liar and a racist who might have planted the gloves to frame Simpson.

Taking the stand in March, Fuhrman offered a methodical account of his movements after the crime, an account designed to show he couldn't have tampered with the evidence. Fuhrman coolly parried defense attorney F. Lee Bailey and repeatedly denied having made racist statements about "niggers"—which quickly became known to the TV audience as the "N word"—claiming that he had not used the epithet in the past 10 years. He also denied suggestions that he had planted the glove to frame Simpson.

In May the prosecution introduced the allegedly incriminating results of DNA blood tests. Forensic scientists Robin Cotton and Gary Sims testified that blood drops found at the crime scene, in O.J.'s Bronco and at his estate matched Simpson's—with only a 1-in-170 million chance of error. In addition, they said, blood found on a sock at Simpson's estate matched his slain ex-wife's, with an even smaller margin of error. But the defense hammered away at the possibility that the blood used in the tests might have been contaminated or planted to frame Simpson.

As the prosecution team slowly moved to its conclusion, it committed its greatest blunder. Christopher Darden, Marcia Clark's second-in-command, had been told by his supervisors not to make a show of the gloves. But impetuously he asked Simpson to try them on. The defense had anticipated the move and had coached Simpson's response. Simpson at first struggled to pull on the supposedly incriminating gloves, then turned toward the jury, raised his half-gloved hands and proclaimed dramatically, "They're too small." Darden quickly suggested that Simpson was faking his difficulty, then solicited expert testimony that the blood-soaked leather gloves had shrunk. But the

THE JUDGE Lance Ito angered some attorneys when he invited them to watch videotapes of Jay Leno's parodic "Dancing Itos"

MAN IN THE MIDDLE Some blacks accused prosecutor Christopher Darden of being a traitor

WITNESS California-cool O.J. tenant Kato Kaelin became a minor celebrity

JUROR Brenda Moran said the jury needed little time to find the prosecution's case unconvincing

NO! After the verdict, a mainly white crowd in California is shocked

YES! Blacks, hearing the news, celebrate outside the courtroom

damage had been done. A week later, Simpson tried on a pristine pair of gloves, matching the size, make and style of the original pair, and this time they fit. But the image of him struggling to put on the gloves clearly stayed with the jury.

FINALLY, ON JULY 6, AFTER 92 DAYS OF TESTImony, 58 witnesses and more than 400 exhibits, the prosecution rested, and Cochran's team took the offensive. As expected, the defense attorneys attacked each point in Clark's case, arguing that the blood samples and other evidence had been poorly handled and that Simpson's previous abuse of his wife was not relevant to the murder inquiry. But they soon focused in on the character of the prosecution's star witness, Fuhrman.

In September a damning set of tapes was presented by the defense, based on a screenwriter's nine years of interviews with Fuhrman, conducted while she was researching police life for a screenplay. Judge Ito ruled that jurors could hear two relatively tame snippets—out of at least 41 instances—from the interview tapes. The excerpts testified to the detective's vocal hatred of blacks and his repeated use of the "N-word"—the very charges he had denied on the stand.

Earlier, with the jury absent, more excerpts from the tapes had been played, and a shocked courtroom had heard Fuhrman boast, in unrelentingly vile language, of beating suspects and lying about evidence in earlier cases. Ito ruled that those tales largely had no relevance to the Simpson case, but even the excerpts heard by the jury were devastating. Moreover, another witness separately testified that Fuhrman had told her that if he wanted to arrest an interracial couple, he would invent a charge if necessary. The nine African Americans on the jury looked enraged.

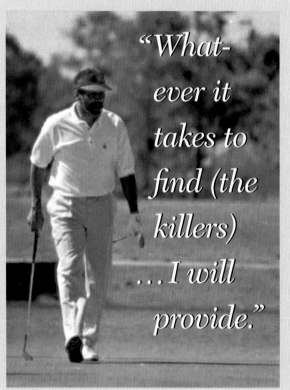

"Whatever it takes to find (the killers) ... I will provide."

FREE AT LAST **But Simpson faced scorn—and civil suits**

With that triumph the defense rested, and even those few Americans who had somehow managed to ignore the circuslike trial now tuned in as prosecutor Clark and defense attorney Cochran delivered their closing arguments. Clark dropped Fuhrman hard in her closing remarks, vehemently repudiating him as a racist and a liar, but standing by her tale of the gloves. She ended her summation with the chilling sounds of Nicole Brown Simpson's pleading 911 calls to police. While a screen flashed pictures of Nicole's bruised face, followed by pictures of Nicole and Ronald Goldman in death, the families of the victims wept.

In his closing arguments, Cochran played off the Darden glove gambit. "If it doesn't fit, you must acquit," he told the jury. Then he played to the black members of the panel by reminding them how often African Americans had been mistreated by racist police and urging them to use a not-guilty verdict to send a message against racism and police misconduct. Later, Robert Shapiro would accuse Cochran of having played the race card, "dealt from the bottom of the deck."

On Monday, October 2, the jurors retired for deliberation—and after less than four hours sent word that they had reached a verdict. The news stunned the country, which had been expecting a much longer deliberation. When the verdict was announced to a breathless nation, the polarization along racial lines was instantaneous. Many white Americans pronounced themselves surprised and bewildered—64% in a CBS News poll taken just before the trial ended said they believed Simpson was guilty. But the black reaction nationwide was epitomized by a hallful of black law students at Howard University who exploded out of their seats, cheering.

Some whites accused the jury of racial bias, but black juror Brenda Moran claimed the verdict had been based strictly on the prosecution's failure to present convincing evidence. Meanwhile, Simpson's return to his estate sparked a huge party, with O.J. joining Johnnie Cochran and others for a rendition of *Amazing Grace.*

O.J. Simpson would need more than grace: he had seen his reputation trashed and had depleted his fortune trying to defend it. Although a pariah among most of his countrymen, he was also a free man who wanted his good name back and his children returned. He faced a fight on both fronts. Simpson was subject to two civil suits—one from Ron Goldman's parents and a second from Nicole's father Louis Brown. The wrongful-death actions carried no threat of jail time, but they could cost millions of dollars to fight and tens of millions in damages if Simpson lost them. The civil suits were scheduled to begin in 1996. Simpson pledged to devote himself to finding his wife's real killer, but his critics delighted in pointing out that his quest seemed to center on golf courses.

The endless questions raised by the case—about Simpson's guilt or innocence, America's racial divides and its embattled system of justice—would be analyzed for years. But behind all the obscurities loomed a single compelling fact: two people had been brutally butchered, and someone had got away with murder. ∎

MARCHING FOR HOPE

Black men throng the capital to renew their values—and themselves

SOMETIMES IT TAKES A RIOT TO MAKE America think long and hard about itself. Sometimes it takes a flood. This flood was a human flood, and it poured into Washington on Monday, Oct. 16. By the hundreds of thousands, black men of all ages, of every standing and occupation and from every part of the country gathered for the Million Man March. They came together for the stated purpose of condemning racism, declaring their own personal sense of purpose and responsibility and pledging to their families and communities their best efforts to build a more equitable and violence-free society.

HOW LONG? Farrakhan's speech lasted two hours

But there was more to it than that. By the simple fact of their numbers, by the sheer power of the head counts and the wide-angle copter shots that still couldn't capture the whole crowd, they were there to remind Americans that, even in a time of conservatism and backlash, the business of racism and inequality would not be ignored.

Among those who addressed the seven-hour rally were poet Maya Angelou and civil rights activists Jesse Jackson and Rosa Parks. The controversial organizer of the march, Nation of Islam leader Louis Farrakhan, concluded the event with a two-hour, meandering address laced with fiery denunciations of white racism and the white establishment. The National Park Service initially estimated that the march drew 400,000 demonstrators to the National Mall, but later conceded that the count may have been considerably higher. March organizers said it was

HOW MANY? After the rally, March organizers said the National Park Service's crowd estimate was far too low

more like a million and threatened to sue to prove it. Whatever the number, it was more than enough to qualify as a critical mass.

Critical for blacks and whites alike. Coming just two weeks after the verdict in the O.J. Simpson trial, the march was another reminder that race is the inescapable complication of American life. For the black men who were there, it was a moment of profound psychological vindication. In the most heated political and policy debates of recent years, black men have seen themselves cast as the welfare freeloader, the affirmative-action hire, the low end of the bell curve, Willie Horton. The facts are often worse than the stereotypes. For black men the average life expectancy is 65, eight years less than for white males. For young black men, the major cause of death is murder. Nearly 1 in every 3 black men between 20 and 29 years of age is behind bars, on probation or on parole.

In a TIME/CNN poll conducted the week before the event, 56% of blacks questioned did not think discrimination against them would ever diminish. Only 27% of whites agreed. While 65% of whites thought that race relations would eventually improve, only 44% of blacks did.

For one day in October, all that was swept aside by the picture of black males urgently but peacefully demonstrating their strength and capability. It was a mood that even Louis Farrakhan couldn't spoil. His purpose may have been to capitalize on the prominence a successful gathering would confer. For most of those who attended, however, the main point was comradeship, pride and rededication to strong core values. ■

Safe at last, Scott O'Grady celebrates his great escape

RESCUE IN BOSNIA

What a save! On June 8, after surviving on rainwater, insects and grass for six days in Serb-held territory in Bosnia, U.S. F-16 pilot Scott O'Grady emerged from a pine forest with his pistol in hand and fell exhausted through the door of a U.S. helicopter. "Thank you! Thank you!" he yelled before collapsing in sobs. O'Grady had played hide-and-seek from searching Serbs after ejecting from his fighter when it was hit by an SA-6 surface-to-air missile fired from a Bosnian-Serb stronghold. He was located after an extensive search by spy satellites and a host of Air Force jets.

PACKWOOD PACKS IT IN

On September 8, precisely 24 hours after first learning of the unanimous, bipartisan call by the Senate Ethics Committee for his expulsion, Bob Packwood stood on the floor of the U.S. Senate, his voice trembling, and said, "Duty. Honor. Country. It is my duty to resign. It is the honorable thing to do for this country, for this Senate." The Ethics Committee's 10-volume, 40-lb., 10,145-page report lambasted Oregon's junior Senator for dishonoring the Senate. The report detailed three violations of Senate laws and rules, sexual misconduct that involved at least 17 unwelcome advances toward women

Senator and friend, 1969

between 1969 and 1990, improper use of his political office for financial gain, and, most damagingly, obstruction of the panel's inquiry by tampering with portions of his diaries. Women's groups hailed Packwood's fall.

A DEFIANT SHEIK: GUILTY OF CONSPIRACY

After an eight-month trial, Sheik Omar Abdel Rahman was convicted in early October on 48 of 50 conspiracy charges for plotting a terror campaign against the U.S. The blind Egyptian cleric and nine co-defendants were found guilty of conspiring to assassinate political leaders and to blow up the United Nations headquarters building and other New York City targets. The proceedings constituted the biggest terrorism trial in U.S. history. Although the deadly bombing of New York City's World Trade Center in February 1993 was considered to be part of the conspiracy, none of the 10 defendants was charged with carrying out that bombing. Four other militant Muslims had been sentenced for participating in that plot in 1994. Unrepentant to the end, the sheik told TIME in an interview on the eve of his conviction that the trial was unfair and that the U.S. media in general were racist. The sheik, prophet in absentia of the

The blind Sheik claimed to see U.S. injustice everywhere

deadly Muslim fundamentalist movement that has destabilized Hosni Mubarak's Egypt, denounced Mubarak as an "obedient dog of the West." Sentencing for the charges was set to take place in 1996.

....

DR. FOSTER SWALLOWS SOME BITTER MEDICINE

Pleading for confirmation

Succumbing to a lethal combination of abortion politics and presidential aspirants, President Clinton's nomination of Dr. Henry W. Foster Jr. to succeed Joycelyn Elders as Surgeon General died on the Senate floor in late June. Initially, Foster seemed an ideal candidate for Surgeon General; he spent most of his career tending to the poor in the inner city of Nashville and preaching sexual abstinence to teenagers. But the nomination became particularly controversial after Foster, whose practice was obstetrics and gynecology, offered differing accounts of how many abortions he had performed in the course of his career. G.O.P. presidential hopefuls Bob Dole and Phil Gramm vied to take credit for scuttling the doctor's nomination.

One N.R.A. aim: legalize TEC-9 assault weapons

BUSHWHACKED

Bull's-eye! The National Rifle Association generally attacks politicians, but this time the tables were turned. Former President George Bush, an ardent hunter, denounced the language in an N.R.A. fund-raising letter that railed against federal agents as "jackbooted thugs … wearing Nazi bucket helmets and black storm-trooper uniforms." Bush resigned his life membership in the organization, noting that a Secret Service man once assigned to his detail had been among those killed in the Oklahoma City bombing only weeks before. N.R.A. executive vice president Wayne LaPierre offered a semi-apology for the letter, declaring,"If anyone thought [our] intention was to paint all federal law-enforcement officials with the same broad brush, I'm sorry." While the N.R.A. was widely condemned for the letter, it was making a powerful comeback. Armed with a combative message that posits a tyrannical government as its main adversary, the 124-year-old organization was at peak power, with revenues and membership surging.

A TOUGH FACE FOR U.S. LABOR

Beset by corporate downsizing and harsh union-busting tactics, America's labor movement has seen its share of the U.S. work force shrink from about 35% in the mid-1960s to just 15% in 1995. But a new day for labor dawned when John J. Sweeney, president of the Service Employees International Union, defeated incumbent Thomas Donahue to become president of the AFL-CIO after a bitterly fought race. Sweeney, 61, promised a more militant voice for unions and pledged to stanch the membership decline. He immediately lent strong support to a 2-month strike by Boeing workers that ended in a victory for the union in December.

WHITEWATER SCENTS

The G.OP. was in power in the Senate—and the search was on for damaging details on Whitewater, the failed Arkansas land deal that had bedeviled the Clintons since they came to the White House. The bloodhound-in-chief: scrappy Senator Al D'Amato of New York, a close associate of presidential hopeful Bob Dole. In November, D'Amato's committee accused Clinton aides of improperly obtaining information in 1993 from federal investigators probing the deal, and demanded the President turn over notes of a meeting on the subject. The White House refused, claiming executive and attorney-client privileges. Shortly before Christmas the President yielded—but, with independent counsel Kenneth

D'Amato is D'ubious

Starr's separate investigation still under way in Little Rock, 1996 promised to be a big year for Whitewater—and for D'Amato.

AN AFFIRMATIVE NO!

For years, conservative Republicans railed without success against America's system of affirmative action, the federal programs that seek to redress decades of imbalance by suggesting race and gender standards in U.S. institutions. But in the wake of their sweeping victory in the 1994 elections, pumped-up G.O.P. opponents of the 30-year-old program set out to deconstruct it. The crusade was a hot button on the campaign trail for G.O.P. presidential hopefuls; even some Democrats put President Clinton on notice that they wanted to overhaul the program, a route that might have threatened the Democrats' support among minorities and women. In July, Clinton surprised many by offering a strong defense of the program, though he conceded that reforms were necessary. His proposed solution: "Mend it, don't end it." ■

Rallying California janitors won recognition for their union

SOLDIER *of* PEACE

The assassination of Prime Minister Yitzhak Rabin strikes at the soul of Israel and threatens its contentious quest for peace

S *hir Ha-Shalom.* The song of peace. In a rare moment of elation for the dour leader, Yitzhak Rabin tucked a leaflet with the lyrics to *Shir Ha-Shalom* into his breast pocket and sang along with the 100,000 people who had gathered to support him one Saturday evening in November on Kings of Israel Square in the heart of Tel Aviv. Such moments came all too infrequently to the embattled Premier in 1995, when Arab and Jewish extremists, equally intent on murdering the tenuous accords between Israel and the Palestinians, held center stage. But this starlit night, the message was different. The 73-year-old Prime Minister of Israel exhorted the crowd to go forward down the road to which he had committed Israel in September 1993. "There are enemies of the peace process, and they try to hurt us," he said. "But violence undermines democracy and must be denounced."

Rabin seemed to be unusually buoyed by the outpouring of support and affection coming from the largest assembly the square had ever seen. Yet watchers could not shake off all their fears. In the course of the rally one man, Meir Doron, walked up to a journalist and asked, "Don't you think Rabin ought to be wearing a flak jacket in a situation like this?" The journalist shrugged, and Doron made his way over to Leah Rabin, the Prime Minister's wife, and asked her if she thought her husband was safe. She looked sharply at him, put her finger to her lips and said, "Shhh. Don't say such things. I don't believe any-one is capable of doing anything like that."

When the rally ended, Rabin walked off the podium and down a stairway leading to a sheltered area where an armored Cadillac awaited him. Just as the Prime Minister was stepping into the limousine, at 9:40 p.m., a man came up behind him with a .22-cal. pistol in his hand. The assassin, a 25-year-old Jewish militant named Yigal Amir, fired two shots from only eight feet away. The hollow-point bullets smashed into Rabin, who had always refused to wear a bulletproof vest. One ruptured his spleen; the other severed major arteries in his chest and shattered his spinal

MOURNING The Clintons joined world leaders at Rabin's funeral

cord, drenching in blood the leaflet in his pocket, the Song of Peace.

As a phalanx of security personnel grabbed Amir and slammed him up against the wall of an adjacent shopping center, another set of bodyguards cradled the stricken leader into the car, then rushed him to nearby Ichilov Hospital. When Rabin arrived, he had no pulse and no blood pressure; after heroic efforts to stop the massive bleeding, his doctors acknowledged failure. At 11:15 p.m., Eitan Haber, the Prime Minister's chief of staff, emerged from the hospital to announce for all the world to hear: "Rabin is dead!"

In Israel news of the assassination sent thousands to the Western Wall in Jerusalem, the wall that Rabin had helped capture as the Israeli army's chief of staff in the Six-Day War of 1967. Born in Israel in 1922, of Russian descent, Rabin had been a fighter all his life. As a young rebel against British rule, he was invited by the swashbuckling Moshe Dayan to join the Palmach, the élite strike force of the underground army Haganah during World War II. He fought with distinction in the War of Independence of 1948 and spent several years afterward in training, building and equipping the Israeli army, rising to be its chief of staff in 1964. In 1967 Rabin prosecuted the Six-Day War brilliantly: he coordinated maneuvers against Egypt, Jordan and Syria that enabled the army to take so much ground in the Sinai, the western banks of the Jordan River and the Golan Heights that the territory under Israel's control swelled three-fold. Later he served as Israel's ambassador to the U.S. and as Prime Minister from 1974 to 1977.

Rabin was Israel's Defense Minister during the Palestinian *intifadeh,* and he ultimately became convinced— grudgingly—that Israel would never rest while it tried to administer the hostile occupied territories. Elected Prime Minister again in 1992, Rabin soon began the gutsy peace process that culminated in his famous handshake with Yasser Arafat in Washington in September 1993.

Because of the logistical difficulties involved in getting world leaders to Israel within the customary 24-hour period between death and burial, Rabin's state funeral was put off a day—until Monday afternoon. More than 60 world leaders, including President Clinton and former Presidents George Bush and Jimmy Carter, gathered in Jerusalem as Rabin was laid to rest on Mount Herzl, burial ground of Israeli heroes. P.L.O. Chairman Yasser Arafat, who did not attend the funeral, later made a quiet 90-minute visit to Tel Aviv to offer condolences to Rabin's widow.

The first political assassination in the nation's short history left Israelis

❝Enemies of the peace process ... try to hurt us. But violence must be denounced. ❞

in utter shock. First there was the fact of a Jew killing a Jew. In a land where every Jewish life is counted precious, there could be no greater horror. But in the two years after Rabin had embarked on his controversial peace with the Palestinians, the farther reaches of Israel's radical right had grown bold in their threats to subvert the process and preserve their dream of a Greater Israel to the Jordan River. Posters of Rabin in a kaffiyeh, in a Nazi uniform, with blood on his hands, began appearing at rallies protesting the expansion of Palestinian self-rule. For months, Rabin's Labor Party had complained that the opposition Likud, psychological compatriot of the extremists in its dislike of the peace plan, was fomenting an atmosphere in which someone might resort to violence.

That someone turned out to be Amir, a third-year law student at the religious Bar Ilan University. One of eight children raised in an Orthodox family in Herzliyya, a town north of Tel Aviv, Amir was quiet and unprepossessing, except when it came to the subject of peace with the Arabs. He fraternized with members of a right-wing group called Eyal, also known as the Fighting Jews. According to a friend, Amir once said he felt he had to do something to stop the peace process, but the friend dismissed Amir's words as an empty threat.

Police discovered a large cache of weapons and explosives at Amir's home. He told authorities he acted alone, but Israeli police questioned many people as suspected accomplices in the case. In December, Amir was charged with murder, and his brother Hagai and their friend Dror Adani were charged with conspiring in the deed.

Rabin's departure had profound implications, for it was his leadership that made the peace process possible. Was his removal sufficient to still it? Likud leader Benjamin Netanyahu condemned the assassination, saying "We must vomit from among us those who do not abide by one of the most basic rules of society: Thou shalt not kill." Yet he reaffirmed his virulent opposition to the peace accords, showing no signs of conciliation.

But Shimon Peres, Rabin's ally in the quest for peace and the new head of the government, confirmed his commitment to Rabin's policies in a television address after the murder. Referring to the Song of Peace, Peres said, "He put this song in his pocket, and the bullet went through this song. But the song of peace ringing in our ears will not end." Stirring words. Yet even as Peres spoke, anthems of war were ringing in other ears, from the right-wingers in Israel to the hard-liners in the West Bank and the Gaza Strip. ∎

ASSASSIN: Yigal Amir in police custody

MOVE OUT! M.J. Begosh, a land mine victim and the first U.S. G.I. wounded in Bosnia, is evacuated

■ THE BALKANS

NATO TO THE RES

Bill Clinton sends in the troops in a gamble to bring peace to Bosnia

OR THE FIRST AMERICAN G.I.S ENCAMPED IN TUZLA, A town of some 460,000 in the republic of Bosnia and Herzegovina, there was no need to dream of a white Christmas: a deep snow had accumulated all around their tents. The treetops may have glistened, Muslim children may have listened—but the Christmas dinner was the T-rations the grunts despised, the carols were sung to the hum of noisy electric generators and the frosty air was filled with the stench of diesel fumes.

The U.S. soldiers would never be mistaken for angelic messengers, but their mission was suitable for the season: they were peacekeepers, and they heralded the arrival of 20,000 American forces dispatched by President Bill Clinton to help end the gruesome war in the Balkans.

In 1995, after 44 months of relentless fighting that left tens of thousands dead and nearly 3 million homeless, the promise of peace had come at last to the brutalized republics of the former Yugoslavia. The opportunity arose because the United States and its NATO allies had conducted a strong, two-pronged offensive—on the battlefield and at the bargaining table. Their efforts culminated in the December signing of a peace pact in Paris by the Presidents of the three republics involved in the carnage: Slobodan Milosevic of Serbia, Franjo Tudjman of Croatia

and Alija Izetbegovic of Bosnia and Herzegovina.

The pact was a personal triumph for Bill Clinton and for the high-flying U.S. diplomat who brokered it, Richard Holbrooke. Yet America itself was deeply divided about the ransom it required: the detachment of U.S. soldiers into an arena distinguished for its deep racial and religious hatreds, its history of "ethnic cleansing" and its savage use of rape and civilian atrocities.

Through the first half of 1995, peace seemed as elusive as ever for the three nations, which had known little but war since 1991, when the provinces of the federated state of Yugoslavia began seceding to become independent republics. The Serbs, an Orthodox ethnic group outnumbered by Muslims and others in the republic of Bosnia and Herzegovina, were still fighting to escape becoming a permanent minority inside an independent, Muslim-led Bosnia. Led by ex-psychiatrist Dr. Radovan Karadzic and General Ratko Mladic and supported by their comrades in Milosevic's Serbia, the rebel Serbs inside Bosnia controlled 70% of the nation's territory. The Roman Catholic Croats had entered into a surprising alliance with the Bosnian Muslims in 1994, but had seen relatively little fighting. Then a sequence of events that began in midsummer altered the balance of power with stunning rapidity and ended in the peace treaty.

First, several Muslim areas designated as "safe havens" by the U.N. peacekeeping force in Bosnia fell to the Serbs in July, convincing Clinton to adopt a firmer stance. Next came a crucial meeting in London that resulted in a shift of authority in the field from the U.N. to NATO. Finally, in early August, Tudjman's Croats launched a scorching assault on the Serbs aimed at regaining former Croatian territory lost earlier in the war. Suddenly, the Serbs were on the defensive.

The turning point came in a single remarkable week in late August. On Monday the Serbs mounted a mortar attack on Sarajevo, Bosnia's besieged capital, that killed 43. On Wednesday NATO launched the largest combat operation in its history, finally pounding the Serbs with bombing sorties after years of fruitless bluffing. By Friday, a diplomatic breakthrough had occurred, with all parties agreeing to meet in Geneva in September to talk. A cease-fire reached in Geneva led to 21 days of "proximity talks" at Wright-Patterson Air Force Base near Dayton, Ohio. Those talks, in turn, led to peace—and to American troops singing Christmas carols in Tuzla.

THE MARCH TO PEACE BEGAN WITH THE FALL OF TWO U.N.-designated "safe areas" for Muslims, Srebrenica and Zepa. The double defeat was an immense public humiliation for America, its NATO allies and the U.N., which had designated six such sanctuaries in 1993: Zepa, Gorazde and Srebrenica in the east, Tuzla and Bihac in the north, and the capital, Sarajevo. But the drastically undermanned U.N. force defending the two havens wilted as the Bosnian Serbs overran them. Two days after the Serbs took Srebrenica, all but a few of its 42,000 Muslims had been expelled. The conquering general of the Bosnian Serbs, Ratko Mladic, swaggered in triumph among the defeated, issuing orders, while his troops butchered some 4,000 Muslim men and raped Muslim women. A few days later the Serbs overran Zepa, 10 miles southwest of Srebrenica, where 16,000 Muslims were harbored. The inability of the United Nations and NATO to do anything to limit the Serbs' brutality was searing.

Galvanized into action, the NATO allies met in London and agreed to scrap the so-called dual-key arrangement with the U.N., which had given Secretary-General Boutros Boutros-Ghali veto authority over NATO air strikes. The allies eventually agreed on a plan that called for "substantial and decisive air strikes" should the Serbs threaten the sanctuaries. For three weeks the Serbs avoided testing the NATO ultimatum—they had other problems on their mind.

In a stunning blitz beginning on August 4, Franjo Tudjman's Croatian army took only five days to conquer Krajina, the crescent-shaped region of Croatia whose Serb majority had seceded from Croatia in 1991 with the help and encouragement of the Serbs' Milosevic. The defeat set some 150,000 Serbs fleeing, the largest exodus of refugees since the Balkan wars began. The Bosnian Serbs had suffered a terrible setback. Critically, Milosevic had not come to their aid: his interests had turned toward peace as his nation suffered in the grip of a crippling U.N. economic embargo. Division had come to the Serb camp.

Then, on August 28, Bosnian Serb forces in the hills surrounding Sarajevo had fired a mortar shell into a market in the Bosnian capital, killing 43 people and wounding 80. Certain they faced "a test of the London rules," NATO allies agreed on a retaliatory attack. On Wednesday morning NATO planes began bombing Bosnian Serb positions near Sarajevo. Artillery units on the ground joined the attack. The air raids lasted for two weeks, and ultimately some 2,000 sorties were flown. But they achieved their most important result. After meeting for only seven hours in Geneva, the foreign ministers of the warring nations agreed, in a one-page document, on the division of Bosnia and Herzegovina into a Serb republic and a Muslim-Croat federation. But the Geneva pact was only a starter's gun for the U.S.'s Holbrooke. Under his energetic hectoring, the warring sides agreed to a cease-fire and attendance at a peace conference near Dayton under U.S. patronage.

In isolated Dayton, the mediators endured negotiations for twenty hours a day under virtual house arrest. After 21 days, succumbing to the tag-team ministrations of Holbrooke and U.S. Secretary of State Warren Christopher, the three rival Presidents emerged with a treaty. It called for Bosnia and Herzegovina to be divided into two republics: a Muslim-Croat federation occupying 51% of the former republic and a Serb state occupying 49%. The two halves of the new Bosnian nation would be brought under the umbrella of a central government, with a collective presidency. Sarajevo would remain, at least in name, an "undivided city," but would be partitioned into nine self-governing ethnic zones. The peace accord would be enforced by an Implementation Force (I-FOR) of 60,000 NATO troops, including 20,000 U.S. soldiers.

Clinton had forcefully asserted U.S. leadership in the Balkans. There was only one problem: the American people were actively hostile to the notion of American leadership if it required risking American lives. Though his commitment of troops did not require congressional approval, the President wanted the legislature's benediction before he sent in the troops. He went on nationwide television to call for support, saying that the U.S. needed to halt a bloody and destabilizing war in Europe and to maintain its leadership in the world and in NATO. He promised that U.S. troops would remain in Bosnia no longer than the one year required under the peace pact.

BUT AMERICA REMAINED DUBIOUS. A TIME/CNN POLL showed 55% of those questioned opposing the policy. Clinton's critics seemed mainly concerned by the possibility of the kind of "mission creep" that had ended in death for American troops on a similar mission in Somalia, and by the lack of a sound "exit strategy" for the U.S. forces. But Senate majority leader Bob Dole, Clinton's would-be opponent for the presidency in 1996, gave his cautious support. The Senate grudgingly passed a resolution supporting the troops but not necessarily their mission. The House voted against the Administration's policy, though it failed to pass a motion to cut off funding for it.

In late December the first U.S. forces began arriving in Tuzla, the headquarters of their patrol sector; ultimately they would be joined by troops from 32 other nations in Operation Joint Endeavor. They faced danger not only from hostile locals, but also from land mines—more than 2 million had been sown in the former Yugoslavia. Military policeman Martin John Begosh of Rockville, Maryland, became the first American injured when he drove over a land mine. Meanwhile, heavy snows and floods slowed the arrival of the Americans, even as they halted fighting in the region. As Christmas came to Tuzla, it seemed that even Mother Nature wanted peace in Bosnia. ∎

BRITISH SECTOR
Some 13,000 British soldiers, 4,500 of whom are already serving in Bosnia as peacekeepers, will oversee the implementation of the treaty here. More than 2,000 Dutch and 850 Czech troops will join them.

AMERICAN SECTOR
This is where the U.S. will deploy most of its 20,000 troops. A Nordic brigade, consisting of soldiers from Denmark, Finland, Norway, Latvia, Estonia and Poland, will also serve in this sector, while 1,800 Russian troops will patrol the dangerous Posavina corridor.

LAND MINES
The 2 million to 6 million antitank and antipersonnel mines scattered throughout the former Yugoslavia pose the greatest threat to the troops in Bosnia. Many of the mines are made of plastic, which hinders detection. Their fuses may contain enough metal to enable sensitive equipment to locate them, but snow makes this task especially difficult.

PMA–2 Antipersonnel

▨ MINED AREAS

⊙ SECTOR HEADQUARTERS

FRENCH SECTOR
About 10,000 French troops—6,800 of them current peacekeepers—and 5,000 soldiers from Portugal, Spain, Italy and Ukraine will patrol this area. NATO rapid-reaction forces and some American troops will also set up headquarters in Kiseljak. Along with Sarajevo and Gorazde, this is perhaps the most dangerous sector of all.

CROATIA
SERB REPUBLIC
Posavina corridor
Bihac
Sanski Most
Doboj
Brcko
Banja Luka
Tuzla
Jajce
SERBIA
CROATIA
REPUBLIC OF BOSNIA AND HERZEGOVINA
Gornji Vakuf
Srebrenica
Kiseljak
Zepa
FEDERATION OF BOSNIA AND HERZEGOVINA
Sarajevo
YUGOSLAVIA
Gorazde
25 mi.
50 km
Source: Defense Department, UN Department of Peacekeeping Operations, State Department
TIME Map by Steve Hart
Mostar
Adriatic Sea

POISONOUS PROPHET

The guru of a bizarre cult
is charged with a deadly,
horrifying nerve-gas attack
on Tokyo's subway system

GAS GURU? Shoko Asahara

O N MONDAY, MARCH 20, ONLY TWO MONTHS after an earthquake devastated Kobe, one of its largest cities, Japan was assailed by the most synthetic of catastrophes: a poison created by man, and a madness that was strictly human. In a painstakingly planned atrocity, a diluted form of a nerve gas called sarin, a weapon of mass killing used by the Nazis, was placed simultaneously in five Tokyo subway cars at the morning rush hour, killing 12 people and sickening thousands more.

The experience of those riding Tokyo's Hibiya line was typical. A man in a surgical mask—not an uncommon sight during Japan's hay fever season—boarded, found a seat and almost immediately began fiddling with a foot-long rectangular object wrapped in newspapers. At the next stop he set the package on the floor and strode briskly from the train. Riders began edging away from a pool of liquid that was forming on the floor near the object, bothered by its offensive smell. By Kamiyacho station, 11 minutes after the strange man had boarded, commuters panicked and ran from the train. But the gas had done its work. Some riders collapsed, vomiting. Others staggered up three flights of stairs to fresh air. The gas temporarily blinded some, turned others mute. Within half an hour, similar scenes had unfolded at five other subway stops on three lines.

The Japanese government did not immediately name a perpetrator. But within days it responded with a morning raid on 25 branches of an obscure sect called Aum Shinrikyo, which translates as Aum Supreme Truth. The sect, which had started as a yoga school, in reality was a cult revolving around a long-haired mystic, Shoko Asahara, 40, a magnetic misfit who preached an apocalyptic message. When police entered the cult's main compound, they found a bizarre spectacle: 50 small cubicles, each containing a cult member lying on a blanket. All were suffering from malnutrition, but most claimed they were fasting voluntarily. Then the police made a yet more dramatic discovery. In a warehouse down a hill from the group's living quarters, they uncovered vast quantities of toxic chemicals, among them many of the constituent ingredients of sarin.

But despite a thorough search, police did not find one thing: Shoko Asahara himself.

Throughout the week, the hidden guru pleaded his innocence via radio broadcast and videotape, then completely vanished. For two months police swept through the extensive factories and businesses of Aum, arresting dozens of lower-ranking members. Meanwhile, Japan lived in fear. On May 5 a cleaning woman in Tokyo's sprawling Shinjuku station found a hydrogen-cyanide gas bomb before it went off. The device had been placed near a ventilation duct that would have spread the gas quickly. It was potent enough to have killed 10,000 people.

The big break came when a 30-year-old doctoral student in organic chemistry was arrested and allegedly admitted he had concocted sarin for Aum just before the subway attack. Then Dr. Ikuo Hayashi, 48, Aum's chief medical official, reportedly confessed he was among the 10 Aum operatives who had placed sarin on the trains. The order, he said, came specifically from Asahara. The police at last put out their own order: hunt down and arrest the guru.

On May 16 they finally nabbed him—hiding in the dark in a space not much larger than a coffin. For four hours they had searched the unlighted interior of a warehouse in an Aum compound near Mount Fuji. Then an investigator tapped on a wall and found a hollow spot. Police cut in with an electric saw and discovered a bearded man in a dark pink pajama suit lying in a compartment about 10 ft. long and 3 ft. high. With him were a cassette player, medicine and a bag containing $106,000 in cash. Followers had apparently sealed Asahara into the hiding place a day or so earlier. "Are you Shoko Asahara?" he was asked. "Yes, I am," Asahara replied. When police started to climb in to remove him, he warned them off. "I'll come out myself. No one, not even my followers, is allowed to touch me."

Japanese authorities did not agree. On June 6, Shoko Asahara was indicted on charges of murder. If convicted, he may be hanged, but a verdict may not come for years. Unlike sarin, Japanese justice moves slowly. ■

THE COMMIES ARE COMING!

Voters prefer the old-timers to Yeltsin's reformers

O N A LATE OCTOBER MORNING AT THE WHITE HOUSE, Bill Clinton and his top national security advisers received a startling assessment from the CIA. Two days before, Boris Yeltsin had met with Clinton in Hyde Park, New York, while visiting America for the U.N.'s 50th-anniversary celebrations. Observing Yeltsin's behavior, U.S. intelligence agents thought they had spotted something amiss with the Russian President. His gait looked awkward; he was walking with difficulty and with his legs spread apart. His skin had taken on a disturbing gray patina, and his face appeared strangely bloated. Yeltsin, the CIA believed, was on the threshold of another bout with his recurring heart problems.

Back in Russia a day later, Yeltsin, 64, was flown by helicopter from one of his dachas outside Moscow and rushed to intensive care at the Central Clinical Hospital. The Kremlin announced that he was suffering from myocardial ischemia, the same blockage of the blood supply to the heart that early in the summer had sent him to the hospital for two weeks and kept him out of work for nearly a month. For the next several days, Yeltsin, who is also believed to have a severe drinking problem, was in virtual isolation, seeing only his doctors, family and bodyguards. Somber aides gave assurances that the President was still in charge, but it was unclear how he could be making decisions when they were forbidden to see him.

Seven weeks later, Yeltsin's health had apparently improved, but his political fortunes had been dealt a serious blow. In December elections for the Russian parliament, the Duma, Yeltsin's foes in the Communist Party thoroughly vanquished their rivals. Voters cast two ballots, one for a party and one for a local candidate. Appealing to impoverished pensioners and others for whom economic reform has failed, the Communists took 22% of the party-preference vote. The ultranationalist Liberal Democratic Party, led by wildman demagogue Vladimir Zhirinovsky, came in a surprising second, but with only 11%, about half its 1993 level. Altogether, the communists were allocated 157 of the Duma's 450 seats; Our Home Is Russia, the party supporting Yeltsin and his Prime Minister, Victor Chernomyrdin, formed the next largest bloc, with only 55 seats. Voters blamed Yeltsin for the continuing war against Chechnya, which flared up again in November, and for

Russia's soaring crime and unemployment. The era of Boris Yeltsin seemed to be coming to an end.

The election's big winner was Communist Party leader Gennadi Zyuganov. His Duma success in hand, Zyuganov was bent on winning the presidency in the June 1996 election, either for himself or for a popular antireform candidate. If he succeeds, the current effort to reform Russia could be choked off in the grip of reimposed central control. The fabric of Russian society and East-West relations could also be damaged.

Zyuganov is a stolid apparatchik; Otto Latsis, a Moscow commentator, says Zyuganov heads "the worst part of the old party apparat, the most reactionary fringe." Indeed, only someone with remarkable tenacity could not only remain a communist in Russia in the 1990s but also manage to maneuver the discredited party back to the brink of power.

Born to village schoolteachers in southwestern Russia, Zyuganov began his career as a full-time party worker in 1967. He was serving as a deputy chief of the ideology department of the Soviet Central Committee in 1990 when he helped found a separate Russian Communist Party to oppose the reformist course of the existing Communist Party of the Soviet Union, then led by Mikhail Gorbachev. Zyuganov proudly takes credit for having been a "leading ideologist" in the failed hard-liner putsch of August 1991 against Gorbachev.

MEET THE NEW BOSS? A recuperating Boris Yeltsin returned to the Kremlin in late December, while Gennadi Zyuganov, above, celebrated the Communists' sweeping election victory

Zyuganov says his party "recognizes a mixed economy, has renounced atheism, and is ready for serious political dialogue to persuade voters." The party opposes privatization, but Zyuganov stops short of saying he would renationalize every industry; he does not want to scare away foreign investors. He would rebuild the shattered armed forces and, perhaps most ambitiously, wants to re-create the Soviet Union or "a great Russian state" of its former republics. Of course, he says, this must be done peacefully, in a "voluntary way, on the basis of elections, referendums and international treaties." As for Stalin's purges, the Gulag and the corruption of the Brezhnev era, they were "mistakes" to be avoided in the future.

Before the Duma election, Zyuganov had said he was uncertain whether it would be better for him to run for President or to help elect an antireform leader who had better name recognition and more appeal across party lines. After the election one such candidate put his name forward: Alexander Lebed, a war hero and retired general. Lebed, who is immensely popular with the public and has a strong nationalist voice, said he would run in June and that he hoped to do so in cooperation with the communists. If Lebed and the communists combined forces, the presidency could be well within their grasp.

But not if Boris Yelstin could help it. During the last week of 1995, the recuperating President returned to work at the Kremlin, strolling around its snowy courtyards in his first public appearance since he was stricken in October. In a staged event, Yeltsin chatted jovially with Russian tourists and journalists and told them he would not allow the communists to end his reform program.

Yet there might not be room on the ballot for Yeltsin in June. The results of the Duma elections suggested that in the first round of voting for President, one of the two winners would be the Communist Party candidate, whether it was Zyuganov or someone else he put forward. But who would be the other contender to emerge from the first round and enter the final runoff? Unless the government and the splintered reform forces managed to unite in support of a single candidate, the other entry might not be Yeltsin or any other reformer. It could be the man whose party was the second favorite among voters in December: the volatile Vladimir Zhirinovsky. ∎

Communist parties were banned in 1991, so Zyuganov joined several nationalist organizations and participated in a drive against Yeltsin, then the President of Russia. When the anticommunist ban was lifted in 1992, Zyuganov re-created his party and became chairman of its Central Committee, the post he still holds. He was an early supporter of the 1993 coup against Yeltsin, although he eventually disavowed violence. By 1995 he was the leader of a party with more than 500,000 members and a political machine with branches in every region of Russia.

A CIRCLE DRAWN AROUND the courtyard of the Beijing bungalow that 91-year-old Deng Xiaoping shares with more than a dozen members of his extended family would cover exactly 165 yards. Until 1994, China's most powerful patriarch would complete this circuit 20 times in the course of his two daily walks, ticking off the rounds each time he finished a lap.

But now the man who survived the persecution and chaos of the Cultural Revolution cannot manage even this modest circumambulation: he can no longer either walk or stand unaided. Filtering through the mist of secrecy in which he is cloaked, reliable reports indicate that the enfeebled Deng is very close to death. He can no longer write, is almost blind and has become so hard of hearing and slurred of speech, it is said, that two of his three daughters are the only people who can interpret his words to the public. Early in 1995 his youngest daughter, Xiao Rong, conceded that her father's health was declining "day by day."

Because Deng's stature in life has been so monumental, his absence in death will reverberate long after he is gone. His authority has held together the two contradictory strands of Chinese life. Even as he spurred the great leap toward a free-market economy, Deng was able to keep China's political system firmly in the hands of an ever more sclerotic Communist Party. When he finally dies, the competing systems will collide.

Deng's ill health obviously troubled a ruling circle determined to hang on to power. Of major concern was Beijing's worsening relations with the U.S., largely the result of the government's continued harsh dealings with political critics, both domestic and overseas. In addition, the June journey of Taiwan's President, Lee Teng-hui, to the U.S., though not a state visit, enraged the Chinese.

Also in June, the government detained the longtime human-rights activist Harry Wu, a U.S. citizen, and later charged him with illegally obtaining state secrets after he tried to cross into China at a remote Kazakhstan border outpost. After strong American protests, Wu was expelled and returned to the U.S. In August two U.S. Air Force officers were expelled on charges of spying. In December the regime sentenced Wei Jingsheng, the most prominent pro-democracy voice in the country, to 14 years in prison.

Anticipating Deng's demise, Communist Party rulers

■ CHINA

DENG'S LAST DAYS

As Deng Xiaoping nears death, the succession battle heats up—and U.S. relations cool down

have been laying the groundwork for a stable transition to a generation of leaders grouped around President Jiang Zemin, who was anointed by Deng in 1989, as the core of a new collective leadership. Jiang, 69, received Deng's mantle five years ago, and since then he has amassed nine major titles in the party, government and military. But monikers do not mean much in Chinese politics; during his retirement, the only title buttressing Deng's influence has been his honorary chairmanship of the China Bridge Association. What does matter is the raw calculus of power, a dynamic that can be as fickle as it is brutal.

So while Jiang's ascendancy may seem ensured, the length of his tenure does not. Viewed by many as weak, he has been working to secure the loyalty of his subalterns, especially the generals in the military. Any of the three men in the powerful triumvirate beneath him could pose a strong challenge.

The standard bearer of the liberal-reform faction, Zhu Rongji, 67, Deng's economic czar, saw his star soar as 1994's GDP grew nearly 12%, to $509 billion. But he has alienated military officers by taking away their commercial enterprises, and party men by tightening up credit for money-losing state enterprises. Durable Li Peng, 67, the widely disliked and authoritarian Premier, may be the least favored of Deng's lieutenants, but he has strong ties to party bureaucrats and the conservative older generation.

The man perhaps best positioned to emerge on top after Deng is Qiao Shi, 71, chairman of the National People's Congress. A "mystery man" because of his service in China's shadowy intelligence service, Qiao commands strategic loyalties among generals, police and party conservatives.

Whoever takes over will find his most daunting tasks defined by the problems that Deng left behind. China's economic explosion has produced the inevitable side effects: income gaps, bankrupt state-owned enterprises and a surge in crime and corruption. In amassing the power required to end the extremism of the Mao era, Deng foreclosed debate on crucial issues like political reform and institutional change. Those questions will now be thrown open. In the short term, the country's stability may depend upon finding a new strongman, one who can offer a gravitational center while the nation struggles with the questions Deng never resolved. ■

NEW HOPE IN HAITI

When he was restored to the presidency of Haiti by U.S. might in October 1994, Jean-Bertrand Aristide vowed he would step down after serving

Ballots, not bullets, in Haiti

out his term. He kept his promise in December, when his close associate René Préval, 52, was elected with 87.9% of the vote. The unpredictable Aristide, 42, a former priest, announced before the election that he would marry Mildred Trouillot, a presidential counselor.

POLES TO WALESA: YOU'RE OUTTA THERE!

Poland's President Lech Walesa described it as "a slap on the cheek," but he was minimizing the damage. Poles refused to re-elect the hero of the Solidarity uprising and chose his challenger, Alexander Kwasniewski, as President, with 51.7% of the vote. A former communist, Kwasnieswki, 41, (at right), campaigned as a pro-Western, reform-minded Social Democrat.

CHIRAC'S FRANCE GOES TO THE BARRICADES

After a tough, come-from-behind campaign in France, Gaullist Jacques Chirac, 62, defeated Socialist candidate Lionel Jospin in May to succeed François Mitterrand, 78, as President. But Chirac's first half year as leader of his troubled nation was tumultuous. When France exploded an underground atomic device at its Polynesian test site, Mururoa Atoll, it set off a furor of antinuclear protest throughout Europe and the South Pacific. Hundreds of rioters in Tahiti, protesting the action of the islands' colonial ruler, fire-bombed the Territorial Assembly in the French Polynesian capital of Papeete and gutted the passenger terminal at the international airport.

Meanwhile a series of

Ex-communist Kwasniewski pledged to uphold reform and democracy in Poland

Strike! French workers wave the red flag of revolution

bombings across France wounded dozens; police believed the four blasts and four attempts were the work of the Armed Islamic Group, Muslim militants who have vowed to punish France for what they claim is its support of Algeria's government in its bloody struggle with Islamic fundamentalists.

But the worst was yet to come for Chirac. In November transport workers led a three-week strike in protest against belt-tightening reforms to the French social security system proposed by Chirac's Prime Minister, Alain Juppé. Supported by students, the strike tied Paris in knots and spread throughout the country, threatening to paralyze the nation. Finally Juppé made a series of concessions that brought the striking workers and other unions back to their jobs.

AN IRISH WELCOME FOR A SON OF THE OLD SOD

Finally, Bill Clinton got a hero's reception—in Belfast. In late November thousands cheered the part-Irish President as a peacemaker. Clinton had annoyed the British in 1994 by welcoming Gerry Adams, president of Sinn Fein, the political wing of the Irish Republican Army, to the U.S., but then helped pressure Adams into a cease-fire. And his end-of-year visit got peace talks between Britain and the IRA moving again.

SADDAM: DESERTED IN THE DESERT

It was a stunning hegira: in August, Lieut. General Hussein Kamel al-Majid, his brother Saddam Kamel and their wives—both daughters of Iraqi strongman Saddam Hussein—conducted a daring overland escape into Jordan. The brothers, critical advisers to Saddam, emerged from the 14-hour trip across the desert with $50 million in cash—and a wealth of information for U.S. intelligence agencies.

CANADA, BY A HAIR

After a boisterous campaign that stirred passions in Canadians from all provinces, French-speaking Quebec chose to remain part of Canada, voting 50.6% against secession and 49.4% for it in a special plebiscite. The razor-thin margin consisted of just 52,448 votes out of almost 5 million cast; the 93.4% turnout was a record. One day later, Quebec Premier Jacques Parizeau, leader of the separatist Parti Québécois, announced he would resign before year's end.

....

A CLOSE CALL FOR EGYPT'S PRESIDENT

Targeted by Islamic fundamentalists for his pro-Western policies, Egyptian President Hosni Mubarak escaped an assassination attempt in June. Conspirators plotting to kill Mubarak had been arrested in 1992 and '93, before they had a chance to act. This time gunmen in Addis Ababa opened fire with AK-47 assault rifles as Mubarak's limousine drove toward the Ethiopian capital. But fast work by security men killed two attackers and drove the others away.

THE U.N. TURNS 50— BUT IT'S FIDEL'S PARTY

Autumn in New York— what a time to fall in love! And who was the hardhearted city swooning over? None other than the bearded bandito of the Bay of Pigs, Fidel Castro. Joining leaders of scores of other countries to celebrate the 50th anniversary of the founding of the United Nations, Cuba's leader was the star of the show. He received more than 200 invitations, broke bread with the Rockefellers, and even made the

Fidel suits up for New York

front pages of the tabloids when he and Yasser Arafat were declared unwelcome at several parties by New York City Mayor Rudolph Giuliani. The purpose of his good-guy gambit: Castro desperately wants the U.S. to end its 33-year-old trade embargo.

Mexico's Zapatista rebels demand their "land and liberty"

HARD TIMES IN MEXICO

Vying with France to be 1995's most troubled nation, Mexico was wracked by economic misery and political scandal. In the wake of the crash of the peso—and Mexico's economy—in late 1994, U.S. and Mexican officials sealed an economic bailout package in February. The U.S. agreed to put up $20 billion in loans and guarantees, while other countries and the International Monetary Fund would kick in enough to bring the bailout fund to $52 billion. In return Mexico agreed to cut federal spending enough to balance its budget and slow the growth of the money supply sharply.

Meanwhile, the saga of disgraced ex-President Carlos Salinas grew darker. President Ernesto Zedillo approved the arrest of Salinas' brother Raul for allegedly masterminding the 1994 killing of a top ruling party official. Later, Raul was accused of amassing some $80 million—perhaps from drug-related deals—in secret bank accounts in Switzerland and other countries.

ALGERIA'S SURPRISING VOTE OF CONFIDENCE

Islamic fundamentalists at war with the Algerian government's Westernizing agenda threatened "blood and bullets" for those who dared to vote in the presidential election. But in November Algerians braved the threats and went to the polls—75% of them, if government figures were accurate. Ex-general and incumbent President Liamine Zeroual was declared victor, earning 61% of the vote and a mandate to bring peace to the badly divided nation during his five-year term.

A security guard in Algiers

Mubarak's would-be assassin died with his AK-47 at his side

ECHOES *of* BATTLE

*A*mericans looked west across the Pacific in 1995, remembering the final days of two very different conflicts. Fifty years

before, in 1945, the Japanese Empire had finally fallen—

beaten into submission by the power of the new atom bomb. Yet only 30 years later, in 1975, the U.S. would know defeat—a humiliation forever captured in the image of Americans scrambling aboard a helicopter to leave Saigon to the enemy.

WAR OF THE
WORLDS

A T THE END, A TRINITY OF BOMBS brought the war in Asia to a close: Jumbo, the device detonated in Alamagordo, New Mexico, to prove that atomic weapons could be made; Little Boy, the uranium titan that vaporized Hiroshima; and Fat Man, the plutonium monster that laid waste to Nagasaki. In the crematory light of those blasts, the world changed—so much death contained in so little, so much of the bloody business of war refined to a bloodless decision. Ultimately it all came down to science, to a matter of buttons. In a flash, Prometheus was one with Genghis Khan.

The philosophical ramifications of Hiroshima and Nagasaki have occupied humankind for a half-century now. What has been obscured is the nature of the war that led to the use of the bombs, a war that possessed its own terrible clarity: that of simple, ferocious hate; of civilization pitted against civilization, race against race, blood against blood. That kind of fighting still occurs: in the Balkans, in Rwanda, in the streets of Los Angeles and Karachi. But the imagination of the world pays little heed to the sensibilities of such conflicts. Minds have been polarized by the cold war and fascinated by the mighty mushroom clouds of 1945—by the imminence of endless death from the radiance of a thousand suns. Nonetheless, in the shadow of that terrifying splendor lurks a history of intense human hatreds, parables we ignore at our peril.

Though paired with the European conflicts of World War II, the immense battles in Asia traced their beginnings back to different histories, different cultures, different fears. The Pacific was a clash of civilizations: the attempt of a modern, non-Western power to carve its place, if not establish its superiority, in a world dominated and colonized by white people. And the war's beginning came long before the attack on Pearl Harbor. The U.S. Naval War College in Newport, Rhode Island, was preparing strategies for a war against Japan as early as 1897. The Japanese saw the war as part of a hundred-year conflict that had begun with the

More than a battle for land or power, the War in the Pacific was a ferocious clash of cultures, fueled by racial fears and a history of hatred

humiliation of the self-satisfied, isolationist Chinese Empire in 1842, after the Opium War, at the hands of the British. Until 1853, Japan was a hermetic, medieval kingdom, but, learning from the foibles of its neighbors and from the technological prowess of the West, it had by 1895 established itself as the dominant Asian power. Japan wanted not only to overtake China as the foremost regional power but also to prove that Asians need never defer to the West. By 1905 it had trounced the Russians in Manchuria, sinking the armada that Nicholas II dispatched from the Baltic Sea to retake the waters around his Pacific port of Vladivostok.

Japan's quest for superiority required not only armaments but also the establishment of a biological prerogative. For a would-be master race, the rights of hegemony must by definition be present in the blood. Japan thus embarked on the creation of a mythology of a chosen people, with the Emperor as the divine icon of the race. Japanese biologists produced studies decrying the apish physical features of other races (hairiness, long arms) and noting the highly evolved characteristics of the Japanese. More important, racial purity derived from loyalty to the Emperor and the protective centuries of isolation, which fostered a spirituality the Japanese believed was possessed by no other people.

It was the American commodore Matthew Perry who, in 1853, had persuaded Japan to open its ports to Western trade, thus initiating an astonishing rush toward modernization. But when the Japanese began flexing their muscle in East Asia, the U.S. realized that its protégé had become a rival. Paranoia followed; by 1924 the American Congress had passed an anti-Japanese immigration act. From the 1890s through the 1940s, the Hearst newspapers were especially rabid about the "yellow peril." When war did come, one Hearst tabloid declared, "The war in the Pacific is the World War, the War of the Oriental Races against the Occidental Races for the Domination of the World."

Many of the American soldiers sent to Asia to pacify the Philippines in 1898 had fought in the Indian wars and described their new foes with white-settler terms for the old. "The only good

GATES OF HELL
U.S. troops landed on Okinawa in April 1945, took it after 83 days

Filipino," said a soldier, "is a dead one." A 1942 article in the New York *Times* Magazine, entitled "The Nips," said, "The Japanese are likened to the American Indian in their manner of making war. Our fighting men say that isn't fair to the Indian. He had honor of a sort." For its part, Japanese propaganda described Americans as racist, sex-obsessed, abortion-loving *yaju* (wild beasts).

For Americans, the Bataan death march was the most infamous example of Japanese cruelty. American and Filipino prisoners from the fall of the Bataan peninsula in 1942 were refused food and water on a six-day, 60-mile forced march to their place of confinement at Camp O'Donnell. Fingers were chopped off to get at West Point rings; decapitated bodies lined the road; by one estimate, there was a body every 10 or 15 paces. The death toll: more than 10,000.

While the majority of Allied soldiers shrank from atrocity, a few were not averse to inflicting on the Japanese the horrors that had been visited on their comrades. In 1946 Edgar Jones wrote in the *Atlantic Monthly*, "What kind of war do civilians suppose we fought, anyway? We shot prisoners in cold blood, wiped out hospitals, strafed lifeboats, killed or mistreated enemy civilians ... tossed the dying into a hole with the dead, and in the Pacific boiled the flesh off enemy skulls to make table ornaments for sweethearts."

The war in Asia was waged mercilessly on all sides. Major General Curtis LeMay, the man who took charge of the B-29 bombings of Japan, once said, "I'll tell you what war is about. You've got to kill people, and when you've killed enough, they stop fighting." The carnage was horrific. In the China theater alone, perhaps as many as 10 million people perished. In the fighting in the central Pacific, some 20,000 U.S. soldiers died. On Saipan, Japanese women and children hurled themselves from cliffs rather than submit to the American invaders. Most Japanese soldiers there either died fighting or took their own lives: 27,040 corpses were found. The toll from Tarawa—984 U.S. Marines and 29 Navy men killed in just 76 hours of fighting—caused normally self-censoring correspondents to send home horror stories that nearly triggered a congressional investigation.

Fueled by their sense of racial supremacy, the Japanese seemed invincible early in the war. But for all its early prowess, the empire had exhausted its resources and skills

EARLY VICTORIES
Japanese troops charge to triumph in the Philippines

four main islands. U.S. bombers set those islands aflame. From March to May, enormous sections of Tokyo, Osaka, Nagoya, Kobe, Kawasaki and Yokohama were incinerated. The raids on Tokyo had to be called off after May because scarcely any major targets were left.

By the end of May, General Douglas MacArthur had been designated to lead the invasion of Japan as commander in chief of U.S. Army Forces Pacific. The plan consisted of two parts. First, Operation Olympic, scheduled for November 1, 1945, would land the largest invasion force in history—nearly 340,000 soldiers and Marines—on the island of Kyushu. Then, as early as March 1946, Operation Coronet, involving up to 2 million men, would target the island of Honshu and the Kanto plain, on which Tokyo lies.

THE EMPEROR'S STRATEGISTS ALSO PREpared for an invasion of Kyushu. Allied intelligence estimates in late April put 84,200 Japanese troops in southern Kyushu. In fact, by late July almost 600,000 imperial troops were on the island. That ratio of Japanese-to-American fighting men portended a cataclysm. The Americans considered a worst-case scenario requiring three attempted landings to achieve victory. Meanwhile, Tokyo had issued orders to its troops that a ferocious repulsion of the invasion was necessary. No one would be allowed to retreat; 13 million civilians were mobilized to fight with sticks and shovels if need be.

U.S. casualty predictions ranged from 31,000 to 220,000. The Joint Chiefs of Staff offered three different sets of estimates. The worst scenario: as many as 500,000 Americans killed or wounded. It was assumed that millions of Japanese defenders, military and civilian, would perish.

As the Allied forces drew closer to Japan, the endgame began. By tradition, the Emperor kept silent during high-level strategy meetings. But on June 22, Hirohito spoke. His words were cloaked in elliptical language, but his meaning was clear: an effort must be made to negotiate an end to the war. The words provided no clear direction for his government. Though officials were eager for peace, few were willing to sue for it, certainly not with Japanese military factions ready to stage assassinations in the face of such a move. Thus, as Japan's peace seekers sought a way out, America's leaders pondered the obstacles to victory.

Already, the empire was ashes. "Nights of strong wind were chosen, and bombs were dropped to windward in great quantity," wrote Foreign Minister Mamoru Shigemitsu in his memoirs. "The area encompassed by a wall of flame then became the target for the next wave, which systematically bombed the whole. The area became a sea of flame."

Shortly after Pearl Harbor, Japanese propagandists had crowed about the empire's people, the "100 million," and a national cohesiveness that could achieve anything it was directed to do: "100 million hearts beating as one ... 100 million people as one bullet," and "100 million advancing like a ball of fire." No one had expected the last to be a prophecy. For Japan, more terrifying wonders would come out of the heavens: the sun turned to darkness, the moon to blood. ■

in order to pull together its victories. Six months after Pearl Harbor, a Japanese armada steaming toward Midway Island was severely pummeled and turned back. In October 1944 the imperial navy was routed in Leyte Gulf in the Philippines, and Japan was virtually eliminated as a sea power. By July 1945 it was cut off from its territory in Southeast and East Asia, losing the raw materials it had gone to war for. The empire in June had just 4,000 aircraft, with only 800 operational. The U.S. had 22,000.

By June 22, 1945, the U.S. had conquered Okinawa, just 350 miles from Kyushu, the southernmost of Japan's

FTER WITNESSING THE SUCCESS-ful test of the first atom bomb— a primordial burst of energy on the predawn New Mexico desert, a man-made fire bright enough to flicker in reflection off the moon—Brigadier General Thomas F. Farrell sought out his immediate superior, Major General Leslie R. Groves. Groves was commander of the top-secret Manhattan Project, which had been commissioned and funded with $2 billion to try to build such a bomb. "When Farrell came up to me," Groves remembered, "his first words were, 'The war is over.' My reply was, 'Yes, after we drop two bombs on Japan.'" This was the morning of July 16, 1945. Within an amazing 30 days, both of these statements would be history.

President Truman heard of the bomb test while in Potsdam, a suburb of bombed-out Berlin, where he was meeting with allies Winston Churchill and Joseph Stalin. The news that the atom bomb had worked promised to solve Truman's most urgent problem in the Pacific: the ordering of a heavy-casualty land invasion of the Japanese home islands, scheduled for November 1.

The question of how to deliver and drop an atom bomb on Japanese soil had been thoroughly studied well before the test in New Mexico. A special Air Force unit had been formed in September 1944, under the command of Lieut. Colonel Paul W. Tibbets, regarded by many to be the service's best bomber pilot. On Tinian, a 39-sq.-mi. island in the Marianas some 1,500 miles south of Japan, U.S. forces had constructed the largest airport in the world, including four parallel, 8,500-ft.-long runways designed for B-29 Superfortresses. On July 26, components of Little Boy, the uranium-based bomb that was scheduled to be dropped first, reached Tinian.

That same day, the Potsdam Declaration was issued by the U.S., Britain and Nationalist China, the three countries at war with Japan. The document's language was blunt: "Following are our terms ... We call upon the government of Japan to proclaim now the unconditional surrender of all Japanese armed forces ... The alternative for Japan is prompt and utter destruction." Only those who had seen or heard of the atom bomb, including Truman and Churchill, could understand what the last words might mean.

The Potsdam text reached Tokyo on July 27; the next afternoon Prime Minister Kantaro Suzuki held a press conference at which he vowed that his government planned to ignore the declaration. On July 30, Secretary of War Henry L. Stimson cabled President Truman at Potsdam, asking for approval of the order to drop the atom bomb. Truman wrote out in longhand a reply: "Suggestion approved. Release when ready."

Bad weather over Japan only delayed what was now inevitable. But the skies gradually cleared. By the afternoon of August 5, on Tinian, Little Boy was being winched into the specially modified bomb bay of a B-29, which Tibbets would christen—in honor of his mother's given names— *Enola Gay.* The 9,700-lb. bomb was 10½ ft. long and 29 in. in diameter. After a midnight briefing, crews of the seven B-29s assigned to carry out the mission— three in the strike team, four in support—had breakfast and then rode by truck to their stations. The *Enola Gay*, with Tibbets as pilot, took off at 2:45 a.m., Tinian time. Only then did Tibbets tell his 11-man crew that they were carrying a new kind of bomb.

Monday, August 6, dawned clear, hot and humid in Hiroshima, a city on the southeastern coast of the main Japanese island of Honshu. In 1942 it had had a population of 420,000, but evacuations had reduced that number to about 280,000 civilians, 43,000 military personnel and 20,000 forced Korean laborers and volunteer workers. Hiroshima housed the offices of the Japanese army's Second General Headquarters. On this summer morning, some 8,900 schoolchildren had been ordered to help clean the city's streets.

An air-raid alert sounded at 7:09—radar had picked up the approach of the strike force's weather plane—and an all-clear followed at 7:31, after the B-29 had departed. Perhaps this apparently harmless sortie lulled the city's civil-defense monitors. In any case, just before 8:15 three more B-29s—the *Enola Gay* and two escorts—could be

A merciless war comes to its appalling crescendo with America's use of the new atom bomb and the instant incineration of two Japanese cities

AUGUST 6, 1945
A mushroom cloud towers over
Hiroshima after the atomic blast

CLOUDS
OF DOOM

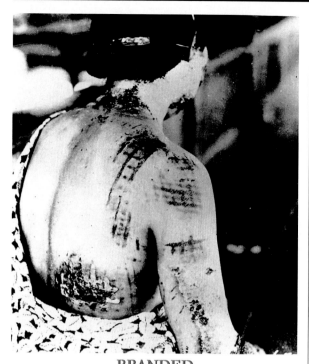

BRANDED
Radiation burned the kimono pattern onto this woman's skin

FLATTENED
**48,000 of Hiroshima's 76,000
buildings were utterly destroyed**

seen and then heard flying some 30,000 ft. over Hiroshima. No alarms sounded in time. The radio announcer on duty had word that three enemy planes had been sighted, but he had paused to check his notes. "Military command announces three enemy planes …" He never finished. Outside, a teacher with a team of schoolgirl laborers said, "Oh, there's a B!" They looked up and saw the eye of death.

Little Boy, which had been dropped from the *Enola Gay* at 8:15:30, exploded 43 seconds later at 1,900 ft. above Hiroshima, creating a blinding bluish-white flash and, for a fraction of a second, unearthly heat. Temperatures near the hypocenter, the ground point immediately below the explosion, surged to figures ranging from 5400°F to 7200°F; within a mile of the hypocenter, the surfaces of objects instantly rose to more than 1000°F. Those people caught in the middle of this maelstrom were the lucky ones. They died instantly, vaporized into puffs of smoke or carbonized into small, blackened, smoking mummies.

People farther away from the source of the thermal wave suffered longer agonies. The intense heat melted the eyeballs of some who had stared in wonder at the blast; it burned off facial features and seared skin all over the body into peeling, draping strips. The survivors who first emerged out of this roiling inferno walked like automatons, their arms held forward, hands dangling. Severely dehydrated, they stumbled toward the riverbanks, some crying out, *"Mizu, mizu!"* (Water, water!). Nature itself seemed deranged by the violence. Whirlwinds tore through the city. Fires jumped rivers with ease. Dark, marble-size drops of water—later called black rain—condensed from the towering cloud of smoke and fell to earth.

After the thermal heat came the blast, spreading out from the explosion's center at an initial speed of 2 miles per second and then subsiding toward the speed of sound. Un-

leashing the equivalent of 12,500 tons of TNT, Little Boy flattened Hiroshima: only 6,000 of the city's 76,000 buildings were undamaged. Practically every window and mirror in the city splintered, hurling shards of glass into the bodies of anyone nearby. An estimated 100,000 died that first day, and the death toll climbed to 140,000 by the end of the year.

Those physicians able to function did so heroically. They would be the first medical experts to observe a new disease: the third effect, after the heat and the blast, of Little Boy. On Tuesday an official of the Red Cross Hospital in Hiroshima discovered that the X-ray plates stored in a basement vault that had survived the blast had all been exposed. The bomb had spread radiation throughout central Hiroshima, with lingering, lethal effects on its survivors that would not be fully understood for years.

The outside world learned of the bomb from a terse White House announcement. The big news was saved for the beginning of the third paragraph: "It is an atomic bomb. It is a harnessing of the basic power of the universe. The force from which the sun draws its powers has been loosed against

MAIMED
Many who survived the blast would face radiation poisoning

those who brought war to the Far East." This was the first public announcement that nuclear weapons even existed.

Japanese radio offered its citizens a more tentative report: "Hiroshima suffered considerable damage as the result of an attack by a few B-29s. Our enemies have apparently used a new type of bomb. The details are being investigated." In truth, Tokyo initially knew almost nothing about what had happened in Hiroshima; all lines of communication had been obliterated. Since the first reports seemed incredible, some Japanese leaders wanted desperately not to believe them. Others decided that even if the U.S. announcement was true, Japan should fight on. "I am convinced," War Minister Korechika Anami told his colleagues, "that the Americans had only one bomb, after all."

Anami was wrong. On August 8, the bulbous Fat Man— nearly 12 ft. long and 5 ft. in diameter, weighing 10,000 lbs.—was loaded into another B-29 at Tinian. The plane and its escorts took off the next morning at 3:47 and headed for Kokura, a city that contained a major weapons arsenal, on the island of Kyushu. Finding Kokura obscured by

clouds and facing a low fuel level on the strike plane, Major Charles W. Sweeney decided to fly over the alternate target on his way to an emergency landing on Okinawa.

Thus did Nagasaki enter history, its ordeal an afterthought. Fat Man exploded 1,650 ft. above the city of some 240,000 people on the western coast of the island at 11:02 on the morning of August 9. The bomb released the equivalent of 22,000 tons of TNT, almost twice the power exhibited by Little Boy. But the devastation in Nagasaki was limited by its topography: the city was divided into two valleys separated by steep hills. The bomb exploded over Nagasaki's northwesterly valley, and the worst of the damage was contained there. The destruction, nevertheless, was infernal. About 74,000 were killed instantly.

Even after learning of the devastation of Nagasaki— and the further news that the Soviet Union had abruptly declared war on Japan—the empire's six-member Supreme War Council remained split down the middle on the questions of whether and how to end the war. But when they met with the Emperor, Hirohito argued that Japan must accept the Potsdam terms. Four more days of fighting and delicate negotiations remained before all sides could agree to stop the killing. Meanwhile, the conventional bombing of Japan continued; by some estimates, more than 15,000 may died during this final spasm.

Finally, at noon Japanese time on August 15, a message recorded by Hirohito was broadcast throughout Japan. Citizens gathered around public loudspeakers, heads bowed in reverence; they had never before heard their Emperor's voice. He told them that "the war situation has developed not necessarily to Japan's advantage ... Moreover, the enemy has begun to employ a new and most cruel bomb, the power of which to do damage is indeed incalculable, taking the toll of many innocent lives." Japan had been defeated. ■

SAIGON
THE FINAL 10 DAYS

As Northern tanks rolled toward the city, America's long involvement in Vietnam ended in the scramble of a frenzied helicopter airlift to safety

PRIL 1975. THE SIGNS OF IMPENDING DOOM HAD BEEN MULTI-plying for at least a month. A headlong bug-out from the Central Highlands in March had signaled that South Vietnam could no longer muster either the strength or the will to hold off the armies sweeping down from the communist North. The fall of Danang late in the month produced scenes of horror that appeared to foreshadow what might happen later in Saigon: panic-mad-dened South Vietnamese soldiers trampling women and children to get aboard the last American 727 to fly out; desperate soldiers clinging to the landing gear of that plane, only to fall off into the South China Sea or be crushed against the undercarriage.

Though any of several dates could be picked as the beginning of Saigon's fi-nal agony, April 20 stands out. For one thing, it marked the fall of Xuan Loc, a small town 38 miles northeast of the capital and the site of just about the last prolonged and bloody battle of the war. If ARVN, the South Vietnamese army, could not hold there, it was unlikely to hold anywhere. In Saigon on that day Graham Martin, the U.S. ambassador to South Vietnam, called at the Presiden-tial Palace for a long interview with President Nguyen Van Thieu. The South Vietnamese leader bore no small share of the blame for the impending cata-strophe: it was his order to the army to withdraw from the Central Highlands without much of a fight that touched off the final rout. In the last few weeks, he had grown increasingly out of touch with aides and allies, and with reality. The communists had repeatedly declared they would never deal with Thieu. If there was to be any hope of a compromise peace, Thieu had to go, and Martin said as much. On his return to the embassy, Martin took a long shower and, with Pon-tius Pilate symbolism, scrubbed with strong soap.

Thieu went, but not quietly. Appearing in an open-necked bush shirt before the National Assembly on the night of April 21, the President delivered a long and at times tearful resignation speech excoriating the United States as "unfair ... inhumane ... irresponsible." Said Thieu: "You ran away and left us to do the job that you could not do." Moreover, Thieu would not turn over power to Duong Van Minh. "Big" Minh, as he was universally known, was a former gen-eral who headed what he described as a neutralist "third force" and was ac-ceptable to the communists. Instead, Thieu yielded power to Vice President Tran Van Huong, who was 71, ailing and nearly blind. Huong's moment in the sun was brief and illusory: his regime lasted seven days before he turned over the reins to Big Minh, who would ultimately surrender to the North.

VICTORY!
On April 30, 1975, Northern tanks surged into Saigon

THE FINAL BATTLE
NVA troops storm Tan Son Nhut, the last U.S. air base, on April 30

Preparations for the final assault of the NVA (North Vietnamese army) were well under way by Thieu's resignation on April 21. Hanoi had sent thousands of trucks racing down the coastal highway loaded with rockets and shells. The push proceeded swiftly and smoothly; by April 26 NVA forces had surrounded Saigon. That night Thieu was persuaded to leave while he still could; Ambassador Martin had him spirited out of the city. The next day, April 27, Saigon was jolted by a series of explosions signaling that the war had finally embraced the capital. The raid was carried out by five captured American jets, flown by South Vietnamese pilots who had defected to the North. The capital obviously was no longer safe. At 10:51 a.m., April 29, in Saigon, Armed Forces Radio burst forth with *White Christmas*. It was a signal: Option IV, a helicopter lift of U.S. troops and citizens as well as pro-U.S. Vietnamese from Saigon to U.S. warships 20 miles out to sea, was on.

The lift ran for about 21 hours, from roughly 11 a.m. on April 29 to almost 8 a.m. on the 30th. Pilots flew for 10 to 15 hours straight; each trip took about 40 minutes in the air and 10 to 15 minutes on the ground loading up. Marine Captain Glynn Hodges landed at the embassy in midafternoon; his H-53 chopper was too big to perch on the roof, so it came down in the compound. "My troops couldn't believe the scene," says Hodges. "People were climbing fences. It was bedlam. We were afraid of the crowds. We had to wear gas masks, though we saw only smoke, no gas. We also wore flak vests. They were hot and heavy. We

were really uncomfortable and scared too." Hodges kept flying for 12 straight hours, well into the night; all his other trips were into Tan Son Nhut, the Saigon airport. "After dark, you could see fire fights coming in from the coast to Saigon," he says. "Air traffic was very crowded [and] we didn't have night goggles. The worst fear I had was of running into another airplane. The Vietnamese I saw, I remember looking at them and they were just confused— how I'd feel if I'd just left my home forever."

THOUGH THE FIRST LOADS FROM THE EMBASSY were mostly Vietnamese, more and more Americans came out as the evacuation progressed. Frank Snepp, a CIA analyst, caught a chopper out at 9 p.m. on April 29. His description: "The roof of the embassy was a vision out of a nightmare. In the center of the dimly lit helo-pad, a CH-47 was already waiting for us, its engines setting up a roar like a primeval scream. The crew ... all wore what looked like oversized football helmets, and in the blinking under-light of the landing signals they reminded me of grotesque insects rearing on their hindquarters."

Kenneth Moorefield, a foreign service officer and former infantry captain who put the dazed Ambassador Martin on one of the last choppers out, climbed aboard one himself shortly afterward. His account of his last look around the embassy: "Hundreds of Vietnamese had swarmed over the walls and were looting the warehouse, the offices, the snack bar. Some were driving embassy cars around and around in almost a maniacal frenzy. On the other side of the walls, crowds were shouting chants against the U.S., celebrating the imminent victory of the communists. In the distance our jets were still flying cover, chased by tracer rounds. Yet the city itself had this unearthly calm. It was pitch black. No movement, no light, no sense of what was coming."

What was coming was the North Vietnamese army, and it did not take long to arrive. At 9 a.m., almost exactly one hour after the last U.S. helicopter left the embassy roof, NVA columns moved into the city from five different directions. The South Vietnamese soldiers confronting them did not just flee; they threw away everything that could identify them as soldiers. Says Bui Tin, an NVA colonel and journalist: "Everywhere you looked on the road, they had left all their military clothing and supplies—canteens, caps, coats, pants, boots, belts. They must have ended up fleeing in their shorts!"

That set the stage for the final, and almost comically unheroic, scene of the war. NVA Major Nguyen Van Hoa, commanding tank No. 843, a Soviet-made T-54, with six other tanks following, had entered Saigon before dawn. His little column ran into a brief fire fight at the Thi Nghe bridge, knocking out two ARVN M41 tanks. Rolling into almost deserted streets, the column kept going toward its target, the Presidential Palace. But where was it? Major Hoa's column split up; at the head of three tanks, No. 843 clattered down a boulevard so lined with leafy trees that, says Hoa, "we couldn't see what was at the end. We met a woman on a motorcycle, and we stopped to ask her where the palace was. It was right there."

By then, says the major, "we had only two shells left. I ordered the gunner to fire one at the gate. But it misfired. So I decided we would just drive through the gates into the palace and raise our flag." Big Minh was at the gates, waiting to greet the NVA troops. He and his entourage, however, scurried inside when No. 843's gunner fired.

Accounts of what happened next differ, but all start with a bit of bureaucratic farce: while Minh waited inside the palace for someone to surrender to, NVA troops milled around outside waiting for an officer of sufficiently high rank to show up and receive the surrender. By one account, Big Minh could not surrender because he could not decipher the writing on a handwritten surrender document, and it had to be rewritten.

At any rate, by noon on April 30 the NVA was broadcasting that it had captured Saigon and renamed it Ho Chi Minh City. There was more to come. For Vietnamese, the communist victory meant "re-education" camps, the flight of the boat people, the gradual softening of a harsh communist regime. For Americans, it was the new sensation of total, undisguisable defeat. But amid all the joy, bitterness, fear and misery, the overwhelming sentiment of Americans was probably the one voiced by Kenneth Moorefield. As his helicopter headed for the U.S. fleet, he says, "I was numb with exhaustion. Physically, I was beyond sensation. But I felt the tremendous weight of all that pressure lift off me. I realized my war, our war, was finally over." ■

Enemies No More

AS HE STEPPED INTO THE EAST ROOM OF THE White House, Bill Clinton looked like a platoon leader venturing into no-man's-land. He did it with his chin up, but quickly—and very carefully. In step behind the President were some of the Pentagon's current and former top officials, and guarding the onetime draft avoider's extremely vulnerable right flank was the operation's point man: Republican Senator John McCain of Arizona, an ex–Navy pilot who had languished for more than five years as a prisoner of war in Hanoi. "Today," said Clinton, "I am announcing the normalization of diplomatic relationships with Vietnam."

And that was it. More words followed from the President about his concern for completing the long, tortuous investigation into the fate of U.S. servicemen in the Vietnam War who are still listed as MIA, or missing in action. Even as he spoke, though, recognition of Hanoi was a reality. A foreign policy initiative that no White House incumbent since 1975 had felt safe enough or accommodating enough to hazard was now Clinton's fait accompli.

Sign of the times: at last, McNamara meets Giap

Would the move backfire? While many families of MIA combatants felt betrayed, the White House knew that the bulk of Americans would approve. The most recent Gallup poll on the issue had found that in the previous two years, support for recognition had risen from 48% to 61%, with just 27% now opposed. When Robert McNamara, Lyndon Johnson's Secretary of Defense in the hottest days of the war, visited Vietnam in November and shook hands with his former nemesis, General Vo Nguyen Giap, the healing of old enmities seemed well under way.

The real anguish remaining at the heart of this vexed relationship will never be easily washed away, of course. The fact that America lost a cause draped in the noblest rhetoric but fought on cynical and divisive terms produced a sense of lingering self-doubt that may never vanish. In a significant way, though, the principles for which the war was waged are ascendant today in Vietnam. The free-market, free-thinking spirit of Saigon is what counts, not the Marxist maunderings of some old men in Hanoi. The Vietnamese, who lost many more lives than Americans did, have put the past behind them. In 1995 the American people moved to join them. ■

Is Bigger

Hooked on constant growth, America's media giants just keep expanding. Is "synergy" hype—or the key to survival?

By JOHN GREENWALD FOR THE TIME ANNUAL

For the $400 billion American entertainment industry, 1995 was the year blockbuster buyouts rivaled any spectacle Hollywood could put on the screen. Indeed, the megadeals sped by at the breakneck pace of James Bond blasting his way through the hit flick *Goldeneye*. At the peak of the action, new owners took over two of the three largest television networks in a single week, and bragging rights to the title of world's largest media company changed hands twice in less than two months.

Pow! In April, Seagram, the Canadian purveyor of whiskey, wine and Tropicana juices, invades Hollywood by agreeing to pay $5.7 billion for MCA, which owns Universal Studios as well as theme parks and record labels. *Bam!* The town is still buzzing about that when, in July, Michael Eisner, the normally tight-fisted chairman of the Walt Disney company, who had vowed to stick to making movies, spends $19 billion for Capital Cities/ABC, transforming Disney into the No. 1 media king. *Wham!* Just 24 hours later, Westinghouse, a conglomerate whose interests range from nuclear reactors to a passel of Group W radio and TV stations, spends $5.4 billion for CBS. *O.K., take that!* Time Warner reclaims the title of media top dog in September by engineering a $7.5 billion buyout of

BETTER?

the Turner Broadcasting System, a company with which Time Warner has long had contentious relations—and hopes that regulators in Washington will approve the complex deal.

The couplings reflected a frantic new world in which a handful of communications giants were vying to command information and entertainment—not only the message, but the medium as well. That called for both owning the means to produce "content," such as films, news and TV shows, and controlling outlets, from satellites to telephone lines, that distribute that content to homes. The acknowledged inspiration for this strategy was Rupert Murdoch, whose News Corp. empire encompasses newspapers and the Fox TV network and movie studio, along with European and Asian satellites that can reach billions of people. "The light bulb has just gone on that the guy is so integrated, he has so many ways to win, that the networks are by comparison pretty narrow companies," said Steven Lerman, a Washington media lawyer.

Congress did its part to spur on the mergers by approving measures that would permit a Murdoch or an Eisner to expand ownership of media outlets, such as cable systems, newspapers and broadcast stations, in a single market. "The landscape for the entertainment industry is completely different now," said John Turo, an analyst with Rodman & Renshaw, a Chicago-based brokerage firm. "From here on we should expect to see continued consolidation within the industry, a consolidation that will move along at a crushing speed."

That is just what bothers some industry watchers, who fear that the mergers could reduce competition for what people see, hear and read. "The good news is, these large companies bring the kind of horsepower, creative force and technological advances that one would hope would create a better universe," said Fred Roberts, president of a Los Angeles investment banking firm that specializes in mergers and acquisitions. "On the other hand, it's going to make individuals and entrepreneurs irrelevant, because no one is going to be able to compete with these behemoths." Massachusetts Representative Ed Markey, the ranking Democrat on the House Telecommunications Subcommittee, put it this way: "For us to allow there to be this concentration of media ownership would make Citizen Kane look like an underachiever."

Not to worry, said other experts, who held that the mergers might breed only sluggish bureaucracies torn by culture clashes and out of touch with fast-changing public tastes. They greeted AT&T's decision in September to split into three separate companies as one more sign that melding supposedly complementary businesses rarely yields the much-hyped "synergy." The bust-up would free AT&T to focus on its lucrative telephone service after it spins off its computer and manufacturing units. "What we keep learning over and over again," says Harvard Business School professor Michael Porter, "is that focus is better than diversity and complexity."

That message was hardly lost on Microsoft chairman Bill Gates and other heavy hitters who put $2 billion behind DreamWorks SKG, making the new studio the other big Hollywood story of 1995. DreamWorks, the brainchild of director Steven Spielberg (*Jaws, Jurassic Park*), former Disney whiz Jeffrey Katzenberg (*Aladdin, The Lion King*) and pop-music impresario David Geffen (Nirvana, Guns N' Roses), plans to make movies, TV shows, records, toys and computer software. The three founders signed up giants like Disney to distribute the products of their fun factory; that would allow the partners to focus on creating the goodies, which is what they know best.

By contrast, few companies strayed farther from what they know than Seagram did in April when it agreed to acquire 80% of MCA from Japan's Matsushita Electric Industrial, which had owned it since 1990. The deal both titillated Hollywood and capped a quest by Edgar Bronfman Jr., 40, chairman of Seagram and grandson of its founder, and a show-biz wannabe who produced his first movie at 17. Bronfman had gone on to invest in Broadway plays, write pop songs, marry a singer-actress and produce a few more films. But when Seagram began buying up blocks of Time Warner stock in 1993, the company feared a takeover and created a poison pill that kept Bronfman from owning more than 14.9% of it.

The setback shifted Bronfman's attention to MCA, which was struggling under Matsushita's yen-pinching ownership. To raise cash to acquire MCA, Seagram first sold most of its 24.1% stake in Du Pont back to the chemical giant for $8.8 billion. That brought howls from some experts on Wall Street, who viewed MCA as a rich man's toy. Said Standard & Poor's analyst Ken Shea: "It doesn't make sense to dump a solid business like Du Pont, which has thrown off good dividends, and take on a much riskier investment in MCA."

Bronfman's faltering first steps at MCA seemed to confirm his image as a muzzy mogul. He ardently courted superagent Michael Ovitz, commonly known as the most powerful man in Hollywood, to run the entertainment company. The choice seemed logical. Not only did Ovitz, 49, represent many of the most sought-after stars, writers and directors in the movie business, but he had also emerged in recent years as Hollywood's pre-eminent dealmaker. Ovitz brought together Sony and Columbia Pictures (which had been owned by Coca Cola) in 1989 and Matsushita and MCA a year later. But Ovitz, who is famed for rising at dawn to practice the Japanese martial art of aikido, spurned the $250 million contract that his friend Bronfman offered and subsequently joined Disney as Eisner's No. 2. A humiliated Bronfman managed to put that rejection behind him by hiring Ron Meyer, Ovitz's partner at the Creative Artists Agency, as president of MCA.

While Bronfman had pined for a piece of the Hollywood action, Eisner had often insisted that his company was a premier provider of content that didn't need to own distribution outlets. "I can't help believing," he said, "that story, emotion, comedy, a beginning, middle and end, identification with characters—that's what counts, and that's what our company is about." Asked to explain his change of heart after Disney agreed to acquire Capital Cities/ABC, Eisner replied, "Being totally consistent is kind of boring."

Boring was the last thing anyone called Disney's Cap Cities/ABC buyout, which was a personal as well as a business triumph for the 54-year-old Eisner. During the previous year he had lost Frank Wells, his revered second-in-

THE MOUSE THAT ROARED

DISNEY	COMPANY	CAP CITIES/ABC
$10.5 Billion	ASSETS	$6.4 Billion
	STRATEGY	

Eisner's "magic kingdom" was strong in theme parks and movies, but weak in TV and cable. Cap. Cities/ABC offered hit television programs, including *Roseanne, Home Improvement* and a strong news division, the cable sports giant ESPN—plus 10 TV stations and 21 radio stations.

1994 FIGURES

command, to a helicopter crash and had forced the departure of Disney studio head Katzenberg, who left when Eisner refused to make him Wells' successor. In the midst of this turmoil, Eisner underwent quadruple-bypass heart surgery, raising questions about the level of his energy and his long-term health. Disney's profits continued to soar, thanks to animated hits like *The Lion King*, but Eisner began to look like an ailing also-ran, too timid or too cheap to do a big deal while rivals like News Corp. charted worldwide distribution ventures.

The deal for Cap Cities silenced those doubts. The merger, the second largest in U.S. history (after the 1988 leveraged buyout of RJR Nabisco), wed Disney's animation and live-action film studios to the ABC network and to cable channels that included sports programmer ESPN. For starters, Disney could promote its movies, TV shows and cartoons on ABC and perhaps create a Saturday morning cartoon block for the network. In the same way, Disney could advertise its films, theme parks and merchandise—from *Lion King* towels to Mickey Mouse T shirts to *Toy Story* figurines—on ESPN programs around the world. "This," sighed Christopher Dixon, an analyst at Paine Webber, "is a marriage made in heaven."

Eisner won more applause by hiring Ovitz and thus succeeding in the talent hunt where Bronfman had failed. The prospect of the two Michaels working together electrified onlookers both in and out of the company. Harvey Weinstein, co-chairman of Miramax Films, a Disney subsidiary, called Eisner and Ovitz "the greatest one-two combination since Sandy Koufax and Don Drysdale—only they're both Koufax." After turning down a quarter-billion dollars from MCA, Ovitz did not come cheap. His pay package reportedly included options to buy 5 million shares of Disney stock, which could net him a $100 million profit over the next 10 years if the company fares even moderately well. Said Ovitz: "It was time to do something different."

But some critics said that the success of the merger was by no means assured. One potential hazard involved that old buzz word synergy—the notion that putting two companies together can create a whole more profitable than the sum of its parts. In Disney's case, skeptics noted that the company could have advertised on ABC before the merger and also put Saturday morning cartoons on the network without having to spend billions of dollars to buy it. And if ABC should restrict its cartoon fare to Disney programs at the behest of the new owner, it could fall behind rivals with a broader range of shows. With such considerations to chew on, Hollywood settled back like a moviegoer with a box of popcorn to see how the merger would play out.

If the ABC deal was a potential triumph for Eisner, the Westinghouse purchase of CBS offered the promise of redemption for Westinghouse chairman Michael Jordan, who had arrived at the company in 1993 billed as a corporate savior. A chemical engineer with degrees from Yale and Princeton, Jordan, 59, joined Westinghouse after nearly two decades at Pepsico, where he had held a variety of executive positions. But Jordan, the first outsider to run Westinghouse since 1929, had got off to a rocky start in his efforts to revitalize the struggling company. After two years on the job, he had failed to swing a major deal, and Westinghouse's earnings and stock price continued to languish.

All the while, however, Jordan was clearly fascinated by Westinghouse's TV and radio ventures, Group W. He had already formed a 1994 alliance with CBS, in which Group W and the network co-owned several stations. The merger made Westinghouse a major media player by bringing it the network and increasing its broadcast facilities to 15 television and 39 radio stations, serving more than one-third of all U.S. households. The buyout, Jordan boasted, would create "a premier, top-notch, outstanding company."

Yet the pitfalls were many. Under former chairman Laurence Tisch, a hard-eyed cost-cutter who acquired control of the network in 1986, CBS sacrificed diversity by selling off its record and publishing companies. Tisch had also stood by as Murdoch outbid CBS for the broadcast rights to pro football, long a staple of the network's sports programming, and then scooped up eight key CBS affiliates around the country. Viewership suffered too, as lackluster shows caused CBS to drop to a distant No. 3 in the ratings race among the three major networks. "Larry's done a marvelous financial job, but he's squeezed everything from CBS

A SURPRISE SUITOR FOR AILING CBS

WESTINGHOUSE	COMPANY	CBS
$8.8 Billion	ASSETS	$3.7 Billion
	STRATEGY	

Michael Jordan at Westinghouse wanted to move out of his stagnating defense and refrigeration operations into entertainment. But Laurence Tisch at CBS had been selling off properties while his competitors were robustly growing—and CBS's prime-time TV programming was flagging.

1994 FIGURES

except the squeal of the hog," said Mario Gabelli, a money manager with major media holdings. "There was nothing left to sell but the company."

Against all this, Jordan seemed to offer mostly more cost cutting. His vision included boosting profits by laying off overlapping personnel at both the network and local-station levels. Many industry watchers thus looked coolly on the future of the merged companies, although not everyone was skeptical. "They said the same thing about GE when it brought NBC," noted Howard Stringer, a former president of the CBS Broadcast Group who headed a consortium of telephone companies developing consumer programming. "What did GE know about broadcasting? It all depends on how Westinghouse manages the network."

Even as Jordan and Eisner unveiled their buyouts, Time Warner chairman Gerald Levin courted Ted Turner in the media summer of '95. Relations between the two men had often been rocky since 1985, when Turner's billion-dollar purchase of the MGM film library left him desperately short of cash. To stay afloat, Turner sold an 18% stake in his company to Time Inc. (which merged with Warner Communications in 1989), and a 21% interest to cable king John Malone's Tele-Communications Inc. (TCI) empire. But now a frustrated Turner, whose outspoken remarks and flamboyant wheeling and dealing had earned him the nickname of "Captain Outrageous," found himself unable to make major moves without the consent of his two largest shareholders. When Levin vetoed a Turner plan to acquire NBC in 1994, Turner railed, "I'm being clitorized by Time Warner."

But the cerebral Levin, 56, who was as low-key as Turner was irrepressible, saw the chance for a major deal that would enhance Time Warner's cash flow and boost its lackluster stock price. A merger with Turner's potent empire promised to achieve both goals. Indeed, so attractive was the news and entertainment powerhouse Turner, 57, had built from three small radio stations that both Murdoch and GE chairman Jack Welch secretly made pre-emptive bids for it during the summer. And Levin, who during the 1970s had been the first to spot the profits HBO movies could generate when they were delivered coast-to-coast by satellite, now saw endless opportunities for linking the brand names in Time Warner's movie, music and publishing divisions to Turn-

er channels like CNN. One of the more tantalizing prospects was meshing the online capabilities of Time Warner and Turner. Another was uniting Turner's library of more than 3,000 films, including *Casablanca* and *Gone With the Wind*, with Time Warner's stable of 3,000 and featuring them on Turner channels. "This," boasted Levin, "is far and away the dream deal."

But it was a dream filled with potential wakeup calls. To win the approval of Malone, whose stake in Turner Broadcasting would be converted to nearly 9% of Time Warner, the merger partners agreed to grant TCI a 20-year contract to cary their cable programs at discounted rates. That brought lawsuits from two Turner directors who operated rival cable systems and insisted that the concessions would give TCI an unfair edge. U.S. West was also suing to block the merger. The Colorado-based phone company, which owned a 25.5% interest in Time Warner's film and cable businesses, claimed to have veto power over the merger, a position that Time Warner vigorously disputed.

A more serious threat to the merger could come from the Federal Trade Commission, which was scrutinizing the deal. Staff members worried that it could increase concentration of power in the cable industry by making Malone, whose TCI was the largest U.S. cable operator, a major shareholder of Time Warner, which ranked No. 2. Any move by the commission to restructure the merger might cause Malone to withdraw his approval and thereby scuttle the deal. But amid widespread speculation about the regulatory outcome, Time Warner and Turner said they remained confident the deal would go through.

Even as these giants girded for battle, the terrain was shifting beneath them. Consumers, for example, had been increasingly switching on computers for information and recreation and thus relying less on TV and movies. The Internet already claimed more than 20 million users, and people were becoming less dependent on traditional means of filling their leisure hours. "There is a growing distrust of one-way, packaged mass media," said Mark Stahlman of New Media Associates. The coming fight for the media dollar would thus involve a showdown between old and new ways of delivering fun and information, along with the clash of the newly merged titans. Now that's entertainment! ∎

TIME WARNER'S HEAD TURNER

TIME WARNER	COMPANY	TURNER
$16 Billion	ASSETS	$2.8 Billion
	STRATEGY	

To its movie, HBO and cable businesses, Time Warner will add Ted Turner's cable properties— CNN and four other channels—along with two movie companies and the Atlanta Braves. Turner will report to Time Warner chief Jerry Levin, but Turner and John Malone, head of the No.1 cable company, TCI, will each control major holdings of Time Warner stock.

1994 FIGURES

MIDAS OF MICROSOFT

Computer tycoon Bill Gates has all the marbles. But does he play by the rules?

ASK BILL GATES, THE FOUNDER AND CHAIRMAN OF Microsoft, about something he wants to talk about—like a new software system or his dream of a railroad trip through China on Chairman Mao's train—and he acts like the teenage boy that he still resembles. He grins. His voice breaks. He tucks his elbows into his lap and rocks back and forth as if to contain his excitement. But press Gates on a subject he doesn't want to talk about—such as the charges of anticompetitive, and possibly illegal, business practices that have turned up over the years, like ex-girlfriends at a wedding party—and he is liable to throw a tantrum. "I challenge your facts!" he shouts when confronted with even a minor allegation. "That's a lie! I never heard of any such thing. What a bunch of nonsense!"

If Gates felt at once cranky and exhilarated in 1995, he had good reason. At 39, he would seem to have achieved the information age's equivalent of the American Dream. Through intelligence, ruthlessness and hard work he dominated a technology so central to modern life that it touched nearly every office, school and desktop. He was very, very rich and so powerful that even his enemies were eager to cut deals with him. Yet in the year when he was supposed to ride the tide of what could be the next personal-computer software standard—the intensely bally-hooed Windows 95 operating system—he found himself under attack on all sides:

▶ From users, who complained that some of Microsoft's mainstay products, like the latest version of Word for the Mac, have become bloated and sluggish. After its release, Windows 95 also came in for criticism from buyers who claimed it was bug-laden.

▶ From the computer press, which had long acted as Gates' head cheerleader but now seemed to delight in reporting Microsoft's every delay, bug and legal setback.

▶ From newly emboldened competitors, who had quietly complained for years about Microsoft's strong-arm business tactics and recently began putting those complaints on the record.

▶ Above all, from government officials, who were concerned that Microsoft had developed a choke hold on a critical industry and who viewed with increasing alarm the prospect of Microsoft's moving into banking, telecommunications, and entertainment.

Early in the year, the Justice Department had derailed Microsoft's $2 billion bid to acquire Intuit and its popular Quicken electronic-checkbook program, a deal that would have helped realize Gates' ambition to make money from almost every commercial transaction in cyberspace. Another team of government lawyers snooped around asking questions about Microsoft Network, the new online service that Gates launched in August. And an antitrust suit that had been hanging over Gates' head for nearly five years—and that he thought he had settled in 1994—left Microsoft in legal limbo for several months, held hostage by Stanley Sporkin, an ornery federal judge. Though Sporkin was eventually removed from the case and the settlement was approved, he succeeded in throwing Microsoft off its stride.

American capitalism likes entrepreneurs to have a gleam in their eye, and even tolerates some clawing and scratching as long as the playing field is level. But it does not take kindly to bullies. When a company gets to be big enough, it invites the kind of scrutiny Microsoft is now getting.

How big is Microsoft? In some respects, the power it wields over the computer industry may exceed IBM's in its heyday. Eight out of 10 of the world's personal computers could not start up if it were not for Microsoft's operating-system software—programs like MS-DOS, Windows and Windows NT. What is even more impressive (not to mention profitable) is that the company also dominates the market for almost every big-ticket application program, like word processing (Microsoft Word), electronic spreadsheets (Excel), filing (Access), scheduling (Project) and the new all-in-one program "suites" (Office).

Financially, the company couldn't be more secure. Microsoft's revenues for 1994 were nearly $5 billion, more than all its competitors' in the PC-software business combined. The company's market value tops $40 billion, more than that of firms 10 times its size.

Gates has amassed a net worth of more than $10 billion, making him either the richest or the second richest man in America, depending on the closing price of his 141 million shares. He was married in 1993 on the Hawaiian island of Lanai and is building a $40 million-plus home on suburban Seattle's Lake Washington. Plans for the estate include video "walls" to display an ever changing collection of electronic art, a trampoline room with a 25-ft. vaulted ceiling where Gates can burn off steam, a 20-car underground garage and a trout stream.

None of which appears to give Gates or anyone else at the Microsoft "campus" in Redmond, Washington, an excuse to relax. One of the most remarkable traits of Microsoft's corporate personality—inherited directly from its restless chairman—is its inability to sit still. The company shifted into its highest gear for the August launch of Windows 95. The new operating system was Microsoft's bid to

BIG DREAMS: Aiming to create more software applications for Microsoft, Gates invested in the start-up of the "dream team" of Jeffrey Katzenberg, David Geffen and Steven Spielberg

rid itself once and for all of its twin albatrosses: the legacy of DOS (a primordial system that is starting to annoy even its most loyal users) and the competition from the Macintosh operating system (which continues to make Windows seem clunky by comparison).

Windows 95, once the bugs were discounted, not only caught up with Macintosh but in some areas outperformed it. It fixed some of the most aggravating aspects of DOS, from plugging in a new printer to communicating over a tangled corporate network. The new system was launched with a heap of hype. To the tune of the Rolling Stones anthem *Start Me Up*, retail stores opened up for 95 minutes of "Midnight Madness" at the first stroke of August 24 to sell copies of the new program; within a few weeks some 450 Windows 95–related books had hit the bookstores. In the first four days of its release, consumers spent $100 million on the new system.

Gates has even bigger plans. In 1995 he invested in a variety of speculative alliances: with Hollywood's Dream-Works troika (Spielberg, Katzenberg, Geffen) to make interactive entertainment products; with cable giant Tele-Communications Inc. to build interactive TV systems; and with cellular-telephone pioneer Craig Mc-Caw's Teledesic Corp. to build a network of low-flying telecommunications satellites.

BUT MICROSOFT'S PRIMARY FOCUS IN 1995 WAS THE INternet. In April 1994 Gates called an off-site meeting of his top staff to talk about a technology that had been around for 20 years but had suddenly exploded. Gates confessed that the Internet "mania," as he called it, had taken him by surprise. Millions of people were communicating via computers using software standards and application programs that Microsoft had no hand in developing. Product managers went back determined to make their programs Internet-compatible. The Microsoft Network , the commercial online service that Gates had cleverly built in ("bundled") with Windows 95, was redesigned to embrace the Internet and eventually steer it in a profitable direction. The goal was to make it easier for people to do everyday transactions over the networks—pay bills, order from catalogs, check bank balances.

Will Microsoft succeed? There are no guarantees. On the rough-and-tumble Internet, in newsgroups like *alt.destroy.microsoft*, the company is routinely excoriated as the great Satan of software. But by bundling the Microsoft Network with Windows 95, Gates got instant access to tens of millions of potential online customers. Although such bundling is standard practice for online-service providers, competitors like America Online president Steve Case are crying foul. "Windows is the dial tone of the digital age. They shouldn't be allowed to do this," said Case.

Gates claims not to understand such talk. Why, he asks in mock frustration, do people complain? Should Microsoft sit back and not make its products any better, so that people will buy from its competitors? Is that what it's all about? In fact, Microsoft's business practices are not that far out of line with most of Silicon Valley's. Even companies that have submitted evidence against Microsoft are ambivalent about inviting the Justice Department to police the industry.

Love Gates or hate him, Microsoft is a national treasure, the undisputed leader in a business now crucial to everybody's life. What Microsoft has yet to discover—and what the world is waiting to learn—is whether the qualities that brought about its triumphs will somehow make it falter. ∎

LEESON: Arriving in Singapore to face trial

■ FINANCE

BILLION-DOLLAR SWINDLES

Rogue traders run amuck, a venerable firm topples, and the world's bankers tremble

THE WEEK BEFORE HE DISAPPEARED, NICHOLAS LEE-son kept throwing up in the bathroom at work. Colleagues couldn't imagine what ailed the star financial trader of the Barings Bank's Singapore office, though he had been working hard, perhaps harder than usual. Then, at the end of trading on Tuesday, February 21, Leeson gathered up his notes, walked off the floor and began his getaway. In his wake lay a venerable 232-year-old British banking empire rendered suddenly and irretrievably insolvent. Half the financial world was reeling in fear, the other half in astonishment.

Barings was utterly undone, sapped of $1.4 billion dollars—nearly twice its available capital—in a few weeks of reckless financial gambling by a single rogue trader. Barings was one of the Queen's banks, and the Princess of Wales is a great-granddaughter of a Baring. But as a result of Leeson's gambles, control of Barings P.L.C. went to the Dutch firm ING in March—for the token sum of $1.60.

Leeson, 28, was a working-class kid from a London suburb. But the hard-partying wunderkind flew high in the financial markets of the East: in 1994, even as Asian markets sagged, he may have made as much as $36 million for Barings. Leeson was buying and selling the simplest kind of derivatives, futures pegged to the fall or rise of an index of Japanese stocks and bonds. Eventually, he began to gamble, telling his superiors he was making his large buys for a wealthy client. But there was no client—his bets were not covered. In the futures market traders only have to put a small percentage on the table—in Singapore at the

time it was 6%—so losses can exceed the ante many times. Yet Barings kept funding its young star's gambles, going as far as taking out an $850 million loan. When the Tokyo market index failed to reach the level Leeson had bet it would, Barings couldn't cover the debt. On March 1, a fleeing Leeson was detained in Germany as he flew back toward England. He was extradited to Singapore in November and pleaded guilty to 11 counts of fraud and forgery. He will serve 6½ years in a Singapore prison.

Financial firms around the globe claimed that the Barings debacle was an anomaly. But in September, Toshihide Iguchi, 44, a trader in U.S. government bonds at the New York office of Japan's Daiwa Bank, was charged with criminal fraud by a U.S. Attorney in New York City. In an effort to cover up a $200,000 loss, authorities said, Iguchi allegedly began forging documents that ultimately concealed more than 30,000 unauthorized trades and a deficit of $1.1 billion. Daiwa, one of the world's 15 largest banks, had enough capital to absorb the shortfall. But Iguchi testified to a U.S. judge that when he reported his frauds to senior executives in July, they asked him to keep the matter a secret while they held their own inquiry. The case—still under investigation at year's end—damaged the reputation of the Japanese banking community. ■

IGUCHI: Daiwa drain

SMART'S the Word

The Big Three are inventing autos that think for themselves and even

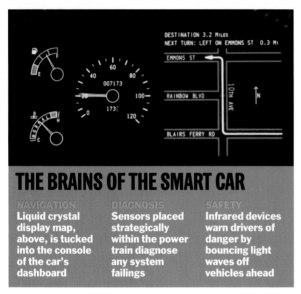

DESTINATION 3.2 MILES
NEXT TURN: LEFT ON EMMONS ST 0.3 MI

EMMONS ST

RAINBOW BLVD

10TH AVE

BLAIRS FERRY RD

007173

173%

THE BRAINS OF THE SMART CAR

NAVIGATION
Liquid crystal display map, above, is tucked into the console of the car's dashboard

DIAGNOSIS
Sensors placed strategically within the power train diagnose any system failings

SAFETY
Infrared devices warn drivers of danger by bouncing light waves off vehicles ahead

FIVE MINUTES AFTER MIDNIGHT: LARRY IS BARRELING along the freeway at 65 m.p.h., his car in cruise control. He is drowsy, his attention drifting, and he fails to notice the dimly lighted truck ahead of him. Suddenly, as he closes in on the truck, his car automatically slows to 50 m.p.h., maintaining a safe distance between the two vehicles.

Jolted into awareness, Larry decides to pass the truck. He does not see another car just beginning to overtake him, hidden in the blind spot on his left. But as he moves toward the passing lane, a warning light flashes on his dashboard, a buzzer sounds, and he quickly swings back, narrowly avoiding yet another collision.

Now fully attentive, Larry checks his location, pinpointed by a glowing dot moving along a map displayed on a dashboard screen, then exits the freeway and reads instructions on an adjoining screen. Finally, as he nears his destination, he is guided further by a computer voice that intones, "Turn left on Cherry Street."

This scenario, which sounds a bit like science fiction to most Americans, is already accepted as fact by the motor moguls in Detroit, where a remarkable technological transformation is occurring. Gone are the days when Detroit's machines were regarded as handsome and powerful but basically dumb brutes. Today the buzzwords in the Motor City are "smart cars," vehicles that literally think for themselves, diagnose their own problems and compensate for their drivers' frailties and failures, while ensuring a safer, more comfortable ride.

Industry executives who not long ago stubbornly fought the federal imposition of seat belts, airbags and emission controls are taking the lead in pushing high-tech innovation. "The automotive industry is finally moving from the Iron Age to the Silicon Age," says Timothy Leuliette, president of ITT Automotive, which produces electronic and structural components for the Big Three. "No one should think of Detroit anymore in terms of steel stampings and iron castings. It's the largest consumer-electronics industry in the world."

Detroit's Big Three have assembled some 50,000 engineers and scientists, and they are hiring more almost daily. Many of them are clustered at General Motors' huge, $2.5 billion technical center in the Detroit suburb of Warren. Chrysler spent $1 billion for its new technical center in Auburn Hills, Michigan, and in late 1994 Ford opened a spanking-new scientific-research laboratory in its campus-like engineering-and-design center in Dearborn, Michigan.

At Ford's new research lab, a car of the future was being brought to life in early 1995. At that stage it was not corporeal, only a ghostly, glowing, laser-generated hologram that looked like a solid, three-dimensional auto but offered no resistance to a hand or other objects passing through it. But for Neil Ressler, Ford's vice president of advanced vehicle technology, the intangible model was as good as there. "We can predict quite accurately how the vehicle is going to sound, from the engine's accelerating right down to the doors' and trunk latches' closing," he said. "We can turn on the

in Detroit

make up for their drivers' failings

wipers and switch on the headlamps. It's now possible to crash-test this car before we even build it."

This kind of high-tech research is speeding the development of the onboard sensors and diagnostic systems that will constitute the central nervous systems of the brainy new cars. For example, the blind spot that was not visible in Larry's side-view mirror will be monitored by a tiny infrared sidelight on the driver's door. A passing vehicle will send a reflection of that light back to a receptor, triggering the dashboard warning light and buzzer.

A forward-looking, infrared, radar-like device will perform a similar function, bouncing light waves off objects in front of the vehicle, then timing the arrival of the reflected waves and signaling when it senses danger. That signal will set in motion actions that disengage cruise control, throttle the engine and, in the case of another car's cutting too close in front, even apply the brakes. More sensors,

placed within the power train, will diagnose any system failings. If a faulty connection disables an electrically controlled coolant system, for instance, those sensors will detect it and signal a computer to connect the system elsewhere—while the car is under way—thus preventing a breakdown.

MORE THAN A PRETTY FACE The 1995 Lincoln Continental has 24 features that adjust automatically to a driver's preferences

Still other sensors will track the wear on the car's parts and systems, alerting the driver to potential trouble, and will even flash a warning when pressure in the tires becomes too low. Self-diagnosis becomes easier for an auto that has multiplex central wiring, introduced in the 1995 Lincoln Continental. Instead of the bunches of colored wires visible under the hood of most contemporary cars, the Continental has what Ford's Ressler describes as a "central nervous system, one continuous-wire system making a complete circle with a separate address for every function. It means fewer wires, fewer connections and fewer things that can go wrong."

With this kind of wiring, Ressler says, it was easier to incorporate Continental's "personalizing" features. With a turn of the ignition key, 24 different features—from seat and steering-wheel positions to interior temperature—automatically adjust themselves to a motorist's preferences. The driver can even adjust ride suspension and steering effort.

One of the more remarkable developments in sensor technology is the Automotive Stability Management System under development by ITT and already proved on frozen test tracks in Sweden and on the upper peninsula of Michigan. Using a coordinating system of seven sensors that detect the sideways momentum, steering-wheel position and cornering rate of the car along with the rotation of each of its wheels, the ASMS makes skidding virtually impossible even on ice covered lightly by snow.

Also down the road for drivers: auto-navigation systems being developed by Rockwell, among others. To use the Rockwell system, the motorist types the address of his destination on a dash-mounted keypad and reads his instructions on an adjoining screen. Using a small computer in the trunk to process signals from the military's satellite global-positioning system, the automatic navigator will track the vehicle's progress and regularly update instructions, including the name of the street where the next turn should be made. As the motorist nears the intersection, a computer voice directs him to "turn left" or "turn right."

Of course, getting smart costs money, as do the growing number of federally mandated improvements, and Detroit is passing on a good part of that cost to consumers. In 1994, average spending on a new car exceeded $20,000 for the first time ever, and Ford economists predict this cost will rise to $30,000 by 2002.

For that reason and others, Detroit is exercising caution in introducing smart features; the industry is testing and retesting them to ensure that they live up to their promise and is carefully gauging the degree of consumer demand for each item. It remembers only too well such failures as the talking dashboard ("Your door is ajar") and the tiny electrical wipers on side-view mirrors.

While reservations are almost always expressed—as they should be—about the introduction of new technologies, only experience can provide the answer. It was just a few years ago, for example, that a columnist described airbags as, essentially, explosives aimed at the driver's face. Yet time has proved that the bags can frequently be life savers and are therefore well worth the extra cost. Detroit is betting that smart cars will be similarly judged. ■

TOP 20		BOTTOM 20	
Australia	$835,000	India	$4,300
Canada	704,000	Nigeria	4,100
Luxembourg	658,000	Mali	4,000
Switzerland	647,000	Kenya	3,800
Japan	565,000	Cambodia	3,500
Sweden	496,000	Burkina Faso	3,500
Iceland	486,000	Gambia	3,500
Qatar	473,000	Niger	3,200
U.A.E.	471,000	Bangladesh	3,100
Denmark	463,000	Mozambique	2,900
Norway	424,000	Sierra Leone	2,900
U.S.	421,000	Guinea-Bissau	2,900
France	413,000	Rwanda	2,900
Kuwait	405,000	Vietnam	2,600
Germany	399,000	Tanzania	2,400
Austria	394,000	Uganda	2,300
Suriname	394,000	Malawi	2,200
Belgium	384,000	Burundi	2,100
Netherlands	379,000	Nepal	1,600
Italy	373,000	Ethiopia	1,400

Natural bonus: The Great Barrier Reef

Source: The World Bank

■ ECONOMIES

THE REAL WEALTH OF NATIONS

The World Bank ranks rich and poor nations by a "greener" set of standards

WHO ARE THE RICHEST PEOPLE ON EARTH? THE Americans? Japanese? Swiss? No, the surprising answer is the Australians, according to a provocative new study by the World Bank. Australia, a largely suburban, middle-class nation of 18 million, has never been known for great financial wealth, but the Land Down Under came up tops after the bank's economists decided to count natural treasures—ranging from minerals to farmland and even protected zones like the Great Barrier Reef—as assets. The analysis ranked 192 countries in all, using a novel yardstick for gauging the wealth of nations and the potential for economic development.

Downgrading such traditional measures as gross domestic product, the study gives new weight to natural resources, environmental protection, education, social flexibility and other generally undervalued assets that can be important instruments of long-term growth.

"This new system challenges conventional thinking by looking at wealth and not just income," explains Ismail Serageldin, the World Bank official who oversaw the study. "And it expands the concept of wealth beyond money and investments." The new approach awards the highest rankings to countries with small, comparatively well-trained populations and abundant natural resources. After Australia, the list's per capita tally puts Canada in second place, followed by Luxembourg, Switzerland, Japan and Sweden. The U.S., usually regarded as the world's richest nation, comes in a mere 12th. Ethiopia, Nepal and Burundi rank as the world's poorest nations.

The study assigns a dollar value to three kinds of national wealth. The first is "produced assets," such as machinery, factories, roads and other infrastructure. Then comes natural bounty, counting not only minerals but land, water and other environmental resources. Third, people power is measured, employing criteria like nutrition and educational levels. The economists who ran the study concede that its quantitative estimates resulted from a "complex chain of educated guesses" that may eventually have to be revised.

World Bank officials argue that their aim is to begin changing the way people and governments think about development. Two-thirds of the wealth of most countries can be found in their population, the report says, while produced assets, such as manufactured goods, represent only about one-fifth of the total. "Richer countries are generally those that invest more in human resources," concludes the report. And they zealously guard their natural wealth: "Good environmental policies are good economic policies and vice versa."

Those weren't always the views of the World Bank, which has long been criticized for doing little to improve the lot of the poor and doing much to damage the environment—by financing giant dams, for example. But with the appointment in June of American investment banker James Wolfensohn as its new president, the institution has been trying to be greener and more people friendly. That, according to the new calculations, is the best way to promote growth that is not only robust but also sustainable. ■

5,000 REASONS FOR WALL STREET TO CHEER

Wall Street offered its thanks for a prosperous year in 1995 in appropriate fashion: after hovering near the magic 5,000 mark for weeks, the Dow Jones industrial average surged past the barrier on the day before Thanksgiving. The close for the week: 5048.84. But the bulls on the Street kept running, boosting the index to over 5,200 before a one-day decline of more than 100 points

Celebration on the Street

cooled things off—for 24 hours. The next day, the bulls were running again.

....

WATCH THOSE CURVES: DETROIT'S NEW LOOK

For the auto industry, 1995 was the year of the oval, with soft lines and curves distinguishing the styling of most of the new cars on American roads. The epitome of the new look was the re-designed Ford Taurus, whose softly rounded contours had caused it to be dubbed a "jelly bean" and a "flying spud" when the first version was intro-

duced in 1986. The year's soft new designs contrasted with the sharp-edged, boxy look long favored by the industry. Early sales of the new Taurus were slow, but the lasting triumph of the car's styling could best be seen in its imitators, from the new Buick Rivera to the Oldsmobile Aurora.

....

INVESTORS' DARLINGS: HI-TECH STOCKS

Technology stocks boomed in 1995, leading some to predict that a bust lay ahead. Netscape, a maker of Internet software, debuted in August and astounded the market by moving from its predicted introductory price of $14 a share to a high of $71 in only 90 minutes. The volatile stock later went as high as $172¼ before declining 28¾ points in a single day. Pixar, an animation company, went public in November just as its film *Toy Story* became a box-office blockbuster. Apple computer co-founder Steve Jobs was a big winner in the Pixar debut: he had bought the company in 1986 for $10 million, and made a neat $1 billion on paper from its initial public offering.

....

A TRADE WAR AVERTED

It was almost a dooms-day for trade: by midnight on June 28 the

Artist's view of Steve Jobs as Buzz Lightyear in *Toy Story*

U.S. was poised to impose 100% tariffs on 13 makes of popular Japanese luxury cars, including Lexus and Infiniti, potentially costing their companies nearly $6 billion a year in lost sales. Japan could have retaliated by limiting imports from the U.S., perhaps starting a spiral that might have shattered financial markets in both countries. But with half a day to go before the deadline, an agreement was reached that averted a crisis: Japan would build more cars in the United States and use more U.S.-made parts—but no numerical targets would be set for the purchase of U.S.-made cars by Japanese buyers. After the last-minute deal, spokesmen for each nation hastened to claim their side had emerged the winner.

FEWER, BIGGER BANKS

The merger mania that has realigned America's banks in the 1990s only increased its pace in 1995. The trend, which had reduced the number of U.S. commercial banks from 12,345 in 1990 to 10,450 by 1994, gathered momentum as banks joined forces to cut overlapping costs, enter new markets and meet domestic and foreign competition. Among 1995's biggest mergers: New York City's Chase Manhattan and Chemical Banks merged to become the nation's largest, and the Bank of Boston and Baybank teamed up in a $2 billion deal. Meanwhile, Wells Fargo launched the largest hostile takeover bid in banking history, hoping to acquire First Interstate Bancorp, but found itself in a bidding war against First Bank System Inc. ■

The spud flies again: a 1996 Ford Taurus

SHOULD

Many Americans are working to make marriages

THIS MARRIAGE

more permanent—and divorce more difficult

BE SAVED?

O N A CHILLY MONDAY NIGHT IN THE WINTER OF 1995, LAURA RICHARDS and Mark Geyman are sitting in a living room in Jeffersonville, Indiana, their hands clasped tightly together in Laura's lap. This attractive, clean-cut couple had met the previous May through a mutual friend and got engaged in November, and they are happy to tell John and Patti Thompson, their mentors in the St. Augustine Catholic Church's marriage-preparation program, all about their wedding plans. It will be a big June affair, Laura says, with eight bridesmaids and eight groomsmen, two flower girls, a ring bearer and two priests. Patti Thompson cuts through the chatter. "How much time have you put into your marriage?" she asks, adding pointedly, "Your wedding is just one day. Your marriage is the rest of your life."

The conversation grinds to a brief, awkward halt, then takes a turn into the wilderness—into the thicket of this young couple's most intimate concerns and darkest fears. Patti tells Laura, a 29-year-old department store salesclerk, that in her opinion it is O.K. to take birth-control pills on the advice of her doctor to help with PMS. Then John, coordinator of family ministry at St. Augustine, says, "Is either one of you jealous?"

"Yeah," Mark admits, laughing. He adds, "Laura gets jealous of some of the girls in the office." Laura smiles nervously, fidgets with a pen and says nothing. Soon the Thompsons hit upon other prickly topics: Mark's compulsive neatness and Laura's worry that her future mother-in-law has reservations about the pending nuptials.

After Mark and Laura leave, the first of four 90-minute sessions completed, the Thompsons—who have been married 31 years and have raised four children—offer an assessment of this couple's chances at marital harmony. It is based on gut impressions as well as on a computer printout of the couples's "premarital inventory"—more than 100 questions about everything from the number of children they want to whether they are com-

THE LAWYER: LYNNE GOLD-BIKIN

Encouraging role-playing high school students to argue over "household chores"

fortable being naked in front of each other. Mark and Laura should do just fine, says Patti, but "there are just some things that smack you in the face that say they've got some work to do."

Working on a relationship, of course, is an activity that everyone—save for perhaps the most wildly romantic and misguided among us—has come to regard as a sometimes thrilling, sometimes infuriating but always necessary exercise. But Mark and Laura, with their lives ahead of them and their family values just taking shape, are actually on the cutting edge—even if it is an old blade. Although the Catholic Church has always required engaged couples to undergo pre-Cana counseling—usually just one day of talks between a priest and a married couple about finances, communication and family planning—a more intensive form of preparation is emerging, not only among Catholics but also among churchgoers of all denominations across America.

If this new marital gravitas were simply a church-based phenomenon, it would not be a phenomenon at all; the clergy has traditionally attempted to shore up the moral foundations of people's private lives. But a growing recognition that marriages are not to be entered into—or dissolved—lightly because of the enormous social costs is crossing political lines. Conservatives who espouse "family values" have long lamented the trend toward throwaway marriage and quickie divorce; now Democrats like President Clinton are joining in. An increasing number of marital therapists—and even lawyers—believe it is their job to save a relationship rather than simply help each party pursue his or her chosen path.

The number of divorces began soaring in the mid-'60s and has declined only slightly since peaking at a little over 1.2 million in 1981. Thus, despite sporadic cheers about falling divorce rates, couples have not got much better at staying together—not yet anyway. The institution of marriage underwent a particularly rebellious and dramatic shift when women entered the work force. "People don't have to stay married because of economic forces now," explains Frank Furstenberg Jr., co-author of the 1991 *Divided Families* and a sociology professor at the University of Pennsylvania. "We're in the midst of trying to renegotiate what the marriage contract is—what men and women are supposed to do as partners." But the facts remain that 1) the chips in these negotiations are often young children, emotionally fragile and economically vulnerable; and 2) despite their work outside the home, most women still suffer a severe income drop after divorce. The by-product of what remains the world's highest divorce rate is millions of children thrown into poverty, millions more scarred by bifurcated lives and loyalties.

ALMOST NO ONE DISPUTES THAT THERE ARE many valid reasons for divorce—among them domestic violence, child abuse and substance abuse. Mere incompatibility seems reason enough, if no children are involved. But the breakup of families is increasingly seen not only as a personal tragedy but also as a social crisis. That may be why, suddenly, so much attention is being paid to preventing divorce. Marital therapy has certainly become big business in the past decade. Some 4.6 million couples a year visit 50,000 licensed family therapists, up from 1.2 million in 1980. Thousands of couples swear by such programs as PAIRS (Practical Application of Intimate Relationship Skills), the semester-long relationship class offered by the PAIRS Foundation in 50 U.S. cities (and 16 other countries), or Retrouvaille, a church-sponsored program in which couples who have weathered their own marital difficulties run seminars for other troubled couples.

THE COUPLE: MARK GEYMAN AND LAURA RICHARDS
They did a "marriage inventory" before their wedding

THE ANALYST: JUDITH WALLERSTEIN
She aims to document the lasting wounds of divorce

"People are poorly trained for marriage today," says Joyce Clark, a coordinator for Retrouvaille in Youngstown, Ohio. From her 34-year marriage she recognizes all the stages of matrimony: romance, casual irritation, then total disillusionment. Clark suffered through five years of misery after discovering her husband Pat had had an affair. Then she and Pat attended a Retrouvaille weekend and learned how to forgive, how to get over it—and how to fight. "Now," says Joyce, "*we* work in the movement."

The newest recruits in the battle against divorce are lawyers like Lynne Gold-Bikin, a divorce attorney in Norristown, Pennsylvania, who is the chair of the family law division of the American Bar Association and founder of the Preserving Marriages Project. In October 1994, she took her project—to which some 3,200 lawyers contributed time and money—to more than 50 high school classrooms around the country. Gold-Bikin's long-term goal is to create a marriage-preservation program for corporations, which she claims suffer tremendous productivity losses because of divorce.

All such efforts are applauded by Judith Wallerstein, the California clinical psychologist who first raised public consciousness about the lasting damage of divorce. After studying 131 children of divorce over a span of 15 years, she found them to be at higher risk for depression, poor grades, substance abuse and intimacy problems. "We started to report this," she says, "and people got angry. They said, 'Impossible! If it's good for the parents, it's good for the children.' They wanted to believe that divorce and women's lib would take care of everything." Though Wallerstein's results are debatable, they have seeped into the zeitgeist and

> "We're in a stalled revolution. Marriage then becomes the shock absorber."

affected not only efforts to stay married but also how people approach divorce; more couples now seek to avoid ugly fights over custody, property and money.

On the state level, too, there is a growing belief that divorcing couples should be taught how to terminate their marriage in a reasonable fashion. Bucking the trend to make divorce easier and quicker, Utah and Connecticut now have mandatory education programs for all parents of minor children entering the family court. Six other state legislatures considered such measures in 1995.

Though the Federal Government has no jurisdiction over marriage and divorce, indirectly the impact of federal programs is enormous. Long-standing welfare policy, for example, pays Aid to Families with Dependent Children benefits only when there is no man in the house, thus fueling divorce and abandonment. And in a broader sense, "we do not have a family-friendly society," says sociology professor Arlie Hochschild of the University of California, Berkeley. Better day care, plentiful jobs at decent wages, flex-time and job sharing would all help to reduce the stresses on overwhelmed American households. "I would say we're in a stalled revolution," says Hochschild, author of *The Second Shift*, a landmark study of two-career marriages. "Women have gone into the labor force, but … we have not rewired the notion of manhood so that it makes sense to men to participate at home. Marriage then becomes the shock absorber of those strains." If he is right, while programs that teach couples to enter into marriage with the utmost care and deepest consideration can only be to the good, it may be marriage itself—along with basic institutions like the workplace—that needs refining. ■

"You have sold your souls, but must you debase our nation?"

*—Sen. Bob Dole
Majority Leader*

CARE TO SEE THE CHIEF THEATER OF operations in the culture wars? Just take a stroll through the Sherman Oaks Galleria, a twinkling mall in California's San Fernando Valley. This is where the great outpouring of pop culture comes to market, a market that caters to all the moods of the American disposition, from moonglow to bloodlust. At the Sam Goody's record store, the CD bins are stuffed with amiable releases by Hootie and the Blowfish and Boyz II Men. But they also hold the gangsta rap of Tupac Shakur. Nearby, at the Time Out video arcade, Jordan Trimas, 16, is playing Primal Rage, a game in which dinosaurs tear one another to pieces. "Sure, the violence influences kids," he shrugs. "But nobody can do anything about it." At Taco Bell, 15-year-old Christopher Zahedi will tell you he prefers movies with the rougher stuff. "I liked the part in *Pulp Fiction* where the guy points a gun and says a prayer from the Bible and you hear the gun go *brrrr* and then he kills everybody," he offers. "It's cool."

In their worst nightmares a lot of parents can also hear that gun go *brrrr.* They aren't so sure it's cool, just as they aren't so sure it's cool when they come across the more stomach-turning specimens of pop music in their kids' CD collections. That's why, when Senate Majority Leader Bob Dole went to Los Angeles in May to blast the entertainment industry, he touched a chord that transcended the party politics his remarks were shrewdly crafted to serve. Though popular culture has a long and proud history of offending the squares, during the current decade it has been particularly scabrous and saw-toothed—and most likely it has been brought to you by the major labels and the big studios. For parents, the pervasive electronic culture can start to look like some suspect stranger who hangs around their kids too much, acting loutish, rude and drunk.

It was that anxiety that Dole was speaking to when he accused the powers behind American movies, music and television of flooding the country with "nightmares of depravity." Warning that the more extreme products of pop culture threaten to undermine American kids, he called on the large media companies to swear off the hard stuff. "We must hold Hollywood and the entire entertainment industry accountable for putting profit ahead of common decency," Dole said, then raised the heat considerably by singling out one company, Time Warner, the media giant that includes the largest American music operation, the Warner film studio, and a stable of magazines, including TIME.

One day after Dole's speech, William Bennett, the former Education Secretary and drug czar, sent letters to Time Warner board members asking the company to stop distributing rap with objectionable lyrics. Later Bennett and C. DeLores Tucker, head of the National Political Congress of Black Women, aired their grievances in a private meeting with Time Warner Chairman Gerald Levin. "Are

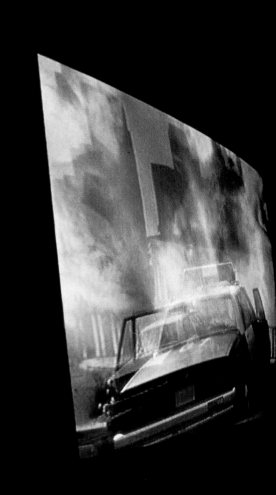

Bob Dole's broadside against the excesses of popular culture sparks a national debate on corporate responsibility

ARE MEDIA SEX & VIOLENCE KILLING AMERICA'S SOUL?

you morally disabled?" Bennett asked Levin, who met the attack with philosophizing and historical perspective.

Many Americans were asking similar questions of the country's large media conglomerates. In a TIME poll conducted after Dole's speech by Yankelovich Partners, Inc., 77% of those questioned said they were very concerned or fairly concerned about violence in the media; 70% said the same about media representations of sex.

"What we need is a national debate over the relationship of liberty to virtue," says Gary Bauer, the former Reagan White House aide who is president of the Family Research Council. "If you expose children to uplifting and noble material, you're more likely to have noble citizens. If children are wallowing in sexual images and violence, that is bound to have an impact on those who are most vulnerable."

Yet the violent and raunchy streak in Western civilization runs deep and long into the past. More teenage boys might be attracted to the classics if they knew about Homer's graphic descriptions of spear points ripping through flesh. As for sex, the lewd posturings in some paintings of Hieronymous Bosch would be rated NC-17 at today's local multiplex.

The rise of capitalism over the past two centuries has meant that all the resources of technology and free enterprise could at last be placed at the disposal of the enduring human fascination with grunt and groan. Early in this century, there emerged in the U.S. an entertainment industry that would prove to be all pervasive and ever more given to decking out our base impulses with sweaty and imaginative detail. It awaited only the youth culture that began stirring in the 1950s to take full advantage of the possibilities in rock, films and TV. In the '60s, skirmishes against such guardians of culture as the network censors who tormented the Smothers Brothers became the stuff of baby-boomer folklore.

The complications set in during the '90s, when the boomers who were once pop culture's most dedicated consumers became the decision makers at media companies—as well as the parents of the next generation. Pulled one way by their lifelong instinct for whatever is sensational or unofficial, they found themselves dragged in the other direction by their emerging second thoughts as citizens and parents.

Yet in the best tradition of Patrick Henry, Americans generally don't have much patience with government in-

"We won't retreat in the face of threats . . . or grand-standing."
—*Gerald Levin*
Time Warner

terference in First Amendment rights of expression, even when they may not much like what's being expressed. In the most prominent attempt in recent years to set the law on pop music, three members of 2 Live Crew were arrested in Florida in 1990 after a live performance. It took a local jury just two hours to acquit them of obscenity charges.

But the First Amendment applies only to attempts by government to restrain expression. It says nothing about decisions made by private media companies, and it does

UNPOPULAR CULTURE

WHILE SOME OF 1995'S FLAP OVER rap music, violent films and other products of pop culture may have been politically motivated, a TIME/CNN poll conducted by Yankelovich Partners in early June revealed that concern with popular culture was widespread. Of those asked, "How concerned are you about the amount of violence depicted in

TV: Ricki Lake talks tacky

movies, television shows and popular music," 77% claimed they were "very" or "fairly concerned." And more than 70% agreed that the depiction of violence in popular culture "numbs people to violence … inspires young people to violence … and tells people that violence is fun and acceptable."

MUSIC: Ice-T tees people off

Sex in the media was of slightly less concern. Still, a strong 70% of those interviewed described themselves as "very" or "fairly concerned" about the amount of sex depicted in popular culture. Results from poll questions on corporate responsibility for sex and violence in the media and possible methods of regulation appear below. ■

MOVIES: Arnold's army likes gore

How much responsibility should the groups listed below have in reducing the amount of sex and violence in entertainment?

	Great deal of responsibility	Some responsibility	Not much responsibility	No responsibility
American consumers who buy, watch or listen to this entertainment	61%	27%	4%	5%
Entertainment companies, like movie studios and record companies	55%	33%	7%	4%
Creative artists, like actors, directors and musicians	47%	38%	8%	6%
The U.S. government	29%	29%	12%	29%

Do you favor or oppose each of the following as a way to reduce the amount of sex and violence in entertainment?

	Favor	Oppose
Tighten parental supervision	93%	6%
Voluntary restraint by companies	81%	15%
Government censorship	27%	69%

As a way to improve the moral climate of this country, would you approve or disapprove of each of the following?

	Approve	Disapprove
Restrictions on TV content	66%	32%
Restrictions on music lyrics	62%	36%
Restrictions on movie content	61%	37%

nothing to prevent them from choosing which songs or programs they will or will not promote. In 1990 Simon & Schuster canceled plans to publish *American Psycho*, the sado-chic novel by Bret Easton Ellis, after advance complaints about passages detailing the sexual mutilation of women. (It was subsequently published by Knopf, a division of Random House.) "It's our responsibility," said Martin Davis, then chairman of Simon & Schuster's corporate parent Paramount. "You have to stand for something." This was just the sort of thing that Dole said he had in mind: self-restraint on the part of producers and distributors.

In a conversation with TIME editors before Dole's speech, House Speaker Newt Gingrich suggested that major radio advertisers band together to boycott stations that play "explicitly vicious" rap. Advertisers balked, but some citizen groups tried it: Dennis Walcott, president of the New York Urban League, organized a protest at the rap radio station WQHT in New York. The prominence of blacks as critics of gangsta rap was a new element in the culture wars. After a woman working at radio station WBLS in New York complained about the lyrics of a rap song, management established a committee to screen the playlist. For station head Pierre Sutton, who is black, it's simply a matter of "not in my house, you don't." Says Sutton: "Artists have the right to say what they want to, and we have the right to decide with regard to the playing of same."

Perhaps Time Warner's Levin was listening: in September he announced that his company would sell its interest in Interscope Records, the Los Angeles label at the heart of the controversy over gangsta rap's violent, anti-police and sexually degrading lyrics.

Score one for the conservatives—who went on to train their sights on the trashy TV talk shows of Ricki Lake and others. But there was a problem for the Republicans: for a party committed to free-market principles, pop culture represents the free market at its freest, meaning most able to make a profitable pitch to the grosser appetites. The most violent American movies are also among the most successful U.S. film exports because their bang-bang simplicities translate easily across cultural divides. Said Democratic Senator Bill Bradley of New Jersey: "The free market that the economic conservatives champion undermines the moral character that the social conservatives desire."

It's also not as simple as it sounds. Some decisions by media companies may seem easy. How many rap songs about slicing women's throats does the world really need? But most other judgments of taste are more difficult calls. Two films that Dole deplored, *Natural Born Killers* and *True Romance*, were written by Quentin Tarantino. He was also the gifted director of *Pulp Fiction*, the great cock-eyed movie where that guy quotes from the Bible and the gun goes *brrrr* and some younger viewers think it's cool—lots of older viewers too. In striving for a kid-friendlier culture, do we want to end up with a sanitized one, free of the excesses of "death metal" but also purged of Tarantino? Or even of the mixed bag of gifts and gas that is Oliver Stone?

Confused? Join the club. The culture wars won't just be conducted in boardrooms and at candidates' debates. For some time to come, they will surely be going on within our families and homes, and within ourselves as well. ■

THE GOSPEL ACCORDING TO

Choirboy? Demon?
Take your pick:
Ralph Reed's
burgeoning and
powerful Christian
Coalition inspires
both zeal and fear

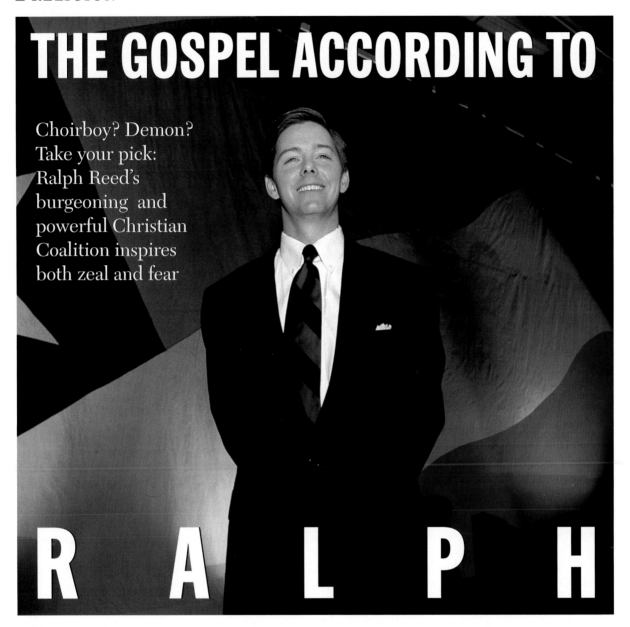

R A L P H

ON SUNDAY RALPH REED RESTS—OR AT LEAST HE TRIES to. But on this night in 1995, his two-year-old Christopher lay awake for hours, badly sunburned from a picnic, leaving Reed little time for sleep in the modern red brick house in Chesapeake, Virginia, that he and his wife Jo Anne had bought not long before. Reed, at 33 the father of three, struggles for time with his family. "I get home as often as I can, even if it's only for a day," he says. Still, as executive director of the Christian Coalition, he had another, more pressing mission. At dawn on Monday he was up and off to catch a 7 o'clock flight to Washington, the beginning of a hectic but typical week of lobbying, socializing and expanding his movement. Tuesday morning he was in New Hampshire, where Governor Steven Merrill joked about Reed's imminent appearance before the state senate: "They want to know that you don't

have two heads, that you don't have horns." Reed, who looks every bit the Eagle Scout he is, responded with a guffaw that was too loud by half for his 140-lb. frame. The New Hampshire senate paid close attention to his message. The ranks of conservative Christians, Reed said, are now "too large, too diverse, too significant to be ignored by either major political party."

Not long ago, the Christian right was dismissed as a group of pasty-faced zealots, led by divisive televangelists like Jerry Falwell, who helped yank the Republican Party so far to the right that moderates were frightened away. But Reed has emerged as the movement's fresh face, the choirboy to the rescue, a born-again Christian with a fine sense of the secular mechanics of American politics.

In 1995 Reed carried off a precarious balancing act: even as he courted centrist voters, he pressed Republican politicians to move toward the Coalition's right-wing policies. Bob Dole's midyear attack on the morals of Hollywood was the result of consultations with Reed.

Reed's cherubic aspect is misleading; behind his cool blue eyes lurks steel. No innocent, he talks tough politics like the late Lee Atwater, a Republican operative of decidedly secular mien. His message, emphasizing such broadly appealing themes as support for tax cuts, has helped make the Christian Coalition one of the most powerful grass-roots organizations in American politics.

For mobilizing eager volunteers down to the precinct (and local church) level and handing out 33 million voter guides—often in church pews—before the November 1994

"A religious person in politics … is working toward more than taking the next election."

GODFATHER: Televangelist Pat Robertson gave Reed his blessing

congressional election, the Coalition is credited with having provided the winning margin for perhaps half the Republicans' 52-seat gain in the House and a sizable portion of their nine-seat pickup in the Senate. The Coalition's 1.6 million active supporters and $25 million annual budget, up from 500,000 activists and a $14.8 million budget in 1993, hold a virtual veto on the G.O.P. nominee for President, and will exert an extraordinary influence over who will occupy the Oval Office in 1997.

REED'S SUCCESS REPRESENTS THE MOST THOROUGH penetration of the secular world of American politics by an essentially religious organization in this century. To some, this ascendancy evokes the 17th century New England theocracies, which were as invasive as they were closed-minded. To Reed's adherents, however, it signifies a bracing and historic spiritual renaissance.

Televangelist Pat Robertson is the founder and guiding spirit of the Coalition. But he has ceded operational control to his young protégé. That transition began when Reed and Robertson sat next to each other at a dinner honoring George Bush's Inauguration. At first

Reed wondered whether the broadcasting tycoon seriously wanted a brass-knuckled pol like himself to run the operation. Reed, then a doctoral candidate in American history at the University of Georgia, was a veteran of Republican headquarters in Washington and the rough-and-tumble campaigns of Jack Kemp and Jesse Helms. But Robertson readily allowed Reed to suffuse the Coalition with a new professionalism. In the meantime, Reed's book, *Politically Incorrect*, became the manifesto of the movement. With Robertson's approval, he is working on a second.

Ralph Reed Jr. was born in 1961, the son of a Navy physician. Nicknamed "Buddy," Reed displayed his nature from the beginning. Asked what her son always aspired to be, his mother told the Atlanta *Journal-Constitution*, "In charge." Raised a Methodist, Reed was an indifferent Christian—though an avid Republican—through his early college years. He wrote a rabid column while at the University of Georgia, taking hawkish positions on gun control and the nuclear freeze. (He resigned from the paper after a reader charged him with plagiarism.) As a student, he ran school campaigns and gained a reputation as a player of dirty tricks.

In 1983, however, shortly before he became the director of a national G.O.P. student committee, Reed not only gave up booze and cigarettes but also found God. He had seen a politician he admired—a "pro-family, traditional-values" type—drinking and fooling around with someone he was not married to. The sight disgusted Reed and led him toward being "born again." He apologized to one of his political victims and started attending an evangelical church. "Since 1983, I haven't been involved with anybody in politics for whom I bear a grudge in my heart," Reed claims. "Which doesn't mean I don't want to win. It means a religious person in politics understands that he's working for goals more universal than taking the next election. I'm asking myself, Where do I want this movement located in the political system in the year 2025? If I fall for the temptation of acting as a power broker within a given party, then 25 or 30 years from now I will be where the labor unions are today."

"By playing hardball [the Christians] may win everything, but hardball also risks losing everything," says Frank Luntz, the pollster behind the Republicans' Contract with America. Reed frankly admits, "If we make this decision the wrong way, 20 years from now we're going to look back and regret it."

Whatever Reed decides—to press for control of the G.O.P. now or to rise above partisanship for a while—the religious right is moving toward center stage in American secular life. The Christian Coalition, says Arthur Kropp of People for the American Way, "won't be content to be background music." They will want the oomph of the big band. And a choirboy will lead them. ∎

■ RELIGION

THE CATHOLIC PARADOX

The U.S. church is healthier than it seems—but fractious

A SATURDAY MORNING IN SUBURBAN BALTIMORE. A group of parishioners of bustling and growing St. Joseph Catholic Church gathers in a member's living room to discuss the Roman Catholic faith. The people from St. Joseph's, a parish of 10,000, speak reverentially about Pope John Paul II, who is about to visit the U.S. for the fourth time, on a trip that will take him to New York City, Newark and—the impetus for their meeting—Baltimore. John Paul II is a familiar figure to them, and at last they may be able to catch a glimpse of him in person, as the first Pope to visit the place where, in 1634, American Catholicism was born.

A few of the parishioners express mild disagreement with positions that John Paul has emphasized during his 17 years as Pontiff. The ban on women in the priesthood prompts a debate. Joseph Lewis, 64, chair of the St. Joseph's parish council, suggests that the omission of women from the ranks of the Apostles may have been historical rather than theological: "You've got to put yourself back to A.D. 25," he says. "Could you picture Christ choosing women Apostles at that time?" But Kevin Coyle, 35, a college student, argues in favor of women in the priesthood: "I look at other faiths and think, Why is our Church different? If women can hold other jobs and are intelligent and capable, why hold them back?"

MASS APPEAL: John Paul greets admirers in New York City. The Pope's flock loves the man—if not his message

Soon the drift of the conversation tugs the parishioners away from dispute and toward shared satisfactions in their faith. Dan Wilson, 62, an insurance salesman who has tickets to a papal Mass, says, "This is a once-in-a-lifetime thing. And I personally admire the Pope and agree with him." Jerry Trees, 56, a financial consultant and chair of the parish pro-life committee, says, "Rome presents the truth, the repository of faith, with a history of 2,000 years, and that puts things in perspective."

Why are these Catholics so happy? Haven't they heard that the church in America is in turmoil and disarray—scolded by John Paul for laissez-faire theology, racked by internal squabbles over moral issues (artificial birth control, abortion, gay and lesbian rights)—and tainted by scandal? The spate of news accounts in recent years about priests accused of sexually molesting children is only the most disturbing sign that something must be seriously wrong within the U.S. church. Another sign, with potential long-range consequences, is the minuscule number of men entering the priesthood and women entering religious congregations.

Yet despite the reasons for gloom or discouragement, 85% of U.S. Catholics say their religion is very important or fairly important in their lives, according to a TIME/CNN poll conducted just before the Pope's visit. A 1994 survey by the Los Angeles *Times* shows that priests and sisters are comparatively satisfied with their vocations. And Father Andrew M. Greeley, an author and sociologist who specializes in analyzing his fellow American Catholics, finds "practically no increase in those born Catholic who no longer identify as Catholic—the defection rate." How does Greeley account for this phenomenon? "They like being Catholic."

THEY ALSO LIKE, ACCORDING to the TIME/CNN poll, to put the dictates of conscience ahead of doctrines, particularly in matters of sexual behavior. The paradox of U.S. Catholicism rests precisely in this freethinking fractiousness among believers, who nonetheless continue to find common ground and fulfillment in the practice of their faith. Some of them advocate change; others resist it. But most have by now realized that change is inevitable, despite the efforts of John Paul to hold it in check. Demographics, immigration, the allure of secular U.S. culture—all these forces and more are reshaping the U.S. church.

While the number of Catholics worldwide passed 1 billion in 1995, the total Catholic population of the U.S. has grown 15% over the past 10 years and stands at just over 60 million. Contributing to this number is the massive immigration of Hispanics, who now account for roughly one-third of the American Catholic population. Some Los Angeles parishes in or near Hispanic neighborhoods must schedule 12 or 14 Masses on Sunday to handle the crowds of worshippers. Who, eventually, will celebrate all those Masses?

Priests are inarguably in short supply—by some estimates there are 2,000 parishes (out of a U.S. total of 19,723) without a resident priest—and the dearth is likely to worsen. Richard Schoenherr, a married former priest and sociology professor at the University of Wisconsin at Madison, in 1994 co-authored a book called *Full Pews and Empty Altars.* He projects that the number of active diocesan priests in the U.S., which stood at 35,000 in 1966, will have fallen 40%, to 21,000, in a decade, and he blames the shortage on mandatory celibacy, a long-standing church discipline that John Paul has refused to reconsider.

Yet some church-watchers doubt that the celibacy rule is responsible for the decline. It was never an easy cross to bear, they point out. Why should it be harder now than

FACE OF THE FUTURE: Hispanic Catholics celebrate a mariachi Mass in East Los Angeles

throughout much of the church's 2,000-year history? "People say the sexual revolution has made sex more attractive for young men," Greeley observes. "I say, Give me a break!"

An alternative theory currently gaining favor is that the ascent of U.S. Catholic families into the middle class has given sons a wider range of career opportunities. Monsignor Paul Cook, 62, pastor of St. Joseph's, says, "Today a young man is in college, and the parents are paying to have him prepare for engineering or law, and he says he wants to be a priest? More often than not, they say, 'You're out of your mind.'" Worldly options for young Catholic women have increased even more dramatically, making it harder to attract them into religious orders.

Despite scattered attempts to revivify the seminary system, hardly anyone expects enough men to enlist in the next few years to make up for the current and projected shortfall of priests. This problem, along with the parallel shortage of sisters and brothers, affects not only local parishes but also the extensive national network of Catholic schools and hospitals, many of which are now staffed overwhelmingly by lay workers. In fact, many Roman Catholics see lay people as the key to the future of the American church. "The church's ministerial character is going to be primarily lay," says Jesuit Thomas Rausch, a theologian at Loyola Marymount University in Los Angeles. "That means that the ordinary ministers of the church tomorrow are not going to be priests and nuns and religious brothers. This is very significant."

If these predictions are correct, then the typical U.S. parish of the future may come to resemble a Protestant-style congregation, directed and administered by members who also have considerable leeway in determining who will preach and conduct services. Would such an independent, grass-roots operation still be recognizable as Catholic? Evangelical Protestant Richard Mouw, president of Fuller Theological Seminary in Pasadena, California, thinks it may not: "A lot of us Protestants wish we had a stronger sense of the teaching and shepherding authority of the church, whereas Catholics are loosening up on that. Many of us worry a little about the breakdown of authority in the Catholic Church. We simply don't want to see them make all the mistakes we've made." President Mouw, meet Pope John Paul II. ∎

a touch of CLASS

ADELECTABLE WHITE JACKET. A sinuous little suit. A shiver of cocktail chiffon. An international parade of pretty, wearable clothes.

It may be the first time a major design trend began on the obituary pages. 1994's fashion spreads offered up the usual chaos: butt-high skirts, little-girl looks, underwear as outerwear, fake furs, fake feathers, fake everything. But the deaths of Audrey Hepburn and Jacqueline Onassis inspired exhilaratingly lovely retrospectives, in magazines and on television. These women always managed to be both sexy and classy—at a grand ball, on horseback, impersonating royalty or playing First Lady to the chandeliers. They had the combination of vitality, faultless grooming and alluring clothes that add up to authentic glamour.

In 1995 it appeared that designers, sick of their own tasteless japes and worried about a retail market that had been sagging since 1992, finally decided to get back to basics. The fall ready-to-wear shows that took place in Milan in March and in New York City in April showed a dramatic shift in direction. In a fashion world that has seemed, in recent years, increasingly remote, self-involved and obsessed with stunts, it was a remarkable about-face. Call it a return to elegance, to wearability, to more realistic apparel with commercial appeal. Most designers, at last, seemed will-

INSPIRATION **Jackie set the tone again**

ing to trade the cutting edge for the cash register.

The movement was broad based and a genuine good-news story for both customers and the industry. At the rich and influential house of Chanel, designer Karl Lagerfeld talked of a "new tendency for beauty to combat ugliness." New York designer Isaac Mizrahi

observed, "People are in a kind of sobering position. In the '80s it was so incredibly over the top. Now it's about how can we express ourselves and still maintain a certain amount of dignity."

Michael Kors, who presented a sleek, sophisticated collection in New York, expressed the fashion industry's new sensitivity to the marketplace: "The plain fact is that it doesn't matter how great it looks on Helena Christiansen. If no one buys what I'm designing, then I really didn't do my job."

Retailers had been waiting to hear this for years. Said Joan Kaner, fashion director of Neiman Marcus: "We have been complaining bitterly for the past few seasons that there aren't enough clothes for women to wear. Now there's a return to quality and beautiful fabrics." Nicole Fischelis, fashion director of Saks Fifth Avenue, observed, "We are seeing a return to elegance, and it is unquestionably commercial."

An early, startling sign of things to come appeared in January at Gianni Versace's couture show in Milan. Versace is more Vegas than Milan, a man who in the past had gloried in vulgarity and pagan displays of naked flesh. But down his catwalk came purring beauties in simple, classic clothes—smart little suits and dresses that Jackie or Audrey, Grace Kelly or Babe Paley would have been delighted to wear. And that is just what Versace intended. "Fashion is once again finding the right equilibrium," he says. "When I was working, I thought of both Hepburn and Kelly." Versace pursued the new look in his ready-to-wear collection a month later, with flattering and practical costumes that featured a real innovation: color. Like dozens of his fellow designers, he favored red and its cousins pink and fuschia. Even more surprising, there were plenty of pastels for cold weather.

The New York collections underscored the trend. Because Seventh Avenue specializes in sportswear, the theme was expressed less dramatically, but it was evident nonetheless. Calvin Klein was true to form with a spare, functional show, mostly in those old standby tones black, brown and white. Geoffrey Beene offered long wool dresses and satin evening frocks—all comfortable silhouettes.

It was in the realm of daytime dresses and suits that Jackie and Audrey most haunted the collections. The biggest surprise came at the Chanel show, its

DE LA RENTA
A glamorous show that
concentrated on his specialty,
heady evening extravaganza

LAGERFELD
He sported shades and fan at the
curtain call, but the powerful designer
got serious on the runway

VERSACE
Man of the hour: he broadcast
the news of elegance without losing
his trademark eroticism

strongest in many seasons. Just a year earlier, Lagerfeld's offerings for Chanel had been a hoot—fluffy, puffy microskirts, silly hats, gold chains and logos attached to just about any surface. Now his about-face was complete. Several of his knee-length suits had no gold trim at all. They were in black or mellow tweeds. Lagerfeld said he was "going back to putting the body first." It was important that Lagerfeld, who presides over France's most successful fashion house, was aboard. Other conservative designers looked good as well. Bill Blass showed tweeds and corduroys in vibrant colors. Oscar de la Renta staged a superglamorous show that concentrated on his specialty: heady evening clothes.

As heartening as fashion's return to elegance was, it called for a lot of rethinking by consumers, and even a little discipline. "The younger generation has been educated to dress in a wild, free way," observed Gianfranco Ferré, the maestro of the house of Dior. Hemlines, for example, seemed to have settled in at knee length. That might be welcome for women frustrated with following the fashion vagaries of the past few years. But knee-length skirts look best with stiletto heels—and few women born since the late '60s have ever worn them. On the runways in the spring, even experienced models teetered perilously, cantilevered over very slender columns.

COLOR **Red and its cousins, fuchsia and pink, attracted designers like Lagerfeld**

The current direction, inspired by the '50s and early '60s, is in some ways a reaction against fashion that had become so extreme it had reached the vanishing point. Skirts—or shorts—could get no shorter, boots no heavier or more aggressive. The entire apparatus of underwear had been exposed. Behind this façade was a highly artificial notion of femininity: butch, heavily lacquered, with lurid makeup and hennaed hair. At its best—when virtuosos like Jean-Paul Gaultier, Karl Lagerfeld or Vivienne Westwood were camping it up—it had rare wit, but the idea was consumed in its own fire. Grunge was another game whose time was up. No need to buy something new when the whole point was to look used.

A FEW DESIGNERS SAT OUT THE CARNIVAL, WHILE making fortunes out of basic, neutral clothes. They included Giorgio Armani, who started the last real revolution in fashion with his destructured jackets, and his colonists: Calvin Klein, Jil Sander and Donna Karan, among others. Now the fashionable cycle had restarted. Versace saw it coming. "You see," he said, "women are changing again. They don't want to look androgynous anymore."

And they didn't want to buy the just-kidding clothes that were being pressed on them. The fashion business was suffering. Howard Davidowitz, a fashion-industry consultant, said that 1994 "may have been the worst year in 20 years for women's clothes." Part of the reason had to do with merchandising rather than fashion. Too many stores were selling the same merchandise, too much of too little. U.S. Commerce Department statistics showed that women were spending their money on other things: furniture, household white goods, cars and even computers. "Women are shopping in their closets" had become a sad and much repeated tag line in the fashion industry.

Beginning in 1995, if designers, retailers and women were to have anything to say about it, sanity—and shopping—had returned to stay a while, along with a touch of class and maybe a whiff of charm. ∎

■ SOCIETY

FALLING THROUGH THE CRACKS

Does America abandon its youngsters during their most critical years?

THE CLOSED DOOR, THE WRONG CROWD, THE BAD grades, the defiant clothes, the sullen demeanor, the telltale scents. These are some of the warning signs of adolescence, signs that parents should heed—but too often ignore. This was the warning delivered in mid-October by the Carnegie Council on Adolescent Development, in a report titled *Great Transitions*. After a nine-year study, the 27-member panel of scholars, scientists, members of Congress and former Cabinet officers concluded that the U.S. is neglecting its 19 million young adolescents to such an extent that half of the kids may be irrevocably damaging their chances for productive and healthy futures. Ten-to-14-year-olds are being abandoned by their governments, communities, schools and parents just when they most need guidance and support. They are in danger of becoming "lifelong casualties" of drug and alcohol abuse, violence, suicide, AIDS, teen pregnancy and failed educations.

The report painted a disturbing portrait of America as a dismissive and preoccupied parent, a country trying to wish away the troubles of its teenagers. "Adolescence is as perplexing for our society as a whole as it is for the individual parent," says Dr. David Hamburg, chairman of the council. "I hope that we have touched a nerve."

The report's statistics were alarming. The suicide rate among young adolescents increased 120% from 1980 to '92; the firearm-homicide rate for 10-to-14-year-olds more than doubled between 1985 and '92; the smoking rate among eighth-graders rose 30% from 1991 to '94; two-thirds of eighth-graders report that they have tried alcohol, and 28% say they have been drunk at least once; pregnancy rates for girls younger than 15 rose 4.1% between 1980 and 1988.

As children enter the physical and emotional turmoil of adolescence, they naturally seek more independence and experiment more boldly. But it is precisely at this phase, the report shows, that parental involvement in school activities—and by extension, parents' influence on their kids' lives—drops off. Seventy-five percent of the parents of nine-year-olds claim high or medium involvement, while only 55% of the parents of 14-year-olds do.

Among the report's prescriptions: 1) educational institutions should create schools better suited to adolescents' developmental needs; 2) parents should re-engage themselves with their children, with the help of more family-friendly policies by employers; 3) health professionals should increase their efforts to educate and treat adolescents; 4) youth organizations should expand and multiply to reach out to the one-third of adolescents who are now ignored; and 5) the media should show more responsibility by discouraging, not glamourizing, violence, sex and drugs.

Acknowledging that the council's—and society's—work only began with the publication of his report, Hamburg quoted Winston Churchill on the Battle of El Alamein: "This is not the end. It is not even the beginning of the end. But it is, perhaps, the end of the beginning." ■

CALLING IT QUITS AT A MALE BASTION

At least 30 other cadets dropped out of the Citadel's freshman class in their first week, but Shannon Faulkner is the only one whose name people will remember. After fighting since 1993 to become the first female cadet in the South Carolina military school's 152-year history, Faulkner floundered for less than five days, most of them spent in the campus infirmary, before deciding to quit. She blamed the 2½-year ordeal to gain entry for her fast withdrawal. The news led to a gloatfest on the part of her male schoolmates, but several other women announced they would try to run the obstacle course.

Cadet Faulkner being braced by a Citadel instructor

DOWN THE TUBES

For America's children, TV's vast wasteland keeps getting vaster faster. In 1995 the broadcast networks all but abandoned the "family hour" between 8 p.m. and 9 p.m. in their prime-time schedules. Kid-oriented shows like *Full House* were canceled, and adult fare like ABC's *Roseanne* aired at 8 p.m.

Yet even as funding for public television was threatened, a study of preschoolers in low-income areas around Kansas City showed that those who regularly watched *Sesame Street* and similar programs performed significantly better on standard verbal and math tests than did children who consistently watched adult programs and cartoons.

Sculptor Neil Estern with a scale model of an F.D.R. statue

REMEMBERING F.D.R.: TRUTH AND FICTION

For decades Americans have argued over plans for a memorial in Washington honoring the longest-serving U.S. President, Franklin Delano Roosevelt. The latest wrangle: disabled Americans were angered that the three F.D.R. sculptures proposed in the latest plans for a memorial had no sign of a wheelchair, leg braces, cane or crutches, all part of his support system. The plans neglected the President's "triumph over his adversity," said a spokesman for the National Organization on Disability, which claims to represent the feelings of 50 million disabled Americans.

A SHAMEFUL DEATH

She was conceived in a homeless shelter in Brooklyn and born addicted to crack. Yet Elisa Izquierdo had an enchanted aura: she even became the special friend of a scion of Greece's old royalty named Prince Michael, who was a patron of her pre-school. But two months before her seventh birthday, the girl was dead, apparently a victim of her mother's savage beatings. A shocked nation was reminded of the horrors of child abuse, especially since New York City authorities had been notified of Elisa's plight several times—but left her with her mother anyway.

GUILTY OF MURDER FOR DROWNING HER SONS

It took a South Carolina jury less than three hours to find Susan Smith guilty on two counts of murder for drowning her sons Michael, 3, and Alex, 14 months, in a lake in 1994. The trial lasted only five days. The jury, which could have found Smith guilty of involuntary manslaughter, sentenced her to life in prison, sparing her the electric chair. ■

Smith: Given life in prison

beyond

a place

Millions of American families will remember 1995 as the year when the virtual world of cyberspace finally emerged from the realm of ballyhoo—and flickered into reality on the computer screen within their home

called hype

PHOTO ROOM

FUN · FUN · FUN
EASY · EASY · EASY
ETC · ETC · ETC

APX 3-11

CYBER

MFMD · HD

IRED

File Edit Mode Image

4587120
NT

■ CYBERSPACE

welcome to
what is it? where is it?

as the big ideas in technology often do, it all began with a science-fiction writer. William Gibson, a young expatriate American living in Canada, was wandering past the video arcades on Vancouver's Granville Street in the early 1980s when something about the way the players were hunched over their glowing screens caught his eye and struck him as odd. "I could see in the physical intensity of their postures how *rapt* the kids were," he says. "It was like a feedback loop, with photons coming off the screens into the kids' eyes, neurons moving through their bodies and electrons moving through the video game. These kids believed in the space the games projected."

That image returned to haunt Gibson. At the time he didn't know much about video games or even computer technology—he wrote his breakthrough "cyberpunk" novel *Neuromancer* (1984) on an ancient manual typewriter—but he knew people who did. And as near as he could tell, everybody who worked much with the machines eventually came to accept the reality of that imaginary realm. "They develop a belief that there's some kind of *actual* space behind the screen," he says. "Some place that you can't see but you know is there."

cyberspace

and how do we get there?

Gibson called that place "cyberspace," and used it as the setting for his early novels and short stories. In his fiction, cyberspace is a computer-generated landscape that characters enter by "jacking in"—sometimes by plugging electrodes into sockets implanted in the brain. What they see when they get there is a three-dimensional representation of all the information stored in "every computer in the human system"—great warehouses and skyscrapers of data. He describes it in a key passage in *Neuromancer* as a place of "unthinkable complexity," with "lines of light ranged in the nonspace of the mind, clusters and constellations of data. Like city lights, receding . . ."

In the years since, there have been other names given to that shadowy space where our computer data reside: the Net, the Web, the Datasphere, the Matrix, the Electronic Frontier, the information super-highway. But Gibson's coinage of *cyberspace* may prove the most enduring. By 1989 it had been borrowed by the online community to describe increasingly interconnected computer systems—especially the millions of computers jacked into the Internet.

Now hardly a day goes by without a news-paper column, political speech, or corporate press release invoking Gibson's imaginary world. Suddenly, it seems, everybody has an E-mail address, from Hollywood moguls to the Holy See. Billy Graham has preached on America Online; Vice President Al Gore has held forth on CompuServe. In Wash-ington cyberspace has become a political hot button of sometimes surprising potency, first pressed during the 1992 presidential campaign by Al Gore and Bill Clinton, who rode to the White House in part on the promise that they would build the so-called information superhighway and route it through every voter's district—if not to his home. The Republicans have also staked a claim. House Speaker Newt Gingrich, a longtime friend of futurists Alvin and Heidi Toffler, proclaimed in a sort of information-age Magna Carta: "Cyberspace is the land of

It's as if some grim

knowledge. And the exploration of that land can be a civilization's truest, highest calling."

Corporations, smelling a land rush of another sort, are scrambling to stake out their own claims in cyberspace. Every computer company, nearly every publisher, most communications firms, banks, insurance companies and hundreds of mail-order and retail firms are registering their Internet domains and setting up sites on the World Wide Web. They sense that cyberspace will be one of the driving forces—if not the primary one—for economic growth in the 21st century. All this is being breathlessly reported in the press, which has seized on cyberspace as an all-purpose buzz word that can add sparkle to the most humdrum development or assignment. For working reporters, many of whom have just discovered the pleasures of going online, cyber has become the prefix of the day, and they are spawning neologisms as fast as they can type: cyberphilia, cyberphobia, cyberwonk, cybersex, cyberslut.

One result of this drum roll is a growing public appetite for a place most people haven't been to and are often hard-pressed to define. In a TIME/CNN poll of 800 Americans conducted in January 1995 by Yankelovich Partners, 57% didn't know what cyberspace meant, yet 85% were certain that information technology had made their life better. The rush to get online, to avoid being "left behind" in the information revolution, is intense.

What is cyberspace? According to John Perry Barlow, a rock 'n' roll lyricist turned computer activist, it can be defined most succinctly as "that place you are in when you are talking on the telephone." That's as good a place to start as any. The telephone system, after all, is a vast, global computer network with a distinctive, audible presence (crackling static against an almost inaudible background hum). By Barlow's definition, just about everybody has already been to cyberspace. It's marked by the feeling that the person you're talking to on the phone is right "in the same room."

Cyberspace, of course, is bigger than a telephone call. It encompasses the millions of personal computers connected by modems—via the telephone system—to commercial online services, as well as the mil-

lions more with high-speed links to local area networks, office E-mail systems and the Internet. It includes the rapidly expanding wireless services: microwave towers that carry great quantities of cellular phone and data traffic; communications satellites strung like beads in geosynchronous orbit; low-flying satellites that will soon crisscross the globe like angry bees, connecting folks too far-flung or too much on the go to be tethered by wires. Someday even our television sets may be part of cyber-

fallout shelter had burst

space, transformed into interactive "teleputers" by so-called "full-service" networks like the ones several cable-TV companies (including Time Warner) are building along the old cable lines, using fiber optics and high-speed switches.

But all these wires and cables and microwaves are not really cyberspace. They are the means of conveyance, not the destination: the information superhighway, not the bright city lights at the end of the road. Cyberspace, in the sense of being "in the same room," is an experience, not a wiring system. It is about people using the new technology to communicate with one another. It can be found in E-mail exchanged by lovers who have never met. It emerges from debates within mailing lists and message boards. It's that bond that knits together regulars in electronic chat rooms and newsgroups. It is, like Plato's plane of ideal forms, a metaphorical space, a virtual reality.

But it is no less real for being so. We live in the age of information, as Nicholas Negroponte, director of M.I.T.'s Media Lab, is fond of pointing out, in which the fundamental particle is not the atom but the bit—the binary digit, a unit of data usually represented as a 0 or 1. Information may still be delivered in magazines and newspapers (atoms), but the real value is in the contents (bits). We pay for our goods and services with cash (atoms), but the ebb and flow of capital around the world is carried out in electronic funds transfers (bits).

Bits are different from atoms and obey different laws. They are weightless. They are easily (and flawlessly) reproduced. There is an infinite supply. And they can be shipped at nearly the speed of light. When you are in the business of moving bits around, barriers of time and space disappear. For information providers—publishers, for example—cyberspace offers a medium in which distribution costs shrink to zero. Buyers and sellers can find each other in cyberspace without the expense of a marketing campaign. No wonder so many businessmen are convinced it will become a powerful engine of economic growth.

At this point, however, cyberspace is less about commerce than about community. The technology has unleashed a great rush of direct, person-to-person communications, organized not in the top-down, one-to-many structure of traditional media but in a many-to-many model that may—just may—be a vehicle for revolutionary change. In a world already too divided against itself—rich against poor, producer against consumer—cyberspace offers the nearest thing to a level playing field.

Take, for example, the Internet. Until something better comes along to replace it, the Internet is cyberspace. It may not reach every computer in the human system, as Gibson imagined, but it comes very close. And as anyone who has spent much time there can attest, it is in many ways even stranger than fiction.

Begun more than 20 years ago as a Defense Department experiment, the Internet escaped from the Pentagon in 1984 and spread like kudzu during the personal-

The Usenet newsgroups are, in their way, the perfect antidote to modern mass media. Rather than catering to the lowest common denominator with programming packaged by a few people in New York, Atlanta and Hollywood and broadcast to the masses in the heartland, the newsgroups allow news, commentary and humor to bubble up from the grass roots. They represent narrowcasting in the extreme: content created by consumers for consumers. While cable-TV executives still dream of hundreds of channels, Usenet

open and a full-scale Mardi Gras parade had come tumbling out

computer boom, nearly doubling every year from the mid-1980s on. Today 30 million to 40 million people in more than 160 countries have at least E-mail access to the Internet; in Japan, New Zealand and parts of Europe the number of Net users has grown more than 1,000% during the past three years.

One factor fueling the Internet's remarkable growth is its resolutely grass-roots structure. Most conventional computer systems are hierarchical and proprietary; they run on copyright software in a pyramid structure that gives dictatorial powers to the system operators who sit on top. The Internet, by contrast, is open (nonproprietary) and rabidly democratic. No one owns it. No single organization controls it. It crosses national boundaries and answers to no sovereign. It is literally lawless.

The Internet is also egalitarian to a fault. Anybody can play (provided he or she has the requisite equipment and access), and everybody is afforded the same level of respect (which is to say, little or none). Stripped of the external trappings of wealth, power, beauty and social status, people tend to be judged in the cyberspace of the Internet only by their ideas and their ability to get them across in terse, vigorous prose. On the Internet, as the famous *New Yorker* cartoon put it, nobody knows you're a dog.

Nowhere is this leveling effect more apparent than on Usenet—a giant set of more than 10,000 discussion groups (called newsgroups) distributed in large part over the Internet and devoted to every conceivable subject, from Rush Limbaugh to particle physics to the nocturnal habits of ring-tailed lemurs. The newsgroups develop their own peculiar dynamic as participants lurch from topic to topic.

But Usenet regulars are fiercely proud of the elaborate communications system they have constructed. They view it as a new vehicle for wielding political power (through mass mailings and petitions) and an alternative system for gathering and disseminating raw, uncensored news.

already has thousands. The network is so fragmented, in fact, that some fear it will ultimately serve to further divide a society already splintered by race, politics and sexual prejudice. That would be an ironic fate for a system designed to enhance communications.

The Internet is far from perfect. Largely unedited, its content is often tasteless, foolish, uninteresting or just plain wrong. It can be dangerously habit-forming and, truth be told, an enormous waste of time. Even with the arrival of new point-and-click software programs such as Netscape and Mosaic, it is still too hard to navigate. And because it requires access to both a computer and a high-speed telecommunications link, it is out of reach for millions of people too poor or too far from a major communications hub to participate.

But the Net is remarkable nonetheless, especially considering it began as a cold war postapocalypse military command grid. "When I look at the Internet," says Bruce Sterling, another science-fiction writer and a great champion of cyberspace, "I see something astounding and delightful. It's as if some grim fallout shelter had burst open and a full-scale Mardi Gras parade had come out. I take such enormous pleasure in this that it's hard to remain properly skeptical."

Sterling is not alone. There is something about cyberspace that sets people's imaginations blazing. Much of what has been written about it tends to swing from one extreme to the other, from hype and romanticism to fear and loathing. It may be that the near-term impact of cyberspace is being oversold. But that does not mean that real change isn't in the works. As a rule of thumb, historians say, the results of technological innovation always take longer to reach fruition than early champions of change predict. But when change finally comes, its effect is likely to be more profound and widespread and unanticipated than anyone imagined—even the guys who write science fiction. ∎

TWENTY MILES NORTHWEST OF THE CHICAGO LAKE front, out in the cottonwoods that mark the skyline of Glenview, Illinois, there is a subdivision called Tall Trees, a winding drive called Sequoia Trail and the brick Georgian-style home of the Weber family: Jack, a vice president of an international sign company; Mary, homemaker and triathlete; Kathleen, Jack Jr., Kerry and Maureen. The center of the Webers' home is the "family room turned office," and in the room—the very heart of the house—sits a stately oak desk. It is here the Webers stop looking like a *Saturday Evening Post* cover and start looking more like something out of *PC World.* Open the bottom-left drawer, and you will find an Image Writer II computer printer. Slide back the rolltop to reveal a Macintosh LC, recently upgraded to a 500-megabyte hard drive. "When we bought this, it came with a 40-megabyte hard drive," says Jack, 43. "We maxed that out."

Welcome to the rest of your lives, folks. Like millions of others, the Webers are barely keeping ahead of a technological tidal wave that is transforming everything about their family life: easing schoolwork, changing the nature of leisure activities, blurring the distinctions between home time and work time, between home and work themselves. But the Webers are unlike the first generation of families to confront a wired world—a generation that, in the triple-time that technology seems to create, may have preceded them by only a few years. They and others like them are feeling a growing familiarity, if not comfort, with the idea of technology in the home. "I have a feeling three-quarters of the residents of Tall Trees have computers," Jack says.

He may well be right. According to a TIME/CNN poll of 1,000 adult Americans conducted by Yankelovich Partners in the fall of 1995, 60% say they're no longer overwhelmed by the new technology, and 72% describe themselves as "comfortable" with it. They know the specs. They can count the RAM. They see, with newly dispassionate clarity, the upside—and the downside—of the machines. They've had the thrill; now they're ready for business. Those who have come to terms with the technology at their fingertips, whether mouse or modem or universal remote, share a determination not to fall behind.

Like many of their neighbors, the Webers are making an active effort to master home technology. Sometimes that process is painful; sometimes it is slow. But the alternative to keeping pace with the computer revolution no longer seems feasible. "I'm already really happy we're getting up to speed," Jack Weber says. "I'd be afraid if we weren't."

The Webers' dependence on technology only begins with the computer in the rolltop desk. Jack's Fujitsu Pocket Commander cellular phone sits charging on a nearby lamp table. He cannot imagine life without it. When expressway construction doubled his morning commute to 1½ hours, Jack resolved to make use of the extra drive time by starting his morning calls from the car. Now, with customers all over the country, he works the time zones

meet the world
How does a family in the American cellular communications and fast

FATHER KNOWS BEST: Determined to keep pace with cyberspace,

like a pro. "It might be 8 a.m. here and 9 there," he says. "If I get phone calls done before I get to my office, I have fewer interruptions when I get to work."

Mary, 39, uses her cell phone to keep track of her far-flung family. Her feelings are not so warm toward the family's home entertainment center. She does a little better with the family Macintosh, especially since last spring, when Kathleen, 15, urged her to take a computer class at New Trier High School. Now Mary is thinking about doing Christmas cards and recipes on the computer, and replacing the color-coded wall calendar that tracks everybody's whereabouts with an onscreen version. She also uses Quicken, a Christmas gift from the family, to manage the household finances, a task that was "aggravating" in the old days.

"They're learning and don't realize it. Nowadays,

wide WEBERS

heartland cope with powerful PCs, new modems? Very well, thanks

he Weber family signs on to America Online for the first time

Jack likes the idea of a computerized family calendar too, especially the prospect of dialing in to check family plans from his office. He uses the family Mac to work at home, running spreadsheets in Excel and writing proposals in Microsoft Word, then transferring files to the office via the newly installed 28.8 fax-modem. (Jack, who describes himself more as a tinkerer than a techie, managed to install the modem himself.) The kids get in their computer time as well: Kathleen and Jack Jr., 13, use it to write reports; Kerry, 8, and Maureen, 6, love Reader Rabbit 2. "The fun part is, they're learning and they don't realize it," Jack says. "Nowadays, playing is sitting at the computer and having fun learning."

The modem has also made possible the Webers' jaunt into cyberspace. It is actually their second try; they gave it a stab a couple of years ago but found the kids were too young to get much out of it. Since then, the rapid expansion of the Internet and the media attention it has drawn have sparked the family's interest again. When Jack and Mary attended a curriculum night at Jack Jr.'s school and heard about how kids from all over the country were tracking monarch butterflies' migration via the Net, they were sold.

On a Thursday night in the autumn of 1995, the Webers—who once thought themselves in the high-tech vanguard because they are a Nielsen family—gathered around the rolltop desk to sign on to America Online for the first time. After a quick overview of the rules ("Don't write swear words"; "Dad had to put this on his credit card, so don't just sit on the thing") they were off. The verdict was mixed. Kathleen was pleased to see the Bulls and Bears online; Jack Jr. found MTV Online "weird"; and, after announcing, "We're lost," Maureen wandered off to find amusement elsewhere. "Is there a book that explains this?" Mary wanted to know. She and Kathleen also wondered aloud about the demands on the family's single telephone line. A sighing Jack sees a second telephone line, even a second computer, in the family's future. One thing that does not appear likely to change: the Webers will still get their news from newspapers and TV. Online services "seem like an expensive way to receive the news," a dubious Jack says.

Mary's general trepidation about going online was only partly relieved when she found she could read *Tri-Athlete* and *Ironman* magazines on the Net. That convenience may not be enough to offset such incidents as the one in which Jack and Jack Jr. camped out in AOL's *Monday Night Football* area the night the family was supposed to be filling out a questionnaire the younger Weber had brought home from school. "Good questions," Mary says, "Like, 'What would you do if you found out one of the kids had been drinking?' I was trying to talk to Jack, and getting nowhere. I finally had to go to bed."

Indeed, the Webers have found that technology raises as many questions as it answers. Mary supports Jack's working at home and communicating with the office via their new fax-modem, but she is worried about the time the kids may spend on the computer. "I feel like our kids are so programmed," she says. "I sometimes worry they don't play enough … pick up a game of softball, take a bike ride." Jack is quick to praise the flexibility the modem allows, but frets about working at home: "I'm stealing time, and I'm going to pay for it down the road. The computer is stretching me away from my family and community."

To help cope, the Webers have started an every-Sunday family night—no TV or computer, just a dinner "where we discuss our week and weekend," Jack says. And in the community the Webers might find extra comfort in this: that they are not the only people to look with some ambivalence on home technology's mixed blessings. They are not the only ones to find that coping with a wired world is taxing—and that, while technology may liberate people from the shackles of the industrial world, it can never free them from the demands of time itself. ■

playing is sitting at the computer and having fun learning."

intimate strangers

Online users keep company in virtual communities where they can be whoever they want to be—up to a point

THE FIRST TIME SHE LOGGED ON TO ECHO, AN EAST coast electronic community, Marcia Bowe dubbed herself "Miss Outer Buro" a handle that facetiously implied beauty queen–like poise, glamour, congeniality. And soon enough, Bowe was enjoying the adulation of fellow "echoids" who posted messages praising her candor and smarts. Such celebrity was heady stuff for Bowe, a free-lance writer who describes herself in real life as shy and wary of emotional encounters. "I became addicted to this constant stream of approval," she says. "It was like a big co-dependency machine."

As Bowe began spending up to 100 hours a month online, however, her life began to take on the burdens of celebrity. "Some people were envious of me," she says. "They accused me of élitism." More disturbing, Bowe began to realize that her own hyperactivity was masking an underlying unhappiness with her life. So she dropped out of ECHO, cold turkey. "I had forgotten that the real world is so complex and fascinating." She's back in cyberspace now, this time in a paid position at ECHO overseeing its 54 conference rooms, but she has learned to navigate online with greater perspective and a thicker skin. That doesn't mean she's become detached, though. "This is an emotional place, not just a communications device," she says.

All of this may sound strangely overwrought to those who have yet to venture into the online world. The Internet, after all, has been touted largely as an unwalled repository of raw data, not of raw emotions. But the truth is that the vast majority of people who troll the Internet's byways are searching for social interaction, not just information. An estimated 80% of all users are looking for contact and commonality, companionship and community—all the conjugations implied by novelist E.M. Forster's famous injunction "Only connect!"

Relationships can be complicated in cyberspace because the very technology that draws most people together also keeps them apart. Over time, the safe sense of distance that initially seems so liberating to newcomers on the Net can become an obstacle to deepening the bonds of friendship, romance and community. At some point, most networkers often find, the only real way to move a relationship forward is to risk personal contact—and then hope the phantom bond will hold up in the 3-D world.

At its best, the sprawling Internet brings together people with mutual interests who, for reasons ranging from ge-ography to social and income disparity, would otherwise never have met. These virtual friendships can lead to physical encounters that may cement lifelong relationships. But dangers also lurk online. The disembodied voices that whisper through cyberspace can often be manufactured identities that disguise, distort or amplify aspects of a user's personality. Fortunately, only a relative few—Lotharios who woo indiscriminately, for example, or pederasts who prey on vulnerable children—have a devious and potentially dangerous intent.

Most Net users are more likely to project aspects of the person they wish they could be. But even unintended distortions can prove bruising. When Christine Rance, 28, struck up a Net relationship with a man she knew as "MyPalJoey," she says, "I told him things I had never told anyone in my life. I was really able to be more open. He was too." After more than three months of furious messaging, the couple had their first F2F (face to face) encounter. About six months later, Rance secured a job transfer from

Cyberspace attracts people who

Chicago to San Francisco, anticipating a trip to the altar. But after six weeks, the couple broke up, crushed by conflicting schedules and personalities.

Dan Marsh, by contrast, knew within five minutes of his first F2F with Audrey that their four years of online

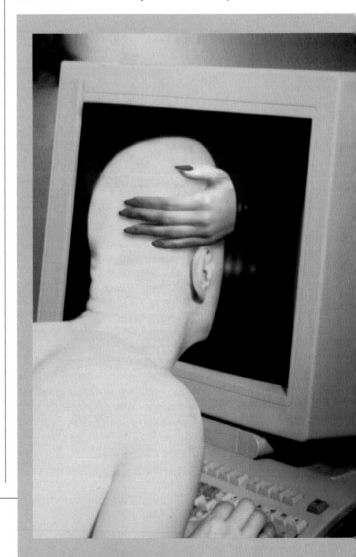

messaging between the West Coast and Pennsylvania had been time well invested. "I don't react well to meeting people in person," says Marsh. "I'm very reserved." But the relative safety of cyberspace had enabled him to be more trusting and vulnerable. In 1993, two years after meeting, they married.

The problems of cementing relationships in cyberspace pale beside the challenges of forging whole enclaves. In fact, among the cyberintelligentsia, debate rages as to whether the concept of "community" even exists in cyberspace. Howard Rheingold, author of *The Virtual Community*, says, "I want to dispel the notion that a computer network is by itself a community—a place where at least some of the people reach out through that screen and affect each other's lives." At some point, Rheingold says, "it requires a further commitment either in real life or in cyberspace from those people to each other."

Rheingold cites the death from cancer last August of Kathleen Johnston, a member of the WELL, a nine-year-old

troll for dates as much as data

Bay Area settlement. Not only did many of the WELL's more than 10,000 subscribers flood Johnston in her waning days with electronic support, but more than two dozen members took turns going to her home, tending to her needs. "Not dying alone," says Rheingold, "that's something a community has." Some found that the feeling of shared loss— even if not shared directly with others—was enough to forge a sense of community.

WELL member Jon Carroll, who participated in the electronic support, believes virtual communities often enjoy a keener sense of connection than physical communities. "Since they are in cyberspace voluntarily," says Carroll, "people are far more interested in participating in the life of the community online."

In most online communities, the esprit is fiercely democratic. Still, there are plenty of élites and hierarchies. Veteran settlers, who look askance at the hordes of newcomers, often form exclusive conferences where they can avoid endless beginner bellyaching about insiderish jokes and jargon. "There are users and superusers," says Steven Jones, editor of *CyberSociety*, a new collection of essays on computer-mediated communications. "There are E-mail addresses that have more status than others."

In other words, the Net is pretty much more of the world we already know: a place both embracing and exclusionary, loving and hurtful. As happened with the telephone and automobile, technology lends to the fragmentation of people's lives and also helps stitch those fragments back together again. "We're not going to bridge anything simply by connecting," warns Jones. "We can build all the bridges we want, but if we don't cross them and mill about, we won't make any kind of connections that count." ∎

Sex and the Infobahn

AS WITH ALL OTHER NEW MEDIUMS, ONLINE draws its energy from the same two timeless topics: radical politics and sexual fantasy. These are the first uses made of any new means of communication when it becomes popular, widespread and affordable, and they recede as the medium matures. The printing press, the photograph, the telephone, the cinema—each medium in its turn was appropriated for illicit communications. Now computer networks are the hot new medium, and they rely on politics and sex as primal energy sources.

In cyberspace there is an ever-expanding menu of places to visit and sexual material from which to choose. Many people like to have electronic sex in real time and become fixated on "chat"—a kind of phone sex pecked onto a keyboard. Others use the medium as a pick-up bar and a place to set up real assignations in the no-tell motels of America. Some roam the networks collecting massive amounts of what, in its more sophisticated versions, is termed erotica, but is more often plain old smut.

It's true that many people fall in love over the Net. But most who venture into the explicitly sexual arenas of cyberspace do so for the freedom it affords them. One of the benefits of cybersex is that they get both to meet and *to be* new people every day. With the proliferating anonymous-posting programs, they don't have to reveal their real name—or even look their best. And the safety of virtual sex is unparalleled: the only viruses that can be transmitted in cyberspace are computer viruses.

The downside is that, especially on the Internet and the adult bulletin-board systems, many people see, hear and read things that are intensely pornographic. And many are offended. At year's end, a House-Senate conference committee agreed in a close vote on tough new prohibitions against transmitting obscenity and "indecent" material over computer networks—though their definition of such material remained hazy. It seemed likely that regulatory legislation of some form would be passed.

A wide range of civil rights groups denounced the vote, saying it violated constitutional rights to free speech. Online information services, including America Online and many newspapers, had endorsed a less-stringent, compromise measure that would have restricted material deemed "harmful to minors." A battle was shaping up on the new online frontier: the marshals in Congress looked to post limits, but the settlers didn't like being fenced in. ∎

a new

The expense of acquiring tomorrow's technologies could fracture American society into computer "haves" and "have-nots"

ANY LINGERING DOUBT THAT THE COMPUTER HAS become ensconced as a member of the American family was dispelled at the beginning of 1995 by some startling statistics. For the first time ever, consumers in 1994 bought $8 billion worth of PCs—just a smidgen away from the $8.3 billion they spent on TVs. The sales record in terms of dollars is bound to fall to the computer soon, though the TV's cheaper price guarantees its dominion in numbers for a while yet.

But in the nation's poorer areas—places like Washington's Anacostia neighborhood, the hollows of Appalachia or Miami's Liberty City—families with IBM Activas, CD-ROM drives, modems and all the other paraphernalia so beloved by computer users are rare indeed. And therein lies one of the most troubling aspects of the emerging information age. In an era in which success is increasingly identified with the ability to use computers and gain access to cyberspace, will the new technology only widen the gap between rich and poor; educated and uneducated; blacks, whites and Hispanics? As Commerce Secretary Ronald Brown put it, "How do you create an environment so that once we've built this information infrastructure, you do not create a society of haves and have-nots?"

The stakes are high. Entry to the information highway may prove to be less a question of privilege or position than of the basic ability to function in a democratic society. It may determine how well people are educated, the kind of job they eventually get, how much access they have to their government and how they will learn about the critical issues affecting them and the country. No less an expert than Mitch Kapor, co-founder of Lotus Development Corp. and now president of the Electronic Frontier Foundation, feels that those who do not have access "will be highly correlated with the general have-nots. Early in the next century the network will become the major conduit through which we conduct our lives. Any disenfranchisement will be very severe."

The fact is that access to the new technology generally breaks down along traditional class lines. Wealthy and upper-middle-class families form the bulk of the 30% of American households that own computers. Similarly, wealthier school districts naturally tend to have equipment that is unavailable to poorer ones, and schools in the more affluent suburbs have twice as many computers per student as their less well funded urban counterparts. All the disparity comes to a head in this statistic: a working person able to use a computer earns 15% more than someone in a similar job who cannot. And that discrepancy could widen.

The debate over how to handle the problem pits the freewheeling techno-cowboys of the computer and telecommunications industries against traditional advocates for the poor. The industry types proclaim a paramount faith in market forces, at least in part because they fear eventual government regulation of access to the infobahn. As they see it, the forces of competition and the marketplace will drive the prices of equipment and online services downward and make both increasingly available to the less affluent.

There is considerable evidence to support that view.

Will the computer revolution create an age of "information

divide

tion networks in more affluent communities, bypassing, at least for the moment, poorer rural and inner-city areas. Representative Ed Markey, a Massachusetts Democrat, calls this separating-out process "information apartheid." A coalition of consumer, poverty and religious groups in May 1995 petitioned the Federal Communications Commission to ban what they labeled "electronic redlining," a term derived from the banking practice of refusing loans to people and businesses in areas considered ghettos.

The information industry is moving so fast that government officials are reluctant to intervene in any way that might slow its dynamism. In a search for creative ways to lessen the technology gap, advocates of wider access are focusing on plans to put computers and Net connections into libraries, post offices and other public places around the country to serve those who do not have home computers.

mANY OF THE EARLY APPROACHES ARE LOCAL and small scale, but they may point the way to the future. The United Neighborhood Houses, a New York City umbrella group of settlement houses, early in 1995 began installing in its project buildings 200 PCs with connections to the Internet. Financed by $1.4 million in federal grants and private donations, the machines help the settlement-house staffs coordinate their work and give neighborhood residents the opportunity to cruise the highway, access government databases, exchange E-mail and otherwise sample cyberspace's many wonders. The city of Santa Monica, California, started a public electronic network, installing 15 public-access terminals in such places as banks, community centers and even grocery stores. Anyone who wants to—including the homeless—can get online information about city services, make E-mail connections to city officials and join discussion groups about contentious local issues like rent control and homelessness.

Mark Cooper, research director of the Consumer Federation of America, argues that there are no panaceas for the emerging gap between the information haves and have-nots. Nor, he believes, will eventual computer literacy and Net access do much to end the blight of poverty, rural isolation and urban decay. "There's always going to be an unequal distribution of income," Cooper says. That's probably true, but at the very least the new technology should unleash all its considerable energies toward the goal of preventing those problems from getting any worse. ■

The newest computer models are far more powerful than their predecessors and are priced lower; presumably, they will continue getting cheaper. Moreover, ever upgrading "heatseekers," who are constantly searching for the latest equipment, are bound to create a vigorous secondhand market. Machines that might otherwise be wasted are instead being sold into the used-computer market, where they can be snapped up by the less advantaged in the same way that poorer people buy used cars instead of new ones.

The problem, as advocates for the poor point out, is that all today's information roads charge tolls, sometimes hefty ones, that effectively bar many, even those who manage to put together the price of a secondhand computer. The situation is further complicated by the tendency of telecommunications companies to place the new informa-

strange sounds & sights

When art and technology mingled, then married in cyberspace, their union produced fresh ways for artists to create, new ways for audiences to tune in

WITH SHOULDER-LENGTH RED DREADLOCKS and an intense gaze, Jaron Lanier is a striking presence, even in the strange universe of performance art. But then he does nothing so routine as, say, recite sonnets while cartwheeling nude across a stage. Lanier is a virtual-reality performance artist. In his piece *The Sound of One Hand,* which has played to packed theaters in Chicago, Toronto and Linz, Austria, he appears onstage framed by the image of a virtual world he enters when he dons special goggles and a DataGlove. His audience sees what he sees—and what he does, which is bend and stretch like some contorted stork. His movements elicit eerie, tinkling notes from the computer-generated virtual instruments he is playing: a Cybersax, a CyberXylo and a Rhythm Gimbal.

Lanier is in familiar territory: he is widely considered to be the father of virtual reality. Though his name is not yet common fare on the cocktail-party circuit of the cultural élite, he is a star of an astoundingly energized new movement of musicians and visual artists who are defining and redefining their work through the use of cybertechnology. "The computer is now an accepted tool," says David Ross, director of the Whitney Museum of Contemporary Art. "In the art world, it is no longer an issue." From the fashionably bohemian precincts of lower Manhattan to London and Los Angeles, the cultural world abounds with computer-aided musicians, CD-ROM virtuosos, painters, photographers and digital artists who are building their own galleries in cyberspace—all in addition to the digitally savvy filmmakers who have already transformed cinema.

Lanier embodies a whole new genre of music that uses computers to create distinctive sounds. Another practitioner on the rise is Italian astrophysicist Fiorella Terenzi, 30, who has been described as a cross between Madonna and Carl Sagan. Terenzi has used audiotelescopes to intercept radio waves from a galaxy 180 million light-years away, then fed them into a computer and applied a sound-synthesis program to convert her data into music. Result: *Music from the Galaxies,* a part New Age, part Buck Rogers sound track, played on an oscilloscope.

The Future Sound of London, one of Britain's trendiest club bands, performed "live" in November 1994 at the Kitchen in New York City—while physically remaining in its studio on Chapter Road in Dollis Hill, London. The group's banks of synthesizers and samplers—and its three-dimensional silicon graphics—were wired through the Internet to speakers and screens 5,000 miles away. The band members promise that by 1997 they will produce a 3-D film of themselves performing in a virtual environment.

Piqued by the possibilities of a new medium, Old Guard rockers are seeking to reinvent themselves cyber-electronically. Veteran songwriters Bob Dylan, Peter Gabriel and Todd Rundgren are venturing into the rapidly growing territory of CD-ROM, which takes the present CD a step further by adding visuals. Dylan's *Highway 61 Interactive* serves as an elaborate audio-visual historiography. Besides Dylan songs and videos, it features an electronic scrapbook that includes the singer's high school photos.

CD-ROMS like Gabriel's *Xplora* and Rundgren's *No World Order* invite viewers-listeners to customize tracks to their own tastes, reassembling images and changing tempo and mood. One of Gabriel's upcoming projects, *Eve,* will allow users to remix sampled sounds while creating their own screen environment from images provided by four collaborating visual artists. While some in the arts might flinch at the notion of forfeiting control of their work, Gabriel champions the idea. Interactivity, he hopes, "will destroy the élite divide between those who can create and those who can't."

Such artistic egalitarianism is a guiding principle on the World Wide Web, which has become the Internet's showcase for visual imagery. Any artist can display his or her images—whether paintings, photos, sketches or other forms—to thousands of viewers at little cost beyond that of a modem and the requisite software to get on the Net. In essence, the Web offers a virtual mall of galleries, each featuring round-the-clock exhibitions, minus the jug wine.

A host of budding Cézannes may yet emerge from the Web's galleries, but for now much of the work remains amateurish. "I haven't been blown away by the online art I've seen," says Sarah Bayliss, the U.S. editor of *World Art,* a new quarterly focusing on emerging artists and electronic media. "A lot of people online are very optimistic; they have an uncynical attitude. And that is what encourages really

PR FOR VR: Virtual

The best web art so far has been designed specifically

reality progenitor Jaron Lanier plays his cyberinstruments

created by computers and designed specifically for them. These are works that would have no place in a traditional gallery or museum. Ross considers the work of conceptual artist Antonio Muntades a paragon of excellence in computer art. Muntades' *File Room* is an ongoing interactive dialogue on censorship featuring images, biographies and discussions of controversial artists like Robert Mapplethorpe and Annie Sprinkle. The Website CitySpace, co-developed by Los Angeles artist Coco Conn and the Ontario Science Center, features virtual metropolises in which visitors may add doors, freeways and parks.

I N THIS MAZE OF INFINITE GALLERY SPACE, WHERE little is for sale yet, even the best artists must figure out how they will survive. Ross envisions a world where Websites are bestowed on worthy artists, who in turn charge visitation fees. In that scheme, an artist might receive a Website as he or she would a grant, and then develop a business. Since popular Websites are visited tens of thousand of times a day, an artist could conceivably make a pretty good living by charging just 25¢ a visit.

Until the mechanics of such a system are worked out and an élite cadre of cyberartists emerges, the most visible pieces of art will be the digitally reproduced museum masterpieces put online by patrons like Microsoft's Bill Gates. His recently formed company, Continuum Productions, is collecting the digital rights to many of the great works of art and creating electronic coffee-table books, available now on CD-ROM and eventually on networks. In September, Gates upped the stakes by acquiring the Bettmann Archive, the legendary collection of historic photographs. Some in the real (as opposed to virtual) art world are concerned that onscreen viewing will deter actual museumgoing. But Markos Kounalakis of San Francisco's Visible Interactive Corp., which produces high-tech interactive museum tours, counters, "Most people understand the difference between viewing a masterpiece with the help of a modem and viewing the real thing at a museum."

The experience that most people associate with computerized art is seeing a movie with elaborate special effects on the big screen. Many of today's most spectacular images are the result of artful digital technology developed at filmmaker George Lucas' studio, Industrial Light & Magic. ILM has revolutionized filmmaking with the kind of digital tricks seen in movies like *Forrest Gump* and *The Mask*.

As old hat as computer-created film effects may have become, they are indicative of the kind of polish and growth that may yet emerge from newer, more experimental digitized art forms. "The predictions for change in the information environment are as profound as they were during the television revolution," says the Whitney's Ross. "We all know we are walking into a dark and foggy room." It is not for the first time. In 1902 Alfred Stieglitz, Edward Steichen and other now venerated American photographers formed a group devoted to convincing doubters that photography was a worthy form of artistic expression. That goal took decades to achieve. In today's accelerated environment, cyberartists may not have to wait so long. ∎

bad art. This 'anyone can be an artist' mind-set is one of the most dangerous things we're seeing."

Part of the problem, contend cyberaesthetes, is that there are no established criteria for judging art on the Internet. "The real issue is how you find, develop and enforce standards in a brave new world," says the Whitney's Ross. "Eventually more critics will begin to develop a vocabulary to say something meaningful about what they're seeing, and critical dialogue will help shape standards. But we're a generation away from that."

The best art on the World Wide Web so far has been

for computers and would have no place in a traditional gallery

ESTROGEN:

America's No. 1 drug is an elixir of youth, but

EVERY WOMAN'S

women must decide if it's worth the risk of cancer

DILEMMA

O n February 13, 1963, a new patient strode into the office of New York City gynecologist Robert A. Wilson. To Wilson, she proved to be nothing less than a revelation or, to be more precise, a walking, talking confirmation of his most deeply held medical convictions. Wilson was a leading proponent of treating menopausal women with the female hormone estrogen. He was convinced that, given early enough and continued throughout life, hormone treatment could actually prevent what he called the "staggering catastrophe" of menopause and the "fast and painful aging process" that attended it.

Wilson's new patient, "Mrs. P.G.," as he later called her, said she was 52 years old, but her body told another story. "Her breasts were supple and firm, her carriage erect; she had good general muscle tone, no dryness of the mucous membranes and no visible genital atrophy. Above all," Wilson noted, "her skin was smooth and pliant as a girl's." When asked about menopause, she laughed and replied, "I assure you, Dr. Wilson, I have never yet missed a period. I'm so regular, astronomers could use me for timing the moon."

Pressed for her secret, the youthful matron revealed that she had been taking birth control pills containing estrogen and a second female hormone, progesterone. That was the very formula Wilson had developed as a means not only to treat menopausal complaints but also to fore-

stall the aging process. Mrs. P.G. was an energetic exemplar of his notion that "menopause is unnecessary. It can be prevented entirely."

Three years later, in a hugely successful book, *Feminine Forever,* Wilson announced the good news to all womankind. "For the first time in history," he wrote, "women may share the promise of tomorrow as biological equals of men ... Thanks to hormone therapy, they may look forward to prolonged well-being and extended youth."

Estrogen is indeed the closest thing in modern medicine to an elixir of youth—a drug that slows the ravages of time for women. It is already the No. 1 prescription drug in America, and it is about to hit its demographic sweet spot: the millions of baby boomers now experiencing their first hot flashes. What Wilson

didn't anticipate, but what today's women should know, is that, like every other magic potion, this one has a dark side. To gain the full benefits of estrogen, a woman must take it not only at menopause but also for decades afterward. It means a lifetime of drug taking and possible side effects that include an increased risk of several forms of cancer. That danger was underscored by a report in the *New England Journal of Medicine* in June 1995 reaffirming the long-suspected link between estrogen-replacement therapy and breast cancer. Weighing such risks against the truly marvelous benefits of estrogen may be the most difficult health decision a woman can make. And there's no avoiding it.

As research reveals the pros and cons of estrogen, the therapy's popularity has flowed and ebbed like some sort of national hormonal cycle. Wilson's book boosted the sale of Premarin (a form of estrogen made from—and named for—a pregnant mare's urine). But estrogen use plummeted after 1975, when studies showed that women taking the hormone had up to a 14-fold increased risk of uterine cancer. Reports of a 30% increased risk of breast cancer scared others away.

Today estrogen in its various forms—pills, patches and creams—is flowing as never before. Cancer risks have been diminished, doctors believe, by lowering the dosages used in hormone-replacement therapy (HRT). The risk of uterine cancer, in particular, can be virtually eliminated, experts say, by adding synthetic progesterone (progestin) to the estrogen prescription, either combined in one capsule or as a separate pill. Meanwhile a raft of studies showing new and unexpected benefits has vastly increased medical enthusiasm for the treatment. Estrogen, it seems, can prevent or slow many of the ravages of aging, including menopausal miseries, heart disease, osteoporosis, mental deterioration, colon cancer and aging skin.

GIVEN ALL THIS, IT'S NO WONDER DOCTORS ARE handing out estrogen prescriptions with almost gleeful enthusiasm. According to researchers at the Food and Drug Administration, estrogen prescriptions in the U.S. more than doubled between 1982 and 1992. About a quarter of U.S. women at or past menopause—roughly 10 million—take the hormone, making estrogen a billion-dollar business. As baby boomers approach menopause, those numbers will skyrocket.

While gynecologists acknowledge the risks of estrogen therapy, they tend to emphasize the pluses. Still, the specter of cancer continues to haunt HRT. With the *New England Journal* report, hope faded that progestin would offer estrogen users protection against breast cancer, as it does against uterine cancer. In fact, it appears that the combined hormones may put women at a higher risk for breast cancer than estrogen alone. This bad news came in the wake of a report in May 1995 suggesting that long-term

> **"Many gynecologists are handing out these hormones like M&M's. We all know there is no free lunch."**

use of estrogen heightens the risk of fatal ovarian cancer.

Even before these disturbing reports appeared, American women were distinctly less exuberant about estrogen than their doctors. A 1987 survey showed that 20% of women given a prescription for estrogen never even fill it. Of those who do begin taking the hormone, more than half quit within one year. For many women there is something fundamentally disturbing about turning a natural event like menopause into a disease that demands decades of medication. And there's something spooky about continuing to have monthly bleeding at age 60, a fairly common consequence of some types of hormone therapy. "Why fight vainly to remain in a stage of life you can't be in anymore, instead of enjoying the stage you are in?" asks Dr. Nada Stotland, an HRT dropout in her 50s. Stotland, a psychiatrist at the University of Chicago, says she is "extra skeptical, because there are powerful forces that aim one toward prescribed hormones, but there is no profit motive in not prescribing something."

Breast-cancer specialist Dr. Susan Love shares her skepticism. "Many gynecologists are handing out these hormones like M&M's," she says. No matter how beneficial estrogen may seem, no drug treatment comes without drawbacks. In biology as in business, she notes, "there's no free lunch."

Estrogen is powerful stuff. Receptors for the hormone are found in some 300 different tissues. Some, including tissues in the urogenital tract, the blood vessels, the skin and the breasts, require estrogen to maintain their tone and flexibility. Estrogen levels begin to rise in girls as early as age 8 in response to a symphony of signals. The hypothalamus, in the brain, is the maestro, spurring the pituitary to release hormones, which in turn prompt the ovaries to churn out estrogen. By age 11 or 12, production of estrogen and other hormones is sufficient to trigger the development of the breasts, growth of body hair and the onset of menstruation. But because these hormones influence so many tissues, they incite adolescent mayhem: oilier hair, blemished skin, moodiness, a growing interest in sex, severe menstrual cramps.

In many ways, menopause is a mirror image of this process. Just as estrogen rises gradually in childhood, so it begins to wane some 25 years later, starting in the early 30s. The effects of the decline are rarely noticeable—except in decreasing fertility—until the early 40s, when women enter the transitional period known as perimenopause. Menstruation becomes less regular, the skin becomes dryer, hair turns more brittle and sparser under the arms and between the legs. Some women feel a loss of libido, and many suffer mood swings analogous to those of adolescents.

Women are often shocked when menopausal symptoms strike in the early 40s: the average age of menopause is 51. Most know little about perimenopause, and their doctors aren't much help. The best therapy for perimenopause is "knowing what it is," says Harvard gynecologist Alan Altman. Exercise, a proper diet and not smoking can also help.

For 85% of women, the symptoms that begin with perimenopause will stop within one year of their final period. But for those who are in too much misery to wait, estrogen can do wonders: halting hot flashes, night sweats and sleeplessness and sometimes alleviating the generalized achiness and mental fogging some women feel. There is a "euphoric effect or general improvement in mental state," says Cleveland endocrinologist Wulf Utian, co-founder of the North American Menopause Society.

But Utian stresses that not every woman should take estrogen. It is not advisable for those with a history or a high risk of breast or uterine cancer. Nor is it recommended for women with clotting problems. Besides, some women feel lousy on hormones, and many are distressed to find they gain weight (though it's unclear that estrogen is really to blame).

ONCE THE STORMS OF PERIMENOPAUSE HAVE cleared, many women stop taking estrogen. Unfortunately, HRT works its preventive wonders only if taken for many years—the longer, the better. Similarly, researchers studying estrogen and heart disease see the greatest benefits in long-term use. Estrogen helps keep levels of LDL cholesterol low and HDL cholesterol high; that's one reason premenopausal women have a much lower rate of heart disease than their male peers. HRT also acts directly on blood vessels, dilating them slightly so that blood flow improves. But these benefits disappear when the patient stops taking hormones.

Given all this, it seems logical to recommend HRT for postmenopausal women with high cholesterol levels or other warning signs of heart disease. Likewise, it is now standard practice to give estrogen to women with a high risk of osteoporosis. But the message emerging from the longer-term data is that prolonged use of estrogen appears to increase the risk of breast cancer and other malignancies. And the longer estrogen is taken, the greater the risks. There may be other risks and other advantages of HRT, but what doctors know is limited by inadequate research.

The good news is that a well-designed, long-term study of HRT is finally under way. Last year, in an attempt to redress a historic shortfall in research on women's health, the National Institutes of Health launched the $628 million Women's Health Initiative. In the HRT portion of the study, which will involve 27,500 women, half will be randomly assigned to HRT, half to a placebo. Researchers will follow the women for at least eight years and compare rates of heart disease, osteoporosis, breast cancer and other ailments. When the results are reported, doctors and patients may finally have some clear picture of the risks and benefits of long-term HRT. Alas, that won't be until 2005.

In the meantime, women are faced with a tough choice. The decision about estrogen should depend on a woman's assessment of her own health; her family history of cancer, heart disease and osteoporosis; and even on personal philosophy. As is so often the case in modern medicine, the most a patient can do is to ask her doctor to lay out the risks, the benefits and the honest fact that the data are inadequate—and then make the choice herself. ■

PROS AND CONS

PROVEN BENEFITS
- Relieves hot flashes, night sweats and other menopausal symptoms
- Reduces bone loss (osteoporosis)
- Relieves vaginal dryness and atrophy

BENEFITS VERY LIKELY
- Reduces risk of heart disease and colon cancer
- Reduces mood swings and memory lapses
- Keeps skin thicker, moister and more youthful

PROVEN RISKS
- Increases incidence of cancer of the uterine lining
- Can trigger return of menstrual bleeding
- May bring on premenstrual-type symptoms (fluid retention, tender breasts, irritability)

RISKS VERY LIKELY
- Higher rate of breast cancer
- Abnormal blood clots
- Weight gain, headaches
- Greater risk of gallstones

THE SEX BONUS

FOR MANY WOMEN THE NO. 1 REASON TO TAKE estrogen after menopause is to improve their sex lives. "Without it, you may soon have no sex life at all," says Dr. Lila Nachtigall, co-author of the handbook *Estrogen: The Facts Can Change Your Life!* (HarperCollins; $11). The waning of estrogen often brings changes that can reduce sexual pleasure. The vagina reverts to its prepubescent shape: narrower, shorter, dryer, less elastic, with thin walls that tear easily and are prone to infection. The libido may also dry up, if only because sex becomes painful.

Nachtigall is a fervent believer in the healing power of estrogen. "Even for women who are already in deep sexual difficulty, the therapy usually reverses the damage in only a few weeks," she writes. Estrogen creams, applied topically, are very effective at rejuvenating vaginal tissues and are probably safer than pills or patches. For those whose sex drive remains stuck in low gear despite HRT, the male hormone testosterone may help, though unless dosages are watched carefully, it can cause a deepening voice, growth of facial hair and other effects.

For the hormone-wary there are other measures. Over-the-counter lubricants can make sex more comfortable, and nonprescription moisturizers can help rehydrate dry tissues. One of the best things to keep the machinery humming is sex itself, says Wulf Utian, co-founder of the North American Menopause Society. As with aging muscles, bones and brain cells, it's a matter of use it or lose it. ■

WEIGHT-LOSS NIRVANA?

A substance that makes fat mice thin just might work for humans too

HOW MANY PEOPLE STRUGGLING MIGHTILY TO KEEP their weight in check wouldn't trade places with the mice in Dr. Jeffrey Friedman's laboratory? Two weeks earlier, these roly-poly fur balls had weighed three times as much as a mouse should, and they still couldn't stop snacking. After daily injections of a new hormone, however, the rodents suddenly started eating less food and burning more fat. They shed excess ounces and trimmed 30% off their bloated size. Even better, their cholesterol readings fell, as did the high glucose levels that had made them mildly diabetic. Virtually overnight, it seemed, the sleek mice were prancing about their cages.

In a country where one in three adults is seriously overweight, the news carried by the journal *Science* in July—that Friedman and his colleagues had discovered a magical potion that melts fat in a matter of weeks—resonated with unusual force. Momentarily, at least, it buoyed the spirits of millions of lifelong dieters such as Barbara Cady, a former teacher from Fairmont, West Virginia, and boosted the stock of Amgen, the biotechnical firm based in California that holds the license on the underlying technology. For if Cady, who has struggled to bring her weight down from 264 lbs. to 195, is any example, the market for such a compound could be huge. "Almost anyone," she wryly observes, "would be sorely tempted to try something that seems to promise Nirvana."

It is too early to predict, however, whether this rare elixir called leptin (after the Greek *leptos,* meaning slender), developed by Friedman and his associates at the Howard Hughes Medical Institute and New York City's Rockefeller University, will be a stunning pharmaceutical

success or just another "miracle" cure that fizzles. Even if all goes well, it could be five to 10 years before leptin is approved for human use. Researchers must first demonstrate that leptin benefits people as well as rodents and that it causes no serious side effects.

What about those side effects? Injections of leptin do not, as one might fear, turn lean mice into starving wretches. After losing weight, researchers from Amgen reported, normal mice stabilize both their food intake and their metabolism. Obese mice likewise reach an optimal leanness, then stop losing weight. The pattern of weight loss is also encouraging. For unlike extreme calorie restrictions, which can weaken muscle, leptin appears to dissolve fat while leaving lean tissue intact. On the basis of such data, Amgen has announced that it hopes to begin conducting human trials as early as 1996.

Many experts find these plans too optimistic. Just because researchers have not noted worrisome side effects yet, critics say, does not mean that none will emerge. Leptin, they point out, is a serious drug, not the easy-to-swallow "thin pill" dieters have dreamed of for so long. To do its work, leptin would probably have to be either injected daily, like insulin, or implanted under the skin for the rest of one's life. In the laboratory experiments reported in July, the obese mice started regaining weight as soon as the injections stopped.

Regardless of what eventually happens in the marketplace, the discovery of leptin is occasion for celebration. It has provided scientists with a new avenue for exploring a still poorly understood metabolic pathway, one that probably consists of many other equally powerful compounds, each of which could lead to new drugs. ■

ATTENTION FOR THE STARVED: Above, Dr. Friedman; at left, two weeks to a healthier, slimmer rodent

Calment shows her mettle

LIFE AT FOURSCORE— AND TWOSCORE MORE

To grasp what it means to be 120 years old, consider this: a woman in the U.S. now has a life expectancy of 79 years. Jeanne Calment of Arles, France, reached that advanced age back in 1954, when Eisenhower was in the White House and Joseph Stalin had just passed from the scene. Yet in early 1995 there she was, charming the photographers and reporters who arrived in droves to mark her 120th birthday.

The woman certified by the *Guinness Book of World Records* as the oldest living human allowed that she was "very moved" by the celebration. Her wit had certainly aged well: asked what kind of future she expected, Calment didn't miss a beat: "A very short one."

In the U.S., the "oldest old"—those 85 and older— make up the fastest-growing segment of the population. The Census Bureau projects that by the year 2040 there will be 1.3 million Americans 100 years or older; some demographers put the figure at 4 million.

ASTHMA, THE KILLER

When 17-year-old model Krissy Taylor was found dead in her Florida home during the summer, authorities were baffled. Her heart seemed fine, and there was no sign of alcohol or drugs in her blood. But a pathologist noted that her bronchioles, the tiniest airways in the lungs, were inflamed and scarred, and said that Taylor, like more than 6,000 Americans each year, died of asthma. Some 15 million Americans suffer from this chronic affliction, which can leave a person suddenly gasping for air. The number with diagnosed asthma has grown by 50% since 1990. The death rate from asthma has also surged—and doctors can't say why.

A BITTER ENDGAME

In hospitals across the U.S., doctors ignore, or are unaware of, the last wishes of dying patients, needlessly prolonging their pain and suffering. That was the disturbing conclusion of a massive study published in November in the *Journal of the American Medical Association.* Among the findings: while

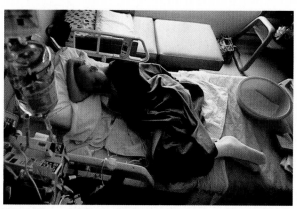

The wishes of dying patients are ignored, a study found

a third of patients had asked not to be revived by cardiopulmonary resuscitation, half the time the order was not written on their charts. Study leaders called for new ways to treat life's final days with dignity and honor for the dying.

FUTURE IMPERFECT

DNA samples in a lab test

It is a paradox of modern medicine: as genetic testing helps physicians predict which diseases patients may develop in the future, they are learning that foreknowledge of disease can create agonizing dilemmas. Fewer than 15% of those eligible took a new test for Huntington's chorea, preferring the anxiety of not knowing their future to the certainty of horror. And such foreknowledge can cause insurers and employers to discriminate. Wisconsin now prohibits health insurers from requiring genetic tests and forbids employers to screen job applicants as well.

IT'S A BIG COUNTRY

The latest results from a long-term study conducted by the federal Centers for Disease Control and Prevention showed that the number of Americans who are seriously overweight, after holding steady for 20 years at about a quarter of the population, jumped to one-third in the 1980s, an increase of more than 30%. According to another report, 58 million people in the U.S. weigh at least 20% more than their ideal body weight—putting millions at an increased risk of diabetes, hypertension, heart disease, stroke, gout, arthritis and some forms of cancer. And the next generation may be even worse off: the number of overweight teenagers, stable at about 15% in the 1970s, had risen to 21% by 1991.

PASS THE PIZZA, MAN!

Men who eat 10 servings a week of tomato-based foods are up to 45% less likely to develop prostate cancer, according to a six-year study of 47,000 males. The tomatoes appear to be more helpful when cooked, as in catsup, marinara sauce—and pizza. ■

Behold

Revealed after 20 centuries, cave

S TANDING AT THE BASE OF A CLIFF IN THE ARDÈCHE region in southeastern France in December 1994, the three middle-aged spelunkers felt a breeze wafting from a pile of rock and debris. "That was a sign that there was a cave beneath it," recalls Jean-Marie Chauvet. With his companions, Chauvet cleared away an opening, then wriggled through a tunnel into a complex of large caves.

Then, in the pale glow of their head lamps, the explorers noticed two red lines on a cavern wall. Chauvet, a government employee who oversees the protection of the many historically important caves in the region, recognized the markings as "characteristic of the Stone Age." What he did not immediately realize—and the world did not know until the French Culture Ministry announced it

in January 1995—was that they had discovered an extraordinarily clear window on prehistoric life, rivalling even the fabled drawings on the cave walls at Lascaux in France and Altamira in Spain.

Restraining their curiosity, the trio crawled back outside and resealed the entrance. "Not only to keep people out," Chauvet noted, "but to return the airflow to what it had been before; a change in the interior climate could ruin whatever was inside." Six days later, they returned with better lighting and plastic sheets that they spread about to avoid disturbing artifacts on the cavern floors.

Probing deeper into the cavern system, the spelunkers began coming upon exquisite, intricately detailed wall paintings and engravings of animals, as well as numerous images of human hands, some in red, others in black pigment. "I thought I was dreaming," says Chauvet. "We were all covered with goose pimples." The art was in pristine condition, apparently undisturbed, as was other evidence of the ancient artists' presence: flint knives, mounds of clay used for making paint and charred fire pits. Scientists soon estimated the art to be 20,000 years old.

The ancient bestiary included lions, bison, deer, bears, horses and some 50 woolly rhinos. One mural shows several horses apparently charging—in a Stone Age mismatch—toward two rhinos. A few species represented on the walls of the Chauvet cave, as it was named, had never before been seen in prehistoric artwork: an owl engraved in rock and a panther depicted in red pigment.

Months later, scientists were electrified to learn that the paintings appeared to be much older than first believed. Radiocarbon dating showed that the images on the wall were not 20,000 years old, but 30,000 years or more—making them the oldest cave paintings ever found. The dating was based on eight paint samples tested at three laboratories. If the finding holds up, said New York University anthropologist Randall White, an expert on prehistoric art, "It's a pretty big shock."

The artwork at Chauvet is far more advanced than the

SPITTING IMAGE **The long-forgotten illustrator of this scene had**

the Stone Age

paintings illuminate the world of our early ancestors

a gifted eye—or mouth. Some scholars say ancient artists achieved their effects by blowing pigment dissolved in saliva on cave walls

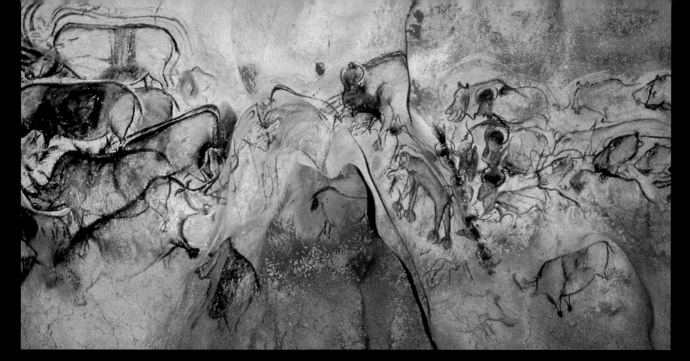

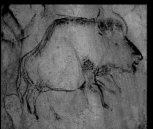

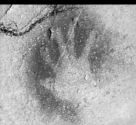

OPTICAL ILLUSION **Above, natural bulges create a 3-D effect**

ON THE HOOF **Far left, extra legs show the bison is running**

THE ARTIST? **Caught red-handed, center**

EUREKA! **Near left, a paleolithic menagerie**

work previously considered the oldest cave art, the crude outline of a human hand found in a cave at Cosquer, near Marseilles, that is believed to be 27,000 years old. If the Chauvet dating proves correct, it suggests that the art of early man did not mature steadily in simple linear fashion.

WHO WERE THE ARTISTS OF CHAUVET? IN THE vast span of human prehistory, the Cro-Magnon people who drew the profusion of animals on the bulging limestone walls of the cave were fairly late arrivals. Human technology—the making of tools from stone—had already existed for nearly 2 million years. Though the dates are vastly generalized, most prehistorians agree that art — communication by visual images—came into existence somewhere around 40,000 B.P. (before present). That was about the time when Cro-Magnons—a species of *Homo sapiens*—reached Europe, having migrated from the Middle East, and began to replace an earlier species, the Neanderthals.

The Cro-Magnons were not the inarticulate Alley Oops of popular myth. They were nomadic hunter-gatherers with a fairly developed technology. They wore animal-skin clothing and moccasins tailored with bone needles, and made beautiful (and highly efficient) laurel-leaf-shaped flint blades. Most striking was their yearning to make art in permanent places—the walls of caves.

The main technique of Cro-Magnon art, according to prehistorian Michel Lorblanchet, director of France's National Center of Scientific Research, involved not brushes but a kind of oral spray-painting—blowing pigment dissolved in saliva on the wall. Lorblanchet, who has re-created cave paintings with uncanny accuracy, suggests the technique may have had a spiritual dimension: "Spitting is a way of projecting yourself onto the wall, becoming one with the horse you are painting. Thus the action melds with the myth."

Stung by the lessons of Altamira and Lascaux, where initial unrestricted access to the caves obliterated archaeological clues and led to the rapid deterioration of artwork, the French Culture Ministry put the Chauvet cave off limits to all but a handful of experts and installed video surveillance cameras and police guards at the entrance. "Our goal," says Patrice Béghain, the regional head of cultural affairs, "is to keep the cave in this virgin state so that research can, in theory, continue indefinitely."

No research is needed to establish one fact: artists of rare talent created the work at Chauvet. "I remember standing in front of the paintings of the horses facing the rhinos and being profoundly moved by the artistry," says Jean Clottes, France's foremost expert on prehistoric rock art. "Tears were running down my cheeks. I was witnessing one of the world's greatest masterpieces." ∎

WHERE DO TOES COME FROM?

Linking fish fins to mouse paws, researchers may have solved an important evolutionary puzzle

ABOUT 360 MILLION YEARS AGO, SOME ADVEN-
turous fish managed to hoist themselves onto
their stubby fins and crawl clumsily out of
the swamps to forage for food. Once
these primeval creatures were on
terra firma, their offspring began to adapt
to their new environment, natural selec-
tion favoring those that developed features
well suited to life on land: paws, hooves,
knees, joints, fingers and thumbs. Thus did
these marine creatures give rise to frogs,
birds, dinosaurs and all the rest.

There's one problem with this familiar version of how our distant
ancestors emerged from the sea: it's
probably wrong. For one thing,
newly assembled fossils—in particular, a 360 million—year-old sala-
mander-like aquatic animal called
Acanthostega—strongly suggest
that toes and feet were developed
before life climbed onto land, not
after. Moreover, in shape and
function, *Acanthostega's* fully joint-
ed toes bear no resemblance to the spiky, fanlike fins of
a fish. How did fins turn into feet like these?

The answer may be in the genes. That's the tantalizing conclusion of a team of researchers from the University of Geneva in Switzerland led by developmental
biologist Denis Duboule. While they have yet to unravel
the complex of genes responsible for turning fins into
toes, they have discovered that genes associated with the
formation of fins in fish are the same ones that orchestrate
the development of paws in mice. "Think of a mouse as a
fish with limbs," says Duboule. "What a mouse does is
take a fin and put something extra on top of it."

That something extra, Duboule and his colleagues
suggested in the journal *Nature*, is provided by a special

A FISH WITH FEET? A model of
a two-foot-long *Acanthostega*

set of genes that act as master
architects in a surprisingly broad
range of animals, from rodents to
roundworms. These gossamer strands of
DNA—known as homoeotic homeobox genes,
or Hox genes for short—lay out the embryo
from head to tail, controlling everything
from the development of limbs to the pat-
terning of the gut and urogenital tracts.

All proteins are coded for by DNA; the
proteins made by Hox genes are
distinguished by the biochem-
ical motif known as a homeobox, a stylized string of 60
amino acids that enables Hox proteins to
stick to DNA like strips of molecular Velcro
and activate still other genes. Hundreds of
genes belong to the extended homeobox
family, but those that are also homoeotic—
associated with changes in body parts—are
the most important. Though they are few
in number, the Hox genes control much of
what happens during embryonic development as they switch on and off in sequence.
Since embryos mature from the top down, a
Hox gene that turns off a bit early, or stays
on a touch longer, can make a dramatic difference in embryo formation. Swans, for
example, have longer necks than chickens.
That's because the Hox genes that
make neck bones stay on longer in
the unhatched cygnet than in
the unhatched chick.

Timing may also explain the
progression of fins to feet. In four-
legged animals, feet do not grow straight out of the leg,
proceeding from the ankle out, but develop in a fanlike
progression that runs from the smallest digit to the
largest. Duboule's team tracked the activity of four Hox
genes in the budding feet of embryonic mice and found
precisely this pattern. By contrast, studies showed that in
the zebrafish, the Hox genes switch off earlier, perhaps to
ensure that a fin ray will form rather than feet.

What would a fish with feet look like? It could easily
resemble the *Acanthostega*.
Mineralized bones of this
strange creature, unearthed
in Greenland in 1987, tend to
confirm the notion that fish
did not crawl onto shore on
their fins, says Michael
Coates, a paleontologist at
University College, London.
Instead they probably de-
veloped limbs and feet that
they used in the water for
millions of years before colo-
nizing the land. ■

Acanthostega's **eight toes
evolved in water, not on land**

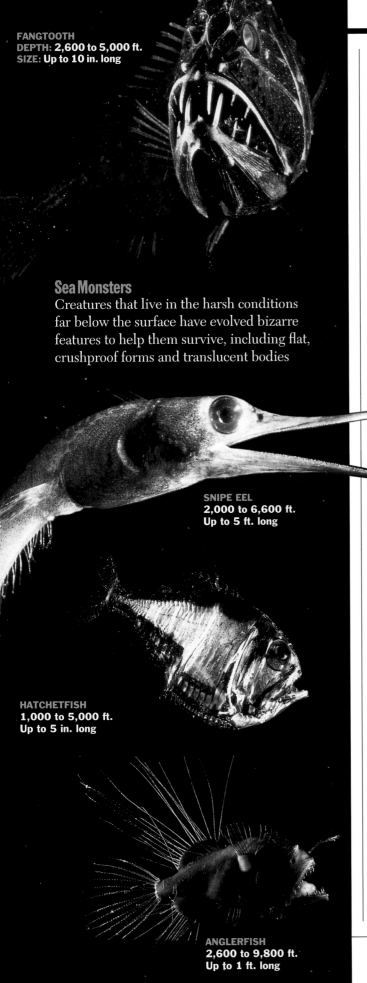

FANGTOOTH
DEPTH: **2,600 to 5,000 ft.**
SIZE: **Up to 10 in. long**

Sea Monsters

Creatures that live in the harsh conditions far below the surface have evolved bizarre features to help them survive, including flat, crushproof forms and translucent bodies

SNIPE EEL
2,000 to 6,600 ft.
Up to 5 ft. long

HATCHETFISH
1,000 to 5,000 ft.
Up to 5 in. long

ANGLERFISH
2,600 to 9,800 ft.
Up to 1 ft. long

SOMETIME IN 1996, A REVOLUTIONARY NEW undersea vessel will be lowered gently into the waters of Monterey Bay for its maiden voyage. Named *Deep Flight I*, the 14-ft.-long, 2,900-lb. vehicle is shaped like a chubby, winged torpedo but should fly like an underwater bird. Compared with the hard-to-maneuver submersibles that now haul deep-sea explorers sluggishly around the oceans, *Deep Flight I* is an aquatic F-16 fighter. It can perform barrel rolls, race a fast-moving pod of whales or leap vertically right out of the sea. With a touch on the controls, a skilled pilot—who lies prone in a body harness, his or her head protruding into the craft's hemispherical glass nose—can skim just below the ocean's surface or plunge thousands of feet below.

But *Deep Flight I* is just a pale prototype of what's to come. Back in their Point Richmond, California, workshop, the craft's designers have already drawn blueprints for its successor, *Deep Flight II*, an industrial-strength submersible capable of diving not just a few thousand feet but as far as seven miles straight down, to the Mariana Trench—the aquatic equivalent of Mount Everest.

■ OCEANOGRAPHY

The Last

In search of great mineral treasures researchers launch new journeys to

More than 35 years after the bathyscaphe *Trieste* took two men, for the first and last time, 35,800 ft. down to the deepest spot in the world—the Mariana Trench's Challenger Deep, just off Guam in the western Pacific—undersea adventurers are preparing to go back. In March 1995 a Japanese robot scouted a tiny section of the bottom of the 1,584-mile-long Challenger Deep crevasse and sent back the first real-time video images of deepest-sea life. And in laboratories around the world, engineers are hard at work on an armada of sophisticated craft designed to explore—and in some cases exploit—the one great unconquered place on earth: the bottom of the sea.

The irony of 20th century scientists venturing out to explore waters that have been navigated for thousands of years is not lost on oceanographers. More than 100 expeditions have reached Everest, the 29,028-ft. pinnacle of the Himalayas; manned voyages to space have become commonplace; and robot probes have ventured to the outer reaches of the solar system. But only now are the deepest parts of the ocean coming within reach.

The unexplored territory includes not only the sea's uttermost depths, but also the still mysterious middle waters three or four miles down, and even the "shallows" a few hundred feet deep. The rewards could be enormous: oil and mineral wealth to rival Alaska's North Slope and California's Gold Rush; scientific discoveries that could change our view of how the planet—and the life-forms on it—evolved; natural substances that could yield new medicines and whole new classes of industrial chemicals. Beyond those practical benefits there is the intangible but real satisfaction that comes from exploring earth's last great frontier.

There is a lot to explore. Oceans cover nearly three-quarters of the planet's surface—336 million cubic miles of water. The sea's intricate food webs support more life by weight and a greater diversity of animals than any other ecosystem, from sulfur-eating bacteria clustered around deep-sea vents to fish that light up like Times Square billboards to lure their prey. Seeing those sights, though, will force explorers to cope with an environment as perilous as outer space. Unaided, humans can't dive much more than 10 ft. down—less than one three-thousandth of the way to the very bottom—before increasing pressure starts to build up painfully on the inner ear, sinuses and lungs. Frigid subsurface water rapidly sucks away body heat. And even the most leathery of lungs can't hold a breath for more than two or three minutes.

Frontier

and major scientific breakthroughs, the undiscovered realms of the sea

The modern age of deep-sea exploration was launched by engineer Otis Barton's 1930 invention of the bathysphere—essentially a deep-diving tethered steel ball—and the invention of scuba (short for "self-contained underwater breathing apparatus") by Jacques-Yves Cousteau and Emile Gagnan in 1943. The *Bathysphere* took Barton and zoologist William Beebe to a record 3,028 ft., off Bermuda, but it wasn't at all maneuverable. Swiss engineer Auguste Piccard solved the mobility problem with the first true submersible, a dirigible-like vessel called a bathyscaphe, which consisted of a spherical watertight cabin suspended below a buoyant gasoline-filled pontoon. (A submersible is simply a small, mobile undersea vessel used for science.)

The *Trieste*, which took U.S. Navy Lieut. Don Walsh and Piccard's son Jacques on their record dive into the Challenger Deep in 1960, was only the third bathyscaphe ever built. But in the wake of *Trieste*'s successful dive, the number of submersibles increased dramatically. The Woods Hole Oceanographic Institution's workhorse, the three-person *Alvin* (still in operation), was launched in 1964. And the first robots-on-a-tether—the so-called remotely operated vehicles, or ROVs—were developed several

DEEP-SEA SHRIMP
DEPTH: 6,600 to 9,900 ft.
SIZE: Up to 6 in. long

CRANCHIID SQUID
1,600 to 6,600 ft.
8 in. long

GULPER EEL
2,000 to 6,600 ft.
Up to 5 ft. long

TUBE WORMS
Average: 7,300 ft.
Up to 8 ft. long.

The recommended recreational depth limit is 130 ft. (40 m), but special equipment can allow for deeper dives.

This tethered metal diving suit maintains atmospheric pressure and enables divers to go as deep as 1,440 ft. (440 m).

Military subs can dive to depths beyond 3,000 ft. (915 m). Information about the limits of their range is classified.

One- or two-person craft with a spherical acrylic hull that gives the pilot a 360° view. They can descend to 3,300 ft. (1,000 m).

A low-cost one-person submersible that will perform like an underwater airplane. The pilot will be able to dive to 3,300 ft. (1,000 m). Deep Flight II, still just a blueprint, will dive 10 times as deep.

This workhorse research sub, completed in 1964, carries a pilot and two scientists as well as lights, cameras, hydraulic manipulators and scientific instruments. Its maximum depth is 14,764 ft. (4,500 m).

These four manned submersibles, which belong to France, Russia and the U.S. respectively, all dive to 20,000 ft. (6,000 m).

Launched from a sled called Medea, the robot Jason can descend to 20,000 ft. (6,000 m). It is tethered to a surface ship.

Japan's five-year-old submersible, which holds three people and can descend to 21,325 ft. (6,500 m), is currently the world's deepest diving manned vehicle.

This bathyscaphe, essentially a metal sphere suspended from a gasoline-filled pontoon, sank to the record depth of 35,800 ft. (10,912 m) in the Challenger Deep of the Mariana Trench in 1960.

PROBING

Sea Cliff

years later. For the first time scientists could systematically collect animals, plants, rocks and water samples, rather than study whatever they could dredge up in collection baskets lowered from the surface.

Thus began a great period of discovery that transformed biology, geology and oceanography. When geologists first visited the mid-ocean range in the late 1970s, their findings supported the then new theory of plate tectonics. According to this theory, the surface of the earth is not a single, rocky shell but a series of hard "plates," perhaps 50 miles thick and up to thousands of miles across, floating on a bed of partly molten rock. The mid-ocean ridges, geologists argued, were likely locations for planetary crust to be created: the new plate material would be pushed upward by forces from below before settling back down to form the sea floor.

Rock samples from the Atlantic section of the range—which, when examined closely, proved to be newly formed—provided striking evidence that the theory is correct. But an even more dramatic confirmation came from the Pacific, where black clouds of superheated, mineral-rich water were discovered spewing from chimney-like mounds on the sea bottom—evidence that the rocks below still carried tremendous heat from their relatively recent formation.

These hot gushers, now known as hydrothermal vents, have since been found in many parts of the world, and because they occur at depths of about 7,300 ft., oceanographers have been able to visit and study a dozen of them. The vents are essentially underwater geysers that work much the same way Old Faithful does. Seawater percolates down through cracks in the crust, getting pro-gressively hotter. The water does not boil, despite temperatures reaching a height of 750°F, because it is under tremendous pressure. Finally, the hot water gushes back up in murky clouds that cool rapidly, dumping dissolved minerals, including zinc, copper, iron, sulfur compounds and silica, onto the ocean floor. The material hardens into chimneys, known as "black smokers" (one, nicknamed Godzilla, towers 148 ft. above the bottom).

If the discovery of the vents was a major surprise, scientists were astonished to learn that at least some of these submerged geysers—whose hot, sulfurous environs bear more than a passing resemblance to hell—are actually bursting with life. Nobody had invited biologists along to study the vents because nobody imagined there would be anything to interest them. But on a dive off the Galápagos in 1977, researchers found the water around a vent teeming with bacteria and surrounded for dozens of feet by peculiar tube-shape worms ranging in size from a few inches to several feet long; clams the size of dinner plates; mussels; and at least one specimen of a strange pink-skinned, blue-eyed fish.

Disbelief was soon replaced by intense curiosity. What were these animals feeding

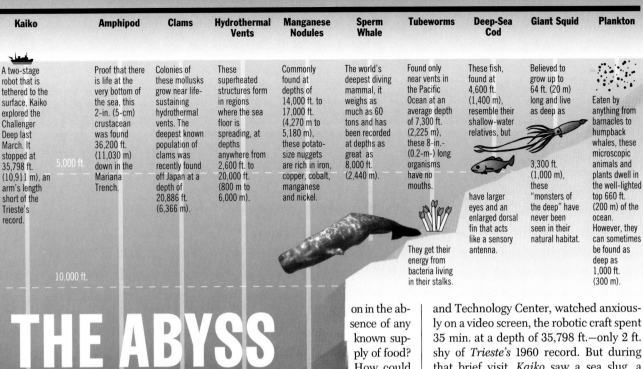

Kaiko	Amphipod	Clams	Hydrothermal Vents	Manganese Nodules	Sperm Whale	Tubeworms	Deep-Sea Cod	Giant Squid	Plankton

A two-stage robot that is tethered to the surface, Kaiko explored the Challenger Deep last March. It stopped at 35,798 ft. (10,911 m), an arm's length short of the Trieste's record.

Proof that there is life at the very bottom of the sea, this 2-in. (5-cm) crustacean was found 36,200 ft. (11,030 m) down in the Mariana Trench.

Colonies of these mollusks grow near life-sustaining hydrothermal vents. The deepest known population of clams was recently found off Japan at a depth of 20,886 ft. (6,366 m).

These superheated structures form in regions where the sea floor is spreading, at depths anywhere from 2,600 ft. to 20,000 ft. (800 m to 6,000 m).

Commonly found at depths of 14,000 ft. to 17,000 ft. (4,270 m to 5,180 m), these potato-size nuggets are rich in iron, copper, cobalt, manganese and nickel.

The world's deepest diving mammal, it weighs as much as 60 tons and has been recorded at depths as great as 8,000 ft. (2,440 m).

Found only near vents in the Pacific Ocean at an average depth of 7,300 ft. (2,225 m),- these 8-in.- (0.2-m-) long organisms have no mouths.

They get their energy from bacteria living in their stalks.

These fish, found at 4,600 ft. (1,400 m), resemble their shallow-water relatives, but have larger eyes and an enlarged dorsal fin that acts like a sensory antenna.

Believed to grow up to 64 ft. (20 m) long and live as deep as 3,300 ft. (1,000 m), these "monsters of the deep" have never been seen in their natural habitat.

Eaten by anything from barnacles to humpback whales, these microscopic animals and plants dwell in the well-lighted top 660 ft. (200 m) of the ocean. However, they can sometimes be found as deep as 1,000 ft. (300 m).

5,000 ft.

10,000 ft.

THE ABYSS

15,000 ft.

20,000 ft.

25,000 ft.

30,000 ft.

35,000 ft.

on in the absence of any known supply of food? How could they survive without any light? Scientists found that bacteria living inside the mollusks and worms were breaking down chemicals into usable food—an ecological niche nobody had suspected they could fill. They were chemosynthetic—as opposed to photosynthetic—getting their energy from chemicals rather than from the sun. Many biologists now believe the very first organisms on earth were chemosynthetic as well, suggesting that the vents may be the best laboratory available for studying how life on the planet began.

Do scientists expect even more surprises as they venture farther below the surface? The question is a crucial one, as both scientists and policymakers debate the finances of deep-sea exploration—and one that only the richest countries can contemplate. The world's deep-sea powers—the U.S., France, Japan and, until economic troubles all but ended its program, Russia—are always aware of who's ahead in the quest for the bottom. At the moment, it's probably Japan, not least because of the triumphant touchdown in the Challenger Deep in March 1995 of its 10.5-ton, $41.5 million ROV called Kaiko. As engineers from JAMSTEC, the Japan Marine Science

and Technology Center, watched anxiously on a video screen, the robotic craft spent 35 min. at a depth of 35,798 ft.—only 2 ft. shy of Trieste's 1960 record. But during that brief visit, Kaiko saw a sea slug, a worm and a shrimp, proof that even the most inhospitable place on earth is home to a variety of creatures.

Japan's latest success adds fuel to yet another debate about deep-sea exploration. Some scientists insist that remote-controlled robotic craft are no substitute for having humans on the scene. But others argue that robots—whether tethered, like Kaiko, or untethered, like the new generation of autonomous underwater vehicles known as AUVS—can do the job. The free-floating AUVS can roam the depths without human intervention for as long as a year, patiently accumulating data. Two American AUVS—a government- and university-funded craft called Odyssey and Woods Hole's Autonomous Benthic Explorer—have just completed tests off the West Coast.

Most scientists think the ideal solution would be to use a mix of all three types of vehicle. There is no shortage of designs. But as government subsidies to science are trimmed around the world, many of those now on the drawing board may never be built. Yet despite the budget cuts, despite the inhospitable environment, despite the pressing danger, there is little doubt that humans, one way or another, are headed back to the bottom of the sea. The rewards of exploring the coldest, darkest waters—scientific, economic and psychological—are just too great to pass up. Ultimately, people will go to the abyss for the same reason men climbed Everest: because it's there. ∎

NEUROLOGY

Glimpses of the Mind

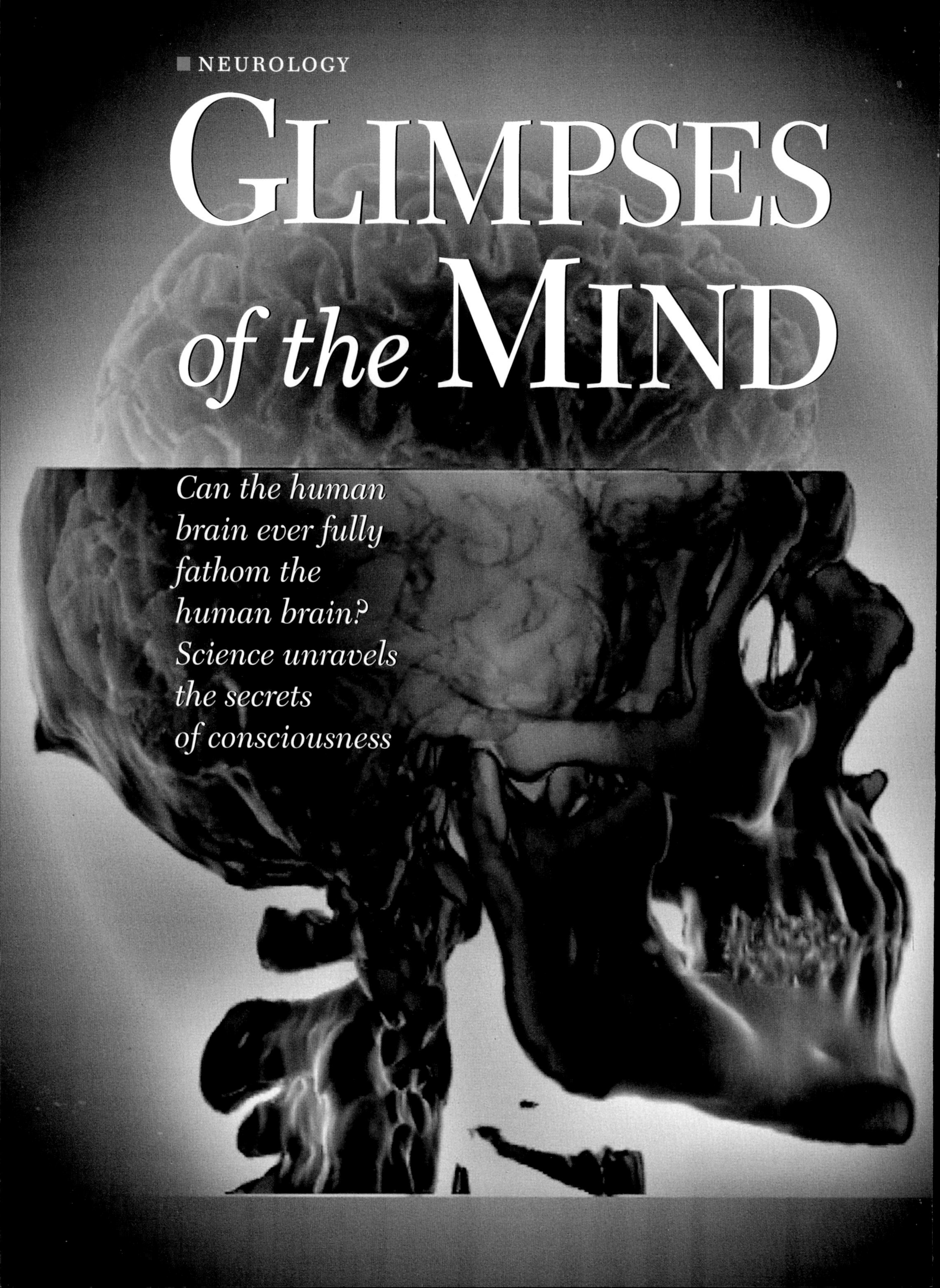

Can the human brain ever fully fathom the human brain? Science unravels the secrets of consciousness

THE MYSTERY IS DEEP, A SET OF INTER-related conundrums perhaps as old as humanity: What, precisely, is the mind, the elusive entity where intelligence, decision making, perception, awareness and sense of self reside? Where is it located? How does it work? Does it arise from purely physical processes—pulses of electricity zapping from brain cell to brain cell, helped along their way by myriad complex chemicals? Or is it something beyond the merely physical—something ethereal that might be close to the spiritual concept of the soul?

Great thinkers have had no shortage of ideas on the subject. Plato was convinced that the mind must be located inside the head, because the head is shaped more or less like a sphere, his idea of the highest geometrical form. Aristotle insisted that the mind was in the heart. His reasoning: warmth implies vitality; the blood is warm; the heart pumps the blood. By the Middle Ages, though, pretty much everyone agreed that the mind arose from the brain—but still had no clear idea of how it arose.

Finally, in the 17th century, the French philosopher René Descartes declared that the mind, while it might live in the brain, was a nonmaterial thing, entirely separate from the physical tissues found inside the head. Furthermore, said Descartes in one of history's most memorable sound bites, *"Cogito, ergo sum"* (I think, therefore I am). His point: consciousness is the only sure evidence that we actually exist.

Until just a few years ago, unraveling the relationship of mind and brain was beyond the realm of observation and experimentation. But science has finally begun to catch up with philosophy. Using sensitive electrodes inserted deep into the gray matter of test animals, researchers have watched vision as it percolates inward from the eye's retina to the inner brain. Powerful technologies such as magnetic resonance imaging (MRI) and positron-emission tomography (PET) have also provided a window on the human brain, enabling scientists to watch a thought taking place, see the red glow of fear erupting from the structure known as the amygdala, or note the telltale firing of neurons as a long-buried memory is reconstructed. "What's so exciting," says Patricia Churchland, a professor at the University of California at San Diego, "is that the philosophical questions raised by the Greeks are coming within the province of science."

In response to this enormous opportunity—not just to clarify the mysteries of consciousness but also to understand and treat such devastating mind malfunctions as Alzheimer's disease, depression, drug addiction, schizophrenia and traumatic brain damage—research projects have multiplied dramatically. Over the past several years, Johns Hopkins has launched the Zanvyl Kreiger Mind/Brain Institute and Harvard has created the

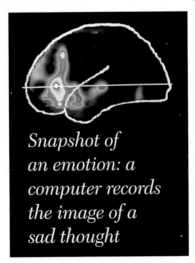

Snapshot of an emotion: a computer records the image of a sad thought

Mind/Brain/Behavior Initiative. And at the urging of the National Institute of Mental Health and other organizations, President George Bush declared the 1990s the Decade of the Brain.

In short, the brain is a hot topic. While a complete understanding of its inner workings will be a long time coming, the surge of interest in things cerebral has already produced tantalizing results. It turns out that the phenomenon of mind, of consciousness, is much more complex, though also more amenable to scientific investigation, than anyone suspected. Descartes was right in one sense: the mind is not a physical object, and while it resides within the brain, it has no particular location. The destruction of any given part of the brain can severely alter the mind in one way or another but not destroy it.

But Descartes was profoundly wrong, it appears, in his assertion that mind and body are fully independent. The mind, argues University of Iowa neurologist Antonio Damasio in his book *Descartes' Error,* is created by the body—specifically by the brain. Utterly contrary to common sense, though, and to the evidence of our own introspection, consciousness may be nothing more than an evanescent by-product of more mundane, wholly physical processes—much as a rainbow is the result of the interplay of light and raindrops. Input from the senses clearly plays a role, and so do body chemicals whose ebb and flow we experience as feelings and emotions. Memory, too, is involved, along with language: the way humans translate concepts into symbolic form. As neurologists gain deeper insights into each of these processes, they come ever closer to the central mystery of consciousness itself.

We think of learning and memory as somehow separate functions; in fact, they are not. Both are processes by which we acquire and store new data in a way that makes them retrievable later on. The storage takes place, according to the current theory, as a pattern of connections among neurons, the nerve cells that serve as the brain's basic building blocks. When information—the image of a new acquaintance's face, for example—enters the brain, it arrives in the form of electric impulses streaming from the retina, up the optic nerve and into the cerebral cortex, the so-called gray matter that houses the brain's higher functions.

The impulses die away within milliseconds, but their passage reinforces the particular set of connections between this particular set of neurons, giving them the ability to re-create the image. The more often the pattern is reinforced—by repeated sightings of the person, by the effort to remember him or by some other mental trigger—the more likely, says Damasio, that the pattern, or image, will not go into short-term memory, but into long-term memory. And from there, barring brain injury, disease or old age, it can be re-created by inducing the neurons to send electric impulses along the optic nerve in the old, by now familiar pattern.

That's the simple version. In fact, almost every memory is made up of many different patterns of neuronal connections, some for sounds, some for sights, some for smells or textures—tens of thousands of neurons firing off minute electric impulses simultaneously. The fact that many overlapping patterns are stored together means that a single stimulus can bring on a flood of remembrance— as Marcel Proust's taste of a madeleine triggered intense memories of his childhood, which in turn inspired him to write his monumental *Remembrance of Things Past*.

Memories of concrete facts and events, which can in principle be retrieved on demand, are coordinated through the hippocampus, a crescent-shaped collection of neurons deep in the core of the brain. Other sorts of memory are handled by other areas. The amygdala, for example, an almond-size knot of nerve cells located close to the brain stem, specializes in memories of fear; the basal ganglia, clumps of gray matter within both cerebral hemispheres, handle habits and physical skills; the cerebellum, at the base of the brain, governs conditioned learning (as in Pavlov's salivating dogs) and some reflexes.

DAMAGE TO ANY ONE OF THESE REGIONS HAS AN effect on the corresponding form of memory. An extensively studied patient known as HM, for example, lost much of his hippocampus in the course of surgery to relieve severe epilepsy. As a result, he could remember everything that happened to him before the surgery, but was completely unable to form new memories. He was stuck forever in the 1950s. Yet HM was able to learn new skills, such as drawing while looking in a mirror.

Physical trauma can distort memory, presumably by destroying all or part of one of these memory-processing structures. But other sorts of shock—strong emotion, for example—can do the same. Posttraumatic stress disorder is a good example of the brain reacting to shock. Whereas the intellectual memory of emotions is routed through the hippocampus, a different, gut-level sort of emotional memory can be involuntarily revived with terrible clarity by abnormal activity in the amygdala. "It's been an eye opener to me that individuals we study who were traumatized 25 years ago still show abnormal brain function," says Dennis Charney, head of psychiatry at a VA hospital in Connecticut. "Severe stress can change the way your brain functions biologically."

It stands to reason that humans would have a specialized region of the brain for processing emotions and memories. What's most surprising is the assertion by the University of Iowa's Damasio that emotion is central to the process of rational thought. His evidence comes from nearly two dozen patients he has treated, including Elliot, a businessman who started behaving irrationally after surgery to remove a brain tumor 10 years ago. Before the procedure, Elliot was a competent adult; now he can't keep appointments, has trouble making decisions and has squandered much of his life savings. Elliot cannot behave rationally, even though his intelligence was unaffected by his tumor. The part of the brain destroyed by invading tissue was in a region of the prefrontal cortex essential to decision making. But what Elliot lost, psychological testing revealed, was the ability to experience emotions like pride or self-confidence. While the amygdala does process fear, his doctors argue from the example of Elliot and other patients, other parts of the brain are also critical to regulating emotion.

In fact, says Damasio, emotion is a key element of learning and decision making. If an investment goes sour, you feel bad about it and act more carefully next time— something Elliot could no longer do after his injury. Observes Damasio: "We can't decide whom we're going

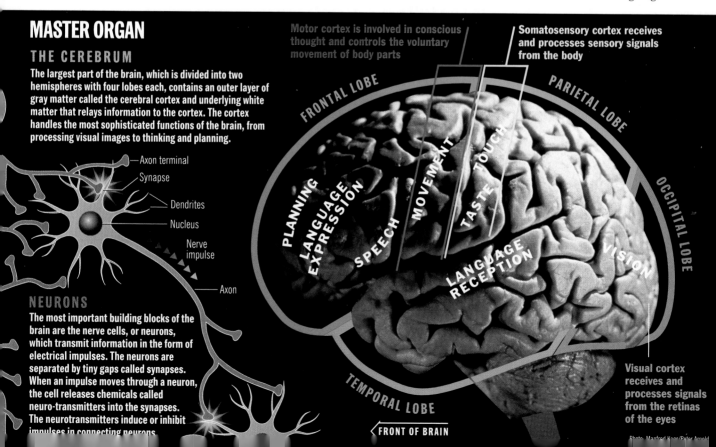

MASTER ORGAN

THE CEREBRUM

The largest part of the brain, which is divided into two hemispheres with four lobes each, contains an outer layer of gray matter called the cerebral cortex and underlying white matter that relays information to the cortex. The cortex handles the most sophisticated functions of the brain, from processing visual images to thinking and planning.

Motor cortex is involved in conscious thought and controls the voluntary movement of body parts

Somatosensory cortex receives and processes sensory signals from the body

FRONTAL LOBE
PARIETAL LOBE
OCCIPITAL LOBE
TEMPORAL LOBE

PLANNING
LANGUAGE EXPRESSION
SPEECH
MOVEMENT
TASTE
TOUCH
LANGUAGE RECEPTION
VISION

FRONT OF BRAIN

Axon terminal
Synapse
Dendrites
Nucleus
Nerve impulse
Axon

NEURONS

The most important building blocks of the brain are the nerve cells, or neurons, which transmit information in the form of electrical impulses. The neurons are separated by tiny gaps called synapses. When an impulse moves through a neuron, the cell releases chemicals called neuro-transmitters into the synapses. The neurotransmitters induce or inhibit impulses in connecting neurons.

Visual cortex receives and processes signals from the retinas of the eyes

to marry, what savings strategy to adopt, where to live, on the basis of reason alone."

The exquisite specialization of neurons for processing very precise sorts of information—moving objects from still objects, the sensation of touch from an amputated finger—is perhaps at its most highly refined when it comes to language. Accordingly, brain-damaged patients can exhibit an astounding range of language problems. Some have trouble using and understanding just nouns. Others have trouble with verbs. Some patients can't produce language but comprehend it perfectly; others can speak normally but can't make any sense out of what they hear.

University of Washington neurosurgeon Dr. George Ojemann has discovered, by probing the brain with electrodes, that some neurons turn on when one is silently naming an object to oneself but not during reading and vice versa. In a bilingual patient he found neurons that were activated by Finnish but not English. In another he discovered neurons that changed activity with English but not Spanish. And, he marvels, "the neurons that are active when you hear a word are not active when you express it."

Until recently, scientists assumed that the brain processed language in two neatly defined boxes: Broca's area (for speech production) and Wernicke's area (for speech comprehension). The picture now emerging is far more complex. Damasio, along with his wife Hanna, also a neurologist, has recently constructed a model for how the brain processes language, based on some 200 unusual case histories. The most prominent among them: a patient code-named Boswell, who has no function in large areas of his brain because of an infection. One consequence is that he has no memory of recent events. Yet he is able to speak and understand language perfectly well—up to a point.

Prompted with "Denver," Boswell responds, "Colorado." Asked to name a city in Colorado, however, he goes blank. Similarly, Boswell recognizes the category "horse" but cannot supply the example "Appaloosa." Somewhere in his brain, the data may still exist, but he can no longer get at them. The reason, argue the Damasios, is that he has lost essential "convergence zones," mental switching stations that provide access to the information and tie it in with other relevant data.

USING AN MRI SCANNER, HANNA DAMASIO HAS EXamined the living brains of hundreds of patients, and she and her husband have identified regions they think may serve as convergence zones in the brain's left hemisphere. An area in the temporal lobe pulls together information about the names of objects, animals and people, for instance, while another in the frontal cortex appears to act as the nexus for verbs. Yet a third oversees the task of assembling nouns and verbs into sentences.

The Damasios suspect that convergence zones—thousands of them, spread through the cortex—do more than just process language. They may also coordinate every other sort of information the brain needs to be fully functional: perception, memory, emotion. And if that's true, the convergence zones, merging disparate pieces of information into a semblance of a whole, could be responsible for that most elusive of brain phenomena: consciousness, the sense of being in the here and now.

Does this mean that science is on the verge of understanding consciousness? Not necessarily. The notion that the human mind can ever fully comprehend the human mind could well be folly. It may be that scientists will eventually have to acknowledge the existence of something beyond their ken—something that might be described as the soul. ∎

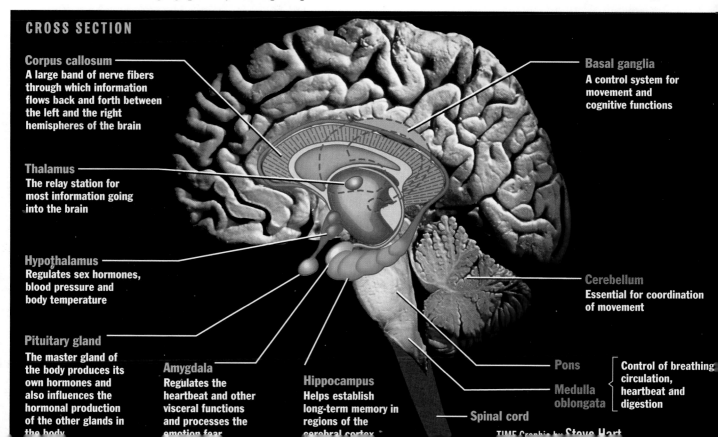

CROSS SECTION

Corpus callosum
A large band of nerve fibers through which information flows back and forth between the left and the right hemispheres of the brain

Thalamus
The relay station for most information going into the brain

Hypothalamus
Regulates sex hormones, blood pressure and body temperature

Pituitary gland
The master gland of the body produces its own hormones and also influences the hormonal production of the other glands in the body

Amygdala
Regulates the heartbeat and other visceral functions and processes the emotion fear

Hippocampus
Helps establish long-term memory in regions of the cerebral cortex

Spinal cord

Basal ganglia
A control system for movement and cognitive functions

Cerebellum
Essential for coordination of movement

Pons

Medulla oblongata

Control of breathing circulation, heartbeat and digestion

TIME Graphic by Steve Hart

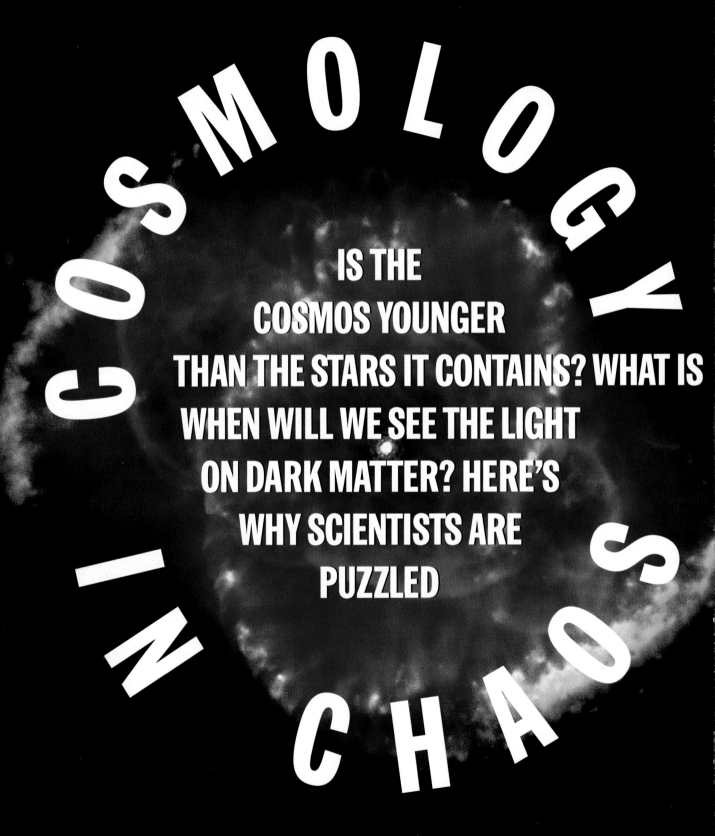

COSMOLOGY IN CHAOS

IS THE COSMOS YOUNGER THAN THE STARS IT CONTAINS? WHAT IS WHEN WILL WE SEE THE LIGHT ON DARK MATTER? HERE'S WHY SCIENTISTS ARE PUZZLED

TENSION BETWEEN THEORY AND OBSERVATION IS part of the normal course of science. It keeps both sides honest, and, at those rare times in history when the two lock horns irreconcilably, it can lead to nothing less than a full-fledged scientific revolution. But what's happening in cosmology—the study of the universe—verges on the bizarre. Astronomers have come up with one theory-busting discovery after another, hinting that a scientific revolution may be close at hand. At stake are answers to some of the most fundamental questions facing humanity: What is the origin of the universe? How old is it? What is it made of?

Stargazers have had to absorb a barrage of bafflements lately. Over the past few years, astronomers have uncovered the existence of the Great Wall, a huge conglomeration of galaxies stretching across 500 million light-years of space; the Great Attractor, a mysterious concentration of mass that is hauling much of the local universe off in the direction of the constellations Hydra and Centaurus; Great Voids, where few galaxies can be found; and galaxies caught in the throes of formation a mere billion years after the Big Bang, when they should not yet exist. The theorists have proposed one mind-stretching idea after another to explain what's going on out there.

Freedman is a highly respected observational astronomer, and so are the 13 others on her space-telescope team. Moreover, theirs is only the latest in a series of measurements that point to a relatively young universe. Just a month before their results appeared in the journal *Nature,* two other sets of astronomers came out with their own young-universe observations. And while a handful of studies have emerged over the past few years arguing instead for an older cosmos, many more have converged on a younger age. The Freedman team's observations are considered by far the most definitive because they are based on the Hubble's extraordinarily clear vision.

Astronomers have known since Edwin Hubble's heyday in the 1920s that you need only two pieces of information to deduce the age of the universe: how fast the galaxies are flying apart and how far away they are from earth. Freedman's team used the new powers of the Hubble telescope to measure the distance to a faraway galaxy called M100, and gauged the Hubble Constant—the cosmic rate of expansion—at 80, indicating a universe between 8 billion and 12 billion years old.

While most astronomers take these numbers very seriously—along with the cosmic paradox they imply—Allan Sandage, Freedman's colleague down the hall, is having none of it. Arguing on the basis of his method of measuring the distance between galaxies—which involves comparing the relative brightness of super-

E AGE OF THE UNIVERSE?

Cosmologists can now say with some confidence that the universe started out in a very hot, very dense state somewhere between 8 billion and 25 billion years ago, and that it has been expanding ever since—the Big Bang in a nutshell. They believe galaxies are strewn around the cosmos not randomly but according to a pattern that includes some patches with many galaxies and others with few. They believe the universe is pervaded by mysterious dark matter, whose gravity has dominated cosmic history from the start.

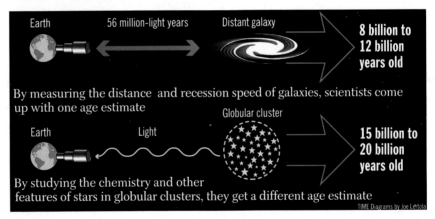

By measuring the distance and recession speed of galaxies, scientists come up with one age estimate

8 billion to 12 billion years old

By studying the chemistry and other features of stars in globular clusters, they get a different age estimate

15 billion to 20 billion years old

TIME Diagrams by Joe Lertola

Beyond that, things get murky. The experts don't know how old or how big the universe is. They don't know what most of it is made of. They don't know in any detail how it began or how it will end. And, beyond the local cosmic neighborhood, they don't know much about what it looks like. Each question is now under study, each bears directly on the others, and each could soon yield to the intellectual and instrumental firepower being brought to bear on it. Assuming, that is, that the universe cooperates.

If Wendy Freedman and her colleagues at the Carnegie Observatories in Pasadena, California, are right, the universe is younger than the stars it contains. They used the Hubble Space Telescope to peg the age of the universe at somewhere between 8 billion and 12 billion years old. But experts insist that the oldest stars in the Milky Way have been around for at least 14 billion years.

novas—he claims, as he has for more than 20 years, that the Hubble Constant is lower, which means the age of the universe goes up considerably. But if Freedman is right and Sandage is wrong, as many cosmic handicappers are betting, then the age crisis won't go away without some fundamental change in the way astronomers understand the cosmos. That means that at least some scientists will have to give up their cherished beliefs about how stars work or how the universe is organized or what it's made of—or maybe even all of the these.

High on the list of concepts that astronomical theorists would hate to lose is that of cosmic inflation. The universe actually makes a lot more sense if you assume that just after it was born, all of space went into overdrive, exploding outward for the briefest fraction of a second. This inflation explains such mysteries as why the universe looks pretty much the same in all directions and how a peanut-butter-smooth distribution of matter in the young

HOW IS THE COSMOS STRUCTURED?

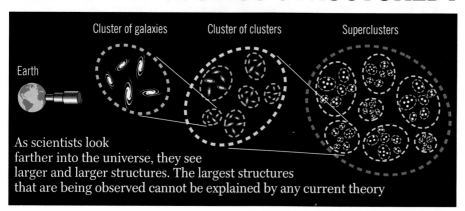

Cluster of galaxies   Cluster of clusters   Superclusters

Earth

As scientists look farther into the universe, they see larger and larger structures. The largest structures that are being observed cannot be explained by any current theory

like objects (known collectively as massive compact halo objects, or MACHOS), they have studied stars for telltale flickers indicating that a MACHO may have passed by. The latest development came in October 1995, when a team at the Los Alamos National Laboratory published findings of strong evidence for neutrino mass, obtained from accelerator collisions. The finding may be of cosmic significance; such mass might account for 10% to 20% of the theorized mass density of the universe, the team said.

cosmos evolved into today's lumpy distribution, with clusters of galaxies surrounded by empty space.

Inflation theory doesn't just explain things; it makes predictions. Chief among them: the blackness of space is only seemingly empty. In fact, it probably abounds with vast amounts of matter—matter that cannot be directly detected because it doesn't shine. If this theory is correct, then there must be precisely enough of this dark matter so that gravity will forever slow the expansion of the universe without ever stopping it, balancing space on a gravitational knife edge between eternal growth and eventual collapse.

Leaving aside theory, the challenge of identifying and understanding the stuff that makes up most of the universe has become one of the most irresistible—and frustrating—quests in science. An early theory held that the missing matter is composed of commonplace particles called neutrinos. One problem with this is that dark matter is massive, and no one knows if neutrinos have mass. Even if they have, in computer simulations they do a poor job of making a recognizable universe. Cold dark matter was another candidate to supply the missing matter ("cold," in physics jargon, means slow-moving; neutrinos, by contrast, are "hot"). Also known as WIMPs, for weakly interacting massive particles, these are hypothetical particles derived from theories. But WIMPs can't account for such new cosmic finds as Great Walls, Great Voids and Great Attractors.

Physicists hoping to observe dark matter directly have searched for objects both large and subatomic. On the theory that the dark stuff is made of an undiscovered particle, they have built all manner of sensitive detectors. On the chance that it is composed of very dim stars or large planet-

the theorized mass density of the universe, the team said.

Neutrinos with mass might solve the dark-matter problem and thus support the inflation theory. But in some ways that would make the crisis worse. The more dark matter there is in the universe, the harder it is to explain the Freedman team's findings about the age of the cosmos. When the team says the universe is between 8 billion and 12 billion years old, its vagueness reflects uncertainty about how much matter the cosmos contains. If there's a lot, as inflation suggests, its gravity would be slowing down the universe's expansion, making the universe younger than it looks. If, on the other hand, there is relatively little matter, the slowing has been minimal, and 12 billion is more like it.

The clash of egos and conflicting claims is a sign that science is alive and well and likely on the cusp of a major new insight. Says astrophysicist John Bahcall of Princeton's Institute for Advanced Study: "Every time we get slapped down, we say, 'Thank you, Mother Nature,' because it means we're about to learn something important." ∎

WHAT IS THE UNIVERSE MADE OF?

Dark matter could be composed of any, some or none of these possibilities

Name	Neutrinos	WIMPs	MACHOs	Black holes
What they are	Subatomic relatives of the electron that have no electrical charge and interact only weakly with ordinary matter	(Weakly interacting massive particles) Also known as cold dark matter	(Massive compact halo objects) Dim Jupiter-size planets or white dwarf stars made of ordinary matter	Objects with gravitational fields so intense that light cannot escape from them
Pros	Known to exist in great numbers	Existence is predicted by theories	The simplest theory	Strongly predicted by general relativity
Cons	May have no mass, cannot account for existing cosmic structure	Are hypothetical	So many would be required that it seems unlikely that all the dark matter could be made of them	Their presence in such abundance should have been detected already

SHAKEN BUT STALWART, GALILEO MEETS JUPITER

Its launch was delayed for years. Its umbrella-like antenna never quite unfolded. Its tape recorder got stuck in rewind. But in December, NASA's gutsy, patched-up little space-craft Galileo settled into its two-year orbit around Jupiter, and a probe it had previously released plunged into the Jovian atmosphere. There it sniffed gases, measured tempera-tures and pressures and carried out other observa-tions before being vaporized by the high temperatures of Jupiter's cloud cover.

REALLY HEATING UP

After years of debate, scientists asserted that global warming is a clear and present danger. Un-less the world takes imme-diate and drastic steps to reduce the emissions of heat-trapping gases, they warned, the so-called greenhouse effect could drive global temperatures up as much as 6°F by the year 2100 and huge swaths of densely populated land could be inundated by rising seas. Sounding the alarm was the Internation-al Panel on Climate Change, a respected group of more than 1,500 leading climate experts from 60 nations.

YEAR OF THE STORMS

Batten the hatches! 1995 was the worst year for tropical storms in the Atlantic region in decades. The year's final tally: 19 tropical storms, 11 hurri-canes, more than 120 dead. Caribbean islands suffered the most damage, but Florida was battered by both Hurricanes Erin and Opal. Experts warned that a 25-year lull in hurricane cycles was ending—and that the region's popula-tion growth could mean a return to the scale of dev-astation seen in the 1950s, when hundreds died in the U.S. and the islands.

New Delhi floods: Our future as the globe gets warmer?

U.S.-Russian rendezvous

EMBRACE IN SPACE

Thursday, June 29, 1995, 245 miles above the earth. U.S. Astronaut Robert ("Hoot") Gibson gently nudged the shuttle *Atlantis* toward the Russ-ian space station Mir, foot by agonizing foot. As mil-lions watched on live TV, six sets of hooks and latch-es locked into place—and an American spaceship and a Russian one were soaring through space to-gether for the first time in two decades. While the spacemen celebrated, their superiors said the future will see more such cooperation, as the budget-cramped space programs from both countries seek to find common ground— where there is no ground.

ANTS IN OUR PANTS

Killer bees, it turns out, are not the most me-nacing marauders to hail from South America. Their less publicized cousins the fire ants—which pack an agonizing, fiery sting—are more widespread in the U.S., more destructive and, so far, deadlier. At least 50 people have died in recent years from allergic reac-tions to fire-ant stings. Antagonistic, moisture-loving and strangely attracted to electric current, the ants have been harassing peo-ple, mostly in the Southern U.S., for decades. The bad news: the ants are on the march. Fire-ant swarms have been found in Arizona, New Mexico, California, Oregon and Washington.

STANDING UP TO BE COUNTED MUCH EARLIER

When did the first manlike creatures begin to walk upright? Scientists believe that hap-pened between 4 million and 6 million years ago, though they did not have enough fossils to back up their hypothesis. But in

A 4 million-year-old jaw

August a team of paleon-tologists led by Meave Leakey from the National Museums of Kenya and Alan Walker of Pennsylva-nia State University an-nounced the best evidence so far that a previously un-known species of hominid strode upright at least 4 million years ago. Their find of jaws, teeth, skull and leg bones from several individuals pushed the emergence of two-legged walking beings 500,000 years earlier than other data had indicated. ■

THE REAL GOLD

Forget the '50s: in 1995 TV's best shows were wittier, more relevant, and more compelling

Criccck! Criccck! Criccck! Was that the rasp of slowly grinding teeth coming from the TV networks' office suites? 1995 had not been the plummiest of fall seasons. By October, overall network viewership was down 9%; none of the record 42 new shows had connected with audiences; and even *Murder One*—everybody's pick as the season's best new series—was in danger of being smothered in the cradle, having to compete first with the closing arguments of the O.J. Simpson trial and then with *ER*. It was almost enough to make you feel sorry for an industry that employs some of the most craven people on earth.

Still, network executives had good reasons to feel their cushy salaries were, to some extent, earned. For one thing, TV remained the nation's dominant medium. Yet despite perennial complaints about TV's formulaic and lowbrow fare—and the religious right's conviction that the medium was shredding the nation's moral fiber—anyone who watched even a smattering of TV would have to agree that there are currently more first-rate programs on the air than at any time in television's 50-year history. Comedies like *The Simpsons* and *Frasier* and *Seinfeld* more than stood up to *I Love Lucy* and *Mary Tyler Moore*; dramas like *NYPD Blue* and *ER* were broadening the scope of narrative art; and heretical as it may sound, the 1990s were television's real Golden Age, the 1950s and Philco TV Playhouse and Paddy Chayefsky and *Winky Dink and You* notwithstanding.

EN AGE IS NOW

Of course, one could go on and on extolling the wonders of CNN, Court TV and American Movie Classics. But discussion here should be limited to old-fashioned prime-time network TV—the fairest way, after all, to draw a comparison with TV's pre-cable Bronze Age. A list of indispensable current series, besides those already mentioned, would include the mighty, acerbic *Roseanne*, still potent after seven-plus seasons; and newer shows now hitting their stride, like *Mad About You, The X-Files, Friends, NewsRadio* and the wonderful *Homicide*, more vivid and biting than its higher-rated rival *NYPD Blue*. Among the season's new shows, *American Gothic, Ned and Stacey* and *The Bonnie Hunt Show* were all fresh and worth watching.

The Larry Sanders Show, with its laugh-trackless verisimilitude, was the best comedy on TV in 1995, probably the closest a sitcom will ever come to perfect pitch (yes, it's on HBO—so much for ground rules). The best drama: *Party of Five*, a *thirtysomething* for teenagers and young adults—with all the pluses (honest, abnormally well-crafted writing) and minuses (too much acoustic guitar in the sound track) that the *thirtysomething* comparison implies. And for pure cheese, Fox's *Melrose Place* was indisputably television's greatest accomplishment—and that's saying something.

None of this boosterism is meant to imply that the 1995 schedule was free from the dreary or the formulaic. Seen from above, prime time's landscape might not even look all that different from its past: acres and acres of precocious kids, man-hungry neighbors and office curmudgeons with hearts of gold; police shows and lawyer shows and doctor shows proliferating like strip malls.

But within familiar genres there has been welcome evolution. Sitcoms have license to deal with more realistic and mature subject matter—not a new trend, it's true, but done with more tact and wit than ever before. Think of the famously sly *Seinfeld* episode about masturbation or *Roseanne's* matter-of-fact treatment of its comparatively many gay and lesbian characters. Shows like *Roseanne, The*

CONTEMPORARY CLASSICS Clockwise from top left, four great reasons not to touch your television dial in '95: *Murder One, Roseanne, ER* and *NYPD Blue*

Simpsons and *Grace Under Fire* also deal frankly with the economic dislocation of the middle class, a sad, mundane fact of modern life largely ignored by the movies as well as by most contemporary literature. And anyone who still doesn't believe television has become more deft and less shrill in its handling of "controversial" topics need only recall an episode—any episode—of *Maude*.

D RAMAS TOO HAVE MORE COMPLEX CANVASES than did their predecessors. One example: compare *ER*—the most popular show on television—with precursors like *Marcus Welby, M.D* or *Medical Center*. *ER* is less concerned with diagnosing the ailment of the week than observing what happens to men and women who are forced to work under almost impossible conditions, how fear and exhaustion both draw them together and repel them from each other.

The current renaissance in programming comes after years of increasing anxiety within the broadcasting industry about the loss of viewers to cable and home video. Not so long ago, the very medium of network television was alleged to be in its death throes. But even with the combined viewership of ABC, CBS and NBC down to an average 57% of the nation's households (at their peak, from the mid-1950s though the mid-'70s, the Big Three were pulling in more than 90%), networks remain lucrative businesses, shabby but sturdy prewar apartment buildings in a rapidly gentrifying neighborhood. Which explains why Disney and Westinghouse were so eager to buy ABC and CBS, and why Time Warner and Viacom were attempting to jerry-build webs of their own with schedules that harked back to the frantic early days of the Fox network.

For the most part, the increased competition kept producers from complacently cranking out the kind of wan, homogenized fare that characterized TV seasons past—and could still be enjoyed on the nostalgia smorgasbord of Nickelodeon's *Nick at Nite* if one was so inclined. The suburban blandness that *Nick at Nite* dines out on is due to the fact that network TV was once the massiest mass medium ever invented. It still is, of course, but thanks to the increasing sophistication of audience-measuring "science," the networks learned they can profit by delivering smaller-niche audiences to advertisers. Which means that *Seinfeld* and *Mad About You* don't have to appeal to everyone in order to make money; they need only reach 18- to 49-year-olds with lots of disposable income to spend on BMWs and Nikes. So producers can create shows that are intelligent and quirky because intelligent and quirky appeals to upscale audiences.

1955 Everybody loved Lucy (and Desi), but they seemed stuck in time

Unfortunately, there are a number of downsides to this phenomenon. One is that some audiences—primarily older folks, younger children and minorities—are being ignored. Another is that some series—the late *Northern Exposure,* for example—end up choking on their own quirky intelligence, crowded with characters who are less than the sum of their arbitrary tics. A third drawback is that seemingly every other character on television is now a young white professional who lives in Manhattan and goes out on unfortunate blind dates; bizarrely, all four of NBC's high-rated Thursday-night comedies (*Friends, The Single Guy, Seinfeld* and *Caroline in the City*) were in that vein.

This demographic obsession was one reason why so many shows had scenes set in coffee bars. Another, more telling explanation is that TV producers, lacking the budgets for car crashes and Bruce Willis, fill up a lot of airtime by having characters sit around and gab. Talk, in production terms, is cheap. A virtue of this necessity is that it allows writers the luxury of exploring the ins and outs of characters and relationships in ways that mainstream feature films rarely do anymore.

This has helped foster an important change from TV's early days, when series characters were largely static from episode to episode, season to season. There was little shading or evolution in Darrin Stephens' nincompoopcy. And Joe Friday—not counting the occasional expression of disgust with punks and hippies—was a tragically repressed emotional cipher. In essence, TV's early characters were subjected to the same drama every week, as if

1959 *Dragnet's* Harry Morgan and Jack Webb were emotional ciphers

1995 *NYPD Blue's* Dennis Franz and Jimmy Smits have frailties—and soul

1995 On *Mad About You*, character growth helps generate the laughs

stuck in a time warp. Would Darrin stop Larry Tate from finding out that Samantha is a witch? Would Lucy come up with a clever scheme to subvert Ricky's wishes? Would McGarrett get to say "Book him, Danno"—or maybe, just once, "Book him, Chin Ho"?

By contrast, characters in today's TV shows are allowed to grow, make mistakes, find themselves—all the touchy-feely things that make real people so endearing and insufferable. Unlike Joe Friday or Barnaby Jones, Sipowicz on *NYPD Blue* has a love life, one he struggles to sustain. Unlike Ricky and Lucy Ricardo's marriage, the relationship between *Mad About You*'s Jamie and Paul Buchman deepens and goes through its rough patches. Set in worlds that evolve from week to week, the best new shows almost seem to take place in real time, accreting day-in, day-out intimacy. Viewers can feel as though they're living with these programs in the way readers live with novels.

What's surprising is that it took so long for creative minds to take advantage of TV's narrative attributes. Inherited from radio, soap operas were originally designed to be messily open-ended—like life, as it happens—in the utilitarian hope that viewers would keep tuning in. Films and plays, by way of contrast, are designed to compress the defining moments of a character's life into a spare and extraordinary couple of hours. Thus the first *Die Hard* movie may have been more gripping than a given episode of *NYPD Blue*, but *NYPD Blue* remains compelling after more than 40 episodes, whereas the *Die Hard* follow-up films—like most movie series—began wheezing halfway through the opening credits of the first sequel.

Once upon a time, TV was Hollywood's sorry stepsibling, creatively retarded by its need to appeal to the lowest common denominator, while movie producers were free to hire David Lean and convince themselves they were making art. Today the bruising economics behind moviemaking has nearly reversed those roles. With Hollywood budgets averaging around $35 million—not including millions in marketing and distribution costs—movies increasingly have to appeal to the broadest audience possible. "Features have turned into exploita-

tion pictures because that's the way to survive," grumbles director Barry Levinson, who should know, having made 1994's *Disclosure*. Fortunately, he's able to find creative fulfillment as an executive producer of TV's *Homicide*.

The truth is, the general run of television series in 1995 was better than the general run of movies—and not just because so many recent films had been based on old TV shows. Not surprisingly, many who work in television agree. "In movies, dumb and dumber is the goal," says Betsy Borns, a writer on *Friends*. "When film people get snobbish and say, 'Oh … you write for TV,' as if it's a step down, I look at them and say, 'It's getting late—you probably have to go home and write your next Pauly Shore film.'"

To some extent, movies' aesthetic woes can be laid at television's door. Producers have to give audiences something on the big screen they can't get at home for free, which has led film away from narrative and toward sheer sensation. Levinson points out a more nefarious problem: "Studio films are now sold to the public with 30-second TV spots … somebody chasing somebody, somebody waving a gun, a lot of music, and then a dramatic voice that says, 'Opens Friday!' If you can't sell a movie in that 30-second spot, your movie won't open. It's hard to sell little, intimate moments where people are just sitting around talking." Of course, people just sitting around talking is a large part of what makes TV worth watching.

A closing cameo: If Marty, the lovelorn butcher from Paddy Chayefsky's classic 1953 teleplay, and his best friend Angie were to step into a time machine and wind up in 1995, they wouldn't have to run through their memorably aimless conversation: "What do you feel like doing tonight?" "I don't know, what do you feel like doing?" Today they'd just turn on *The Simpsons* or *Larry Sanders* or *NYPD Blue* and enjoy the best that contemporary American entertainment has to offer. What they would make of *NYPD Blue*'s famous views of bare-butted cops is harder to say. ■

1955 As Ralph Kramden, Jackie Gleason made his home his castle

1995 *Roseanne* is a '90s female take on the dislocation of the middle class

Mary-Louise Parker, 31

Keanu Reeves, 31

Uma Thurman, 25

GENERATION X

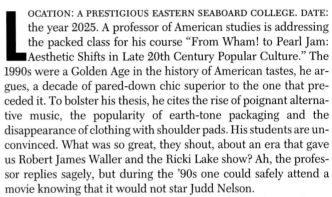

Forget the Brat Pack (please!). Today's

LOCATION: A PRESTIGIOUS EASTERN SEABOARD COLLEGE. DATE: the year 2025. A professor of American studies is addressing the packed class for his course "From Wham! to Pearl Jam: Aesthetic Shifts in Late 20th Century Popular Culture." The 1990s were a Golden Age in the history of American tastes, he argues, a decade of pared-down chic superior to the one that preceded it. To bolster his thesis, he cites the rise of poignant alternative music, the popularity of earth-tone packaging and the disappearance of clothing with shoulder pads. His students are unconvinced. What was so great, they shout, about an era that gave us Robert James Waller and the Ricki Lake show? Ah, the professor replies sagely, but during the '90s one could safely attend a movie knowing that it would not star Judd Nelson.

If the current decade really will be venerated by future chroniclers of pop culture, it may well be because the '90s have produced an appealing stable of new actors who stand in smart contrast to the so-called Brat Pack of the '80s, the cliquish band of young stars that included Nelson, Rob Lowe, Ally Sheedy and various sons of Martin Sheen. The '90s newcomers also provide a downtown alternative to married-with-children superstars like Demi Moore and Tom Cruise. Brad Pitt, Ethan Hawke, Winona Ryder, Uma Thurman and a handful of others, all in their 20s and early 30s, share soulful good looks, unconventional style and a refreshing seriousness about their craft. They typically work with edgy directors in an impressive variety of roles. On screen and off, they convey a beguiling intensity and even a fondness for books. They are a fine lager next to the Brat Pack's Bud Lite.

Consider the group's 1995 successes. Pitt vaulted to star status as a wild-hearted rancher in *Legends of the Fall* early in the year, and his thriller *Seven* was an autumn smash. Ethereal beauties Ryder and Thurman earned Oscar nominations—Ryder for her role as Jo in Gillian Armstrong's *Little Women* and Thurman for her portrayal of a heroin-sniffing Mob wife in Quentin Tarantino's *Pulp Fiction.* Hawke won rave reviews for his role as a charmingly scruffy romantic in *Before Sunrise.* In the meantime, Mary-Louise Parker garnered praise for her performance in the girl-bonding hit *Boys on the Side.* Critics have also been smitten by that other winsome (unrelated) Parker, Sarah Jessica, who plays a witty copywriter in *Miami Rhapsody.*

If today's alterna-stars seem infinitely cooler than their predecessors, it is in part because they are choosier about the roles they accept. It would be hard to imagine Hawke appearing in the equivalent of Charlie Sheen's 1990 trash-collection farce, *Men at Work.* "People my age have an earnestness, a desire to do good work," says Mary-Louise Parker, who appeared in

X-CELLENT

stars would rather shine than whine

Brad Pitt, 32

Winona Ryder, 24

Leonardo DiCaprio, 21

Woody Allen's multiple-Oscar-nominated *Bullets over Broadway.* "There seem to be more people who want to do something worthwhile and different and provocative."

Unlike the Brat Pack, the new group is venturing far beyond movies about youth angst. Significantly, Pitt and Ryder both tried period films on for size during the year. Keanu Reeves, who starred in the 1994 hit *Speed,* appeared in Kenneth Branagh's film version of *Much Ado About Nothing,* then played Hamlet onstage in Canada. Leonardo DiCaprio, first noticed for his portrayal of a retarded boy in *What's Eating Gilbert Grape,* starred as junkie poet Jim Carroll in *The Basketball Diaries* and as Arthur Rimbaud, the gay 19th century French poet, in *Total Eclipse.*

Idealism seems to run in the blood of Hollywood's new junior class, several of whom grew up in counterculture families. Thurman's mother was once married to Timothy Leary—who is also, coincidentally, Ryder's godfather. Thurman's father is a highly regarded scholar of Buddhism. Writer Charles Bukowski was a frequent houseguest at the DiCaprios' when Leonardo was growing up in Los Angeles. Leonardo's best childhood friend was Abbie Hoffman's son. And Sarah Jessica Parker grew up idolizing Cesar Chavez and attending peace marches with her parents.

The interests of this new wave of stars seem to extend beyond the Hollywood club scene. Hawke and Sarah Jessica Parker live quiet lives in Manhattan. In 1993, Hawke started his own theater company, where he presides as artistic director. Ryder collects rare books and owns an edition of James Joyce's *Ulysses* that features original drawings by Matisse. She is also a fan of the obscure, critically lauded Italian-American novelist John Fante.

But despite their urbanity, these actors and actresses have an appealingly childlike quality. Pitt is the sort of free spirit who might woo a girl by popping wheelies in a parking lot. Hawke would be more likely to take her to his dorm room and show off his John Coltrane collection. Rather than overt sex appeal, actresses like the Parkers project the flustered insouciance of college coeds, the smart, pretty girls on campus who keep losing their library cards. Declares Thurman: "I am completely a goofball nerd."

If the new kids have successfully styled themselves away from comparisons to the Brat Pack, they have also distinguished themselves from prior generations of movie stars. They don't have the smoldering rebelliousness of '50s stars like Brando, Clift and Dean. Nor are they throwbacks to the glamorous Hollywood stars of the '30s and '40s. This generation has created its own kind of understated, unaffected sophistication—Bette Davis and Cary Grant in mussed bobs and basketball sneakers. These actors have nothing against grownups; they're just not ready to be them. ∎

LOW VOLTAGE, HIGH POWER

Casting off their electric chains, musicians young and old find fresh inspiration on MTV Unplugged

THE SHOW IS ABOUT TO START, BUT THE BICKERING seems unstoppable. Courtney Love and her punk-rock group, Hole, are on the stage of the Brooklyn Academy of Music in mid-February 1995 preparing to tape a performance for MTV *Unplugged*—the influential TV show in which rock bands cast aside their electric guitars and amplifiers in an attempt to demonstrate their musical talents on old-fashioned acoustic instruments.

The band has been through difficult times lately, and during rehearsals Love and guitarist Eric Erlandson snap at each other. The testy exchange makes one wonder: Can this band pull it together in time to perform? It does—and with impressive results. Love's voice is raw, but the band's ragged sound is perversely charming in this folksy format. The performance is unexpectedly loud, and not completely unplugged—Love and Erlandson gamely pluck away at acoustic guitars and are backed by a harpist, but their instruments are wired to not strictly kosher onstage electric amplifiers. Still, the show has grit and guts.

MTV *Unplugged* has changed the direction of popular music in the '90s. *Unplugged* albums are showing up ever more frequently at the top of the charts, and the unplugged ethos has influenced much of pop music. The very term unplugged has entered the language, connoting that someone has stripped off the gaudy trappings of the disinformation age and gone back to basics. In the spring of 1995 MTV launched a new series of *Unplugged* concerts, featuring some of the hottest acts in pop music. Among them: Grammy winner Sheryl Crow, the tart but sweet Irish pop group the Cranberries, singer-guitarist Melissa Etheridge and the spiritualistic rockers Live. Says Crow: "Honoring the song as opposed to blowing up amps and stuff—I think that's a cool way to reach people." Acknowledging its power as a showcase, Live lead singer Ed Kowalczyk adds: "It's become an important show for bands in their career now."

Unplugged has come a long way since its humble, low-budget beginnings in 1989 , when it debuted with a concert

NO WIRES ATTACHED: Bruce Springsteen and Melissa Etheridge work out on *Thunder Road,* above. Right: Kurt Cobain and his band Nirvana, Eric Clapton and Tony Bennett scored huge sales with *Unplugged* CDs—and Clapton and Bennett won Grammys.

featuring the band Squeeze, Syd Straw, Elliot Easton and Jules Shear. The original goal was high concept, not high ratings: a return to unvarnished, straight-from-the-artist rock after the high-voltage, high-volume entertainment of the '80s. Says *Unplugged* producer Alex Coletti about the show's beginnings: "There were no tricks, no effects. It was a whole reaction to the '80s and the [disgraced lip-synching pop duo] Milli Vanilli mentality."

The TV program gradually began attracting better guests and a bigger following. Irish vocalist Sinead O'Connor was featured in a 1991 show, and progressive rockers R.E.M. appeared later that year. Other A-list musicians—Sting, Eric Clapton, Arrested Development—soon followed. Older performers went on *Unplugged* to revive careers, younger rock-

in New York sold more than 3 million copies. "Some people are just put off by certain genres of music, be it jazz or grunge," says Danny Bennett, executive producer of his father's *Unplugged* album. "But when they hear Kurt Cobain or Tony Bennett stripped down, all they hear is the talent. And then they can connect with it."

To be sure, the folks at MTV did not invent acoustic music. But by championing the sound, *Unplugged* has had widespread impact throughout the music industry. Radio stations have sponsored *Unplugged*-type concerts, and pop stars who have never been on *Unplugged*—soul singer Vanessa Williams, for example—have released albums that echo the show's soft-pop, pared-down sound.

NOT EVERYONE IS PLUGGED INTO THE UNPLUGGED sound. Steve Albini, the combative producer of Nirvana's last studio album, *In Utero,* says record companies have seized on *Unplugged* as a way of repackaging old material. Already own the original? Now buy the unplugged version. "From an artistic standpoint, it's a total joke," says Albini. "You take electric-rock bands and put acoustic guitars in their hands and make them do a pantomime of a front-porch performance. It's not an authentic reading of that music at all. It's like watching a water ballet crossed with an N.F.L. football game."

The homogeneity of the performers on *Unplugged* has also come in for criticism. With a few exceptions, such as Mariah Carey and Mary J. Blige, the acts invited to come on the show have been white rock 'n' rollers. In late 1994 the New York City–based Black Rock Coalition held its own, nontelevised, "unplugged" in New York City to showcase minority talent ignored by MTV. Coletti defends his show's record and argues that rhythm-driven genres such as rap, R. and B. and reggae are often better suited for dance floors than for an acoustic showcase. MTV officials point out that a Stevie Wonder appearance on *Unplugged* is being planned. But critics charge that the show's racial makeup reflects a persistent double standard at the music channel: black musicians are seen mainly as entertainers, while white musicians are more likely to be regarded as "artists" deserving of a serious showcase on *Unplugged.*

Unplugged is not a perfect show. MTV helped create the glitzy, surface-over-substance music-video age, and sometimes *Unplugged* succumbs to the very values it once reacted against. At points the show's naked emotionality feels as false and forced as an arena full of headbangers holding their lighters aloft during a power ballad. Often enough, though, there are flashes of excellence. The best and most transporting performance in the 1995 series of concerts was turned in by Etheridge. She walked onto a bare set with no string section, no drums, no backup—just her and her acoustic guitar filling up the stage.

The concert hit its peak when Bruce Springsteen joined her for a tender, mournful rendition of his classic rock anthem *Thunder Road.* It was a magical moment—spontaneous, liberating, passionate. Near the end of the song Etheridge fumbled the words. So, to the delight of the crowd, she and Springsteen performed the song again—flawlessly. It proved, once more, that you don't need to be plugged in to generate electricity. ∎

ers to boost new ones. When Pearl Jam paid a visit in 1992, it was largely unknown; its *Unplugged* appearance accelerated the band's drive toward megastardom. Aging soulman Rod Stewart scored a hit with his *Unplugged* album. And folk-rock trailblazer Bob Dylan, who enraged music purists when he plugged in his acoustic guitar 30 years ago, came full circle and released an *Unplugged* CD in April 1995.

The performers are growing more eclectic, the sales booming. Tony Bennett's Grammy-winning MTV *Unplugged* was the No. 1 album on *Billboard's* jazz charts for nearly 40 weeks, and Bennett's appearance on the show cemented his appeal to the grunge generation. Although Nirvana became defunct after the death of lead singer Kurt Cobain, the group's posthumously released MTV *Unplugged*

EDWARD HOPPER DIED IN 1967, NEARLY 30 YEARS ago, but he remains one of those artists whose work—no matter how familiar and often repro-duced it has become—comes up fresh whenever you see it. This diffident son of a Nyack, New York, dry-goods merchant had a long working life, almost all of it in America, and a sober style, some of which came from France and particularly from Manet and Daumier. One of his few public utterances—in 1927, to the effect that "now or in the near future, American art should be weaned from its French mother"—used to be taken by cultural America-firsters as a manifesto of secession, but it wasn't. He knew that real originality is made, not born; that it doesn't appear in spasms and tics but rather in a long digestive process, modified by anxiety. And he was a ruminator: placid, some-times, on the surface, but an artist of incalculably deep feel-ing. Along with Jackson Pollock, his polar opposite in every way, he was probably the most original American painter of the 20th century.

The largest collection of Hoppers, some 2,500 paint-ings, drawings and prints, was left to the Whitney Museum of American Art by his widow, Josephine Nivinson Hopper,

MORNING SUN, 1952

when she died a year after her husband. Hopper's name is more closely bound to the Whitney than any other Ameri-can artist's to any American museum, and in the summer of 1995 the Whitney convened a reunion of some 60 of his finest paintings from various collections, including its own. "Edward Hopper and the American Imagination" wasn't a formal retrospective. It was more an evocation of Hopper's world, and its scale felt just right.

Instead of the usual scholarly catalog, the museum opt-ed for a collection of texts, poems and stories by (mostly American) writers, ranging from Paul Auster to very early Norman Mailer, from Ann Lauterbach to William Ken-nedy. These suggested a parallel harmony to the paintings, not art history or criticism, but analogies in writing. (Since, unlike most curators, the writers can write, one can read this *vade mecum* with pleasure after the show.) The idea is to show how pervasive the areas of American experience that Hopper raised have become. The show fell between two more formal Hopper events: the publication of Hopper's *catalogue raisonné*, and a definitive biography,

■ ART

Under the Cr

Hopper saw an America that no other painter had

published in the fall. Both were by the leading Hopper scholar, Gail Levin, and represent 20 years of work.

Hopper's realism had nothing to do with the prevalent realisms of the 1930s and '40s in American painting. It had no persuasive content; it was entirely free from ideology, left or right. He had studied painting with Robert Henri, whose politics were romantically anarchist. But none of the political ferment of pre–World War I New York rubbed off on him, and none shows in his work. The only painting in this show that could be guessed to show an industrial worker was *Pennsylvania Coal Town*, 1947, which shows a bald man raking grass outside in the sunlight, not hewing at the coal face in darkness. No hints of class conflict intrude on Hopper's vision of American society, which he painted one isolated person at a time.

He kept his political views to himself. They were those of a conservative Wendell Willkie Republican who, like his wife—the "Jo" whose presence pervades his paintings—loathed the New Deal and believed Roosevelt was trying to become a dictator. Hopper rejected New Deal cultural pro-grams; he didn't need work from the WPA (his pictures were selling in the '30s for enough money to keep the Hoppers in frugal comfort and privacy, which was all he asked for), but he despised "improving" rhetoric in painting anyway. At the same time, he hated being classed with the equally

EARLY SUNDAY MORNING, 1930

ack of Reality

got right. Now we can't see it without seeing him

rhetorical conservatives of "American Scene" painting, like Thomas Hart Benton. "I never tried to do the American scene," Hopper said. "I think the American Scene painters caricatured America. I always wanted to do myself."

As a result, you won't find a stereotype anywhere in Hopper—though there are certainly figures and nuances of human relationship that recur because they fascinated him, which is not at all the same thing.

He saw an America no one else had got right; and now you can't see it without seeing him. His baking New York rooftops and rows of stumpy brownstones; his blue vistas of the sea at Wellfleet on Cape Cod, where yachts lean with plump sails into the light; and his isolated people gazing from the windows of dull apartments or seedy motels have become part of the very grain and texture of America's self-image. They capture what Hopper called "all the sweltering, tawdry life of the American small town, this sad desolation of our suburban landscape." Sometimes this transcends itself and leads to a sense of epiphany, as when the blond woman in the open blue robe appears in the dark doorway of *High Noon*, 1949, like some secular madonna drawn from sleep by a distant angelic voice.

Moreover, no American painter has influenced popular culture more deeply. A host of vernacular images, some famous (like the palace on the Texas plain in *Giant*, or Nor-

man Bates' gaunt and brooding Victorian house in Hitchcock's *Psycho*), seems to grow from his work. Stage designers love him. Cameramen especially are drawn to what his friend, the critic Brian O'Doherty, called "that slanting, film-noir light." Hopper loved movies and the stage, and was deeply influenced by them. He was capable of an enormous enthusiasm for players, not as stars but as workers in the mine of illusion. In that respect he was like a more demotic Watteau, tracing an American *commedia dell'arte*.

Hopper's theatricality extends beyond his theater scenes. In a great Hopper there is always the moment of frozen time, literally a tableau, as though the curtain has just gone up but the narrative hasn't begun. It gives images of ordinary things their mystery and power, as in *Early Sunday Morning*, 1930, with its long streaks of raking shadow cast by hydrant and barber's pole, its empty but never standardized windows. It's never portentous, as De Chirico's cityscapes could be; you are in the real world but a stranger world than you imagined. The screwdriver slips under the lid of reality and lifts it a crack, no more.

Hopper excelled in painting, discreetly and from without, people who are outsiders to one another. You imagine

AUTOMAT, 1927

him staring from the Second Avenue El as it rattled past the lit brownstone windows, storing the enigmatic snapshots of home and business for later use. These are reconstructed scenes, emotion recollected in tranquillity.

HOPPER GIVES US A CREATED WORLD, NOT ONE that is merely recorded. Everything in it is shaped by memory, sympathy, distance and formal imperatives. Nothing is there merely because it "was there." Mark Rothko hated diagonals but loved Hopper's. Richard Diebenkorn loved diagonals and loved Hopper's too. As well anyone might: the diagonal, the slanting patch (especially of light), becomes a wonderfully expressive element in Hopper, acting both as a structural brace for the actual painted surface and as a sign of fugitive reality in imagined space. In *Morning Sun*, 1952, you are acutely aware that Jo, the long-limbed, middle-aged woman staring at nothing in particular from her bed, will move in a moment, that the patch of light will move too, that nothing will be the same again: but there it is, exactly the same. ■

Being a Nuisance

His work is deliberately off-putting, but Bruce Nauman has become the most influential American artist of his generation

SELF PORTRAIT AS A FOUNTAIN, 1988

SHOULD ART BE SEEN AND NOT HEARD? NOT AT A Bruce Nauman show: the catalog for his retrospective at New York City's Museum of Modern Art in the spring of 1995 had a human ear on its cover. And indeed, no show was ever noisier. Once in, you hit a wall of sound, all disagreeable: moanings and groanings; the prolonged squeak of something being dragged over a hard surface; repetitious rock drumming; voices reciting mantra-like inanities; and (in its own room titled *Clown Torture,* full of TV monitors) the hoarse voice of Nauman, who appeared on the screens dressed as a clown, shrieking, "No, no, no, nonono!" while writhing and jerking on the floor.

Nauman, beyond much dispute, is the most influential American artist of his generation. Though he was born in 1941, the artists whose work he most counts for are younger. It is safe to say that hardly a corner of the mix of idioms at the end of the 1980s, from video to body pieces to process art to language games of various sorts, escaped his influence.

There's no mystery about why this should be so. What Nauman practices is a form of psychic primitivism, or atavism. His art is chiefly about two states: compulsion and regression. Autism is the governing metaphor of his work's "look"—the long-winded rituals of trivial movement, the ejaculatory phrases, the bouts of ungovernable rage. Nauman is good at a particular sort of put-on, a sour clownishness. When it is really silly, the dumbness can be disarming, as in the early photo piece *Self-Portrait as a Fountain.*

Nauman is a kind of guru to artists who seek gnomic "enactments" of pain, are obsessed by splits between private and public identity—including their own feelings of victimization—and treat the body as canvas. Not for nothing does one of Nauman's video pieces feature a bewildered rat in a Plexiglas maze, scuttling about under the bombardment of rock drumming. It's Nauman's idea of the relationship between artist and audience. Rejecting the role of the artist as either hero or social critic, Nauman has cut himself a different role: the artist as nuisance. You didn't so much enjoy this show as endure it; you got through it.

The best piece in the show, both horribly vivid and weirdly distanced, was the room-size *Carousel,* 1988. Four motor-driven arms swing on a pivot. From each hangs what appears to be the flayed carcass of a deer or a wolf. (They are, in fact, hard plastic-foam molds.) These casually suspended mock bodies drag on the floor, producing an unremittingly irksome scraping noise and leaving a silvery circular train behind them. You don't feel empathy with the dead animals—the molds are too blank to evoke much more than the merest ghost of pathos—but you shudder at the gratuitousness of their posthumous torment. It's like a brief glimpse of animal hell, going on forever. ■

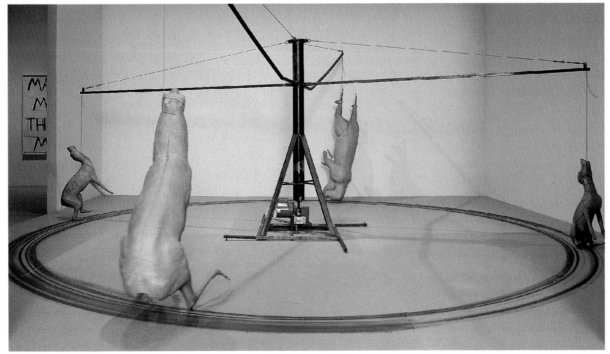

CAROUSEL, 1988

■ BOOKS

Dostoyevsky and a Decaf

Booked for lunch? Lavishly stocked superstores turn book buying into a social scene

VIRTUAL EONS AGO, WHEN PEOPLE STILL SOCIALIZED over martinis and not via modems, reading was a solitary pastime. Call it a paradox of the online age—or maybe a backlash against it—but book reading has suddenly gone aggressively public. The old-fashioned bookstore has been supplanted in many places by new superstores, which provide convivial hang-out spots where customers can get cappuccino, conversation and a cushy chair for perusing the latest Elmore Leonard or the earliest Dostoyevsky.

In a culture where book reading is supposed to be an endangered habit, it is an oddly heartening sight. By the end of 1995, the U.S. had more than 450 sprawling, chain-run book emporiums equipped with reading tables, sofas, club chairs and coffee bars. These superstores, run by such chains as Barnes & Noble, Borders and Media Play, usually stock around 100,000 titles (compared with 20,000 for a typical mall store). Far from shooing away loiterers, these superstores operate on the philosophy that by creating an inviting atmosphere they can lure customers who will linger and eventually plunk down their money.

Leonard Reggio, CEO of Barnes & Noble, pioneered the superstore concept in New York City five years ago and always envisioned it as a local gathering place. "You can't really hang around a Linens 'n Things or a Today's Man," he reasons. "When you go into a bookstore, you are going to meet people like you." Those too shy to approach a potentially special someone in the art-history aisle needn't worry, though. Superstores increasingly play host to organized social events aimed at enticing lovelorn customers. Singles nights are a staple at many Barnes & Noble stores, and other stores offer chess matches, Scrabble and backgammon games, as well as reading groups and open-mike nights for new poets in search of an audience.

In smaller towns superstores are providing a welcome burst of urban energy. Borders opened a store in rural Lancaster, Pennsylvania (pop. 55,550), in late 1992, and it is now the most popular spot in town, with its Saturday-night musical performances. "There are no major museums or galleries here," says Trudi Musselman, a management consultant who used to live in New York City. "When Borders opened, it was a godsend."

Does the lure of a fine patisserie or the whiff of a Tuscan supper translate into greater book sales? They seem to. More than 980 million adult books were sold in the U.S. in 1993 (the last year for which figures are available), 64 million more than the previous year, and superstores report that their sales are growing 15% a year on average. Of course, not everyone is sold on the superstores. Small independent bookshops complain that the national chains have encroached on their trade, driving many out of business. Some book lovers, too, feel that these commercial giants have spoiled things. "It's all too frenzied," says Susan Moriarty, a Denver-based travel writer. "I don't want to get picked up in a bookstore. Bookshops used to be a private thing between you and a book." How quaint. ■

IRON BIRD

More than a throwback, Cal Ripken displayed grit, spirit and skill in his relentless quest for perfection on and off the baseball diamond

CAL RIPKEN, JR., THE 35-YEAR-OLD SHORTSTOP FOR the Baltimore Orioles, played in his 2,131st straight game on September 6, against the California Angels in Oriole Park at Camden Yards. On that night he passed a milestone many thought would never be approached, much less surpassed: the record for playing in consecutive games set by Lou Gehrig, the first baseman for the New York Yankees from 1925 until 1939. Ripken's "Streak," as it came to be called, began on May 30, 1982, when Orioles manager Earl Weaver started Ripken at third base, which was then his position, against the Toronto Blue Jays. The previous day, Weaver had rested the 21-year-old rookie in the second game of a doubleheader.

Ripken is renowned for steadiness, not the spectacular gesture. But on his record-breaking night, he rose to the occasion. Before a home crowd that included President Clinton, Vice President Gore and former Yankee great Joe DiMaggio, Ripken strode to the plate in the fourth inning, took a mighty whack at a 3-0 pitch from the California Angels' Shawn Boskie and deposited a line drive in the left-field seats. It was a dazzling capper to Ripken's 13-year chase of Gehrig, the Yankee's legendary Iron Horse.

Yet fans saved their longest ovation for the moment at the end of the first half of the fifth inning when the game became official and entered the record books. For 20 spine-tingling minutes, the Camden Yards faithful saluted their hero, eventually cajoling him into taking a lap around

the field. Ripken high-fived with fans around the stadium and ended up inside the Angels' dugout, where he was embraced and congratulated by his admiring foes. Opponents and teammates alike hold Ripken in the same awe in which he holds Gehrig.

Ripken never set out to eclipse Gehrig, who he modestly and somewhat mistakenly believes was a much better ballplayer than himself. "I'm not even in Gehrig's league," says Ripken. Offensively speaking, Ripken may be right, although he has had two MVP, Gehrigian seasons (1983 and '91). But defensively Ripken plays a much tougher position than Gehrig did, and he does a much better job of it. As durable as Lou was, he played every inning of every game for only one season; Ripken played every inning of 904 straight games from 1982 to '87—only his father Cal Sr., then the manager of the Orioles, could sit him down. While Gehrig occasionally resorted to artifice to extend his streak, Ripken never did anything untoward to keep his alive, nor played anything less than hard. Gehrig was literally afraid of leaving the lineup; Ripken is in it for the fun.

"There's a joy to Cal's game that never ceases to amaze me," says Mike Flanagan, the Orioles' pitching coach, who has played for Cal Sr. and with Cal Jr. "People who think he's out for glory just don't get it." Indeed, fans who thought Ripken might sit down after No. 2,131 were mistaken. Ripken just kept going, playing in Nos. 2,132, 2,133, 2,134. The Iron Bird.

The Streak had two close calls. The first came during game No. 444 in April 1985, when Ripken sprained his ankle on a pick-off play in the third inning. Although he continued playing, his ankle was badly swollen and discolored after the game. Fortunately, the Orioles had scheduled an exhibition game against the Naval Academy the next day. The second near-miss came as a result of a bench-clearing melee with the Seattle Mariners during game No. 1,790 in June '93. Ripken twisted his knee, and when he woke up the next morning he couldn't put his weight on it. He told his wife Kelly he might not be able to play that night. According to Kelly, "Just before he left for the ball park, I said, 'Maybe you could just play one inning and then come out.' He snapped, 'No! Either I play the whole game or I don't play at all.' I told him, 'Just checking, dear.'"

Ripken did play the full nine innings that night. In

fact, he has played in 99.2% of every Orioles game since the Streak began. The percentage would be even higher had Ripken not been ejected from two games in the first inning. After umpire Drew Coble threw him out on August 7, 1989, for arguing, Coble said, "I felt like I was throwing God out of church."

Characteristically, Ripken didn't go into a shell to protect his privacy during the season; instead he made a concerted effort to satisfy both the media and the fans. At the All-Star game in Arlington, Texas, he worked his way from dugout to dugout in 100° heat, signing everything put in his way. In Baltimore he conducted postgame autograph sessions to make up for lost time and repair the wounds of the 1994 baseball strike.

A Ripken autograph session is illuminating because he doesn't just sign, sign, sign in the joyless way that many other ballplayers do. He talks to baseball fans as one fan would to another. ("Man, did you see the stuff Mussina had tonight?" says Ripken, the fan.) If he sees a child with a rival's hat on, he'll kid him or her and maybe even exchange the cap for one of his own.

AT TIMES RIPKEN SEEMS NOT JUST A THROWBACK but the last true sports hero. He carries the requisite superstar salary—$6 million annually for two more years—but almost none of the other baggage that has come to be associated with the modern-day professional athlete. He has never sulked, malingered, strutted, whined, wheedled or referred to himself in the third person. He has turned down several opportunities to become a free agent, preferring to remain an Oriole and a Baltimorean. He has endorsements, to be sure, but his most famous one is for milk.

If Ripken does have a flaw, it is his temper. He doesn't tolerate incompetence on the part of umpires or teammates. "I'm also stubborn," he says. "I think that's one trait I share with Gehrig." But by and large he conducts himself with consideration, intelligence and good humor. The Orioles' organization has helped: it has a unique tradition of encouraging players to become active in the community. Ripken is particularly involved in an adult-literacy program in Baltimore.

Cal and wife Kelly have two children: Rachel, who was born in November 1989, and Ryan, who was born in July 1993 on—somebody up there likes Cal—an off day. When Ripken is asked how he's changed during the Streak, he responds, "Less and grayer hair." But then he gives a more thoughtful answer: "I'm much better with people, kids particularly. When I was young and fans would give me their babies to hold for a picture, the babies always ended up crying. But now that I have kids of my own, I find it easier not only to hold them, but to talk to them. And they ask—no offense—the best questions. Like 'How come you're not mad you lost the game?' And I tell them, 'I am mad, but I've learned not to show it.' Or they'll ask, 'What's it like to hit a home run to win the game? Is it the best feeling in the world?' And I tell them, 'It *is* the best feeling.' The kids reduce the game to its most basic level, and they remind me why it is I love baseball so much." ∎

CLEVELAND ROCKS!

Longtime RCA record-label mascot Nipper, left, was only one of the celebrities on hand in Cleveland to help open the Rock and Roll Hall of Fame over the Labor Day weekend. The museum boasted an impressive building by architect I.M. Pei (the entire project cost $92 million), with interactive exhibits and an array of music memorabilia. Highlights included the poetry Bruce Springsteen wrote in junior college (excerpt: "Emerald waves crashed upon the shores …") and a list from the Rolling Stones detailing their backstage needs for a 1972 tour (among them: vodka, backgammon set and "apple pie—lots").

60 MINUTES' WORST HOUR

It was a bad day at Black Rock, CBS's skyscraper headquarters in New York. Its flagship news program, 60 Minutes, was scheduled to air an interview with a former tobacco-industry executive seeking to blow the whistle on alleged misdeeds by his former employer. But the interview was killed after CBS lawyers raised concerns about possible lawsuits that the network could face from the tobacco industry if it were to run. 60 Minutes ran a bowdlerized version of the story (without the interview), which ended with correspondent Mike Wallace declaring that he and his colleagues were "dismayed" at management's decision. But a later report revealed that the show had made a number of unusual arrangements with the source that might indeed have compromised CBS.

WEST SIDE GLORY

For at least the 10th time in 38 years, Jerome Robbins returned to West Side Story, this time renewing it as a suite of dances for the New York City Ballet. Resetting Shakespeare's Romeo and Juliet among teenage street gangs in the 1950s was the great showman's most brilliant idea: its tale of star-crossed city kids hasn't dated. It was the first time this classic marriage of Broadway and ballet had been staged strictly as a dance work, and with Robbins, now 77, personally supervising rehearsals, the result was a joyous show that highlighted bravura male dancing—the rumble as ritual.

BROADWAY'S HELLO TO GOLDEN OLDIES

You might call it the "Great White-Haired Way." Broadway theaters played host to a clutch of geriatric thespians— and audiences loved it. Leading the parade was the venerable Carol Channing, reprising her matchless performance as matchmaker Dolly Levi in Hello Dolly. The theater world also said hello to Carol Burnett in a Ken Ludwig farce about a vaudeville couple, Moon Over Buffalo, and to Jerry Lewis, who played the devil in a revival of the classic baseball musical Damn Yankees. And Julie Andrews returned in a new musical based on her husband Blake Edwards' 1982 film, Victor, Victoria.

Carol Burnett

Jerry Lewis

Carol Channing

Julie Andrews

TWIN BLOCKBUSTERS

For art lovers, two blockbuster shows dominated the year. Washington's National Gallery featured 21 of the 35 known paintings by the 17th century Dutch master Jan Vermeer. And the Art Institute of Chicago raked in Monet money with a show of 159 paintings by the beloved French impressionist.

FORGET TUTTI-FRUTTI —HERE'S HOOTIE

Popularity for Hootie & the Blowfish was a long time coming. But it was worth the wait: they became rock's success story of the year with their debut album, Cracked Rear View. The record

Hootie fishes, hits it big

sold an astonishing 11 million albums to become one of the all-time best sellers. Big and guitar-stuffed, their sound was popular with audiences of all ages. The four band members— singer Darius Rucker, guitarist Mark Bryan, bassist Dean Felber and drummer Jim Sonefeld—got together at the University of South Carolina in Columbia in the mid-1980s; all the members are in their late 20s or early 30s. The band's goofy name belied the serious themes covered on their album, including the death of Rucker's mother. And in a year when America's racial stresses came to the fore, the group's quietly interracial makeup struck a welcome note of harmony. ■

Ballet meets Broadway as the Jets get ready to rumble

THE BEST OF

...

From the

Beatles to

Jane Austen,

it was a

year for

looking

back—

way back

...

...

Picking the year's best is always an exercise in nostalgia: looking back a few weeks or months and deciding which people and events are worth remembering. This year the retro spirit took TIME'S critics back far beyond 1995. Jane Austen, Molière and The Beach Boys' Brian Wilson were back, and Bruce Springsteen returned to his roots. But the year held new treasures as well, from the computerized breakthough movie *Toy Story* to TV's *Murder One* and *Party of Five.* So step up, 1995, and take a bow.

...

2 **Crumb** Robert Crumb, the Brueghel of underground comic books, sits uneasily for Terry Zwigoff's blistering documentary portrait. Crumb's images of geeky guys and

rampaging women seem almost normal next to this picture of his middle-class family—a mother and three gifted, twisted sons—all devoured by demons. Appalling and enthralling, *Crumb* is the ultimate situation tragedy.

3 **Wild Reeds** Young love rarely seemed so tormented or rapturous as it does in André Téchiné's memory film. Political rivalries cloud a bucolic French town and Algerian war drums beat, but the main convulsions are romantic. A great date movie for teens with high SAT scores and overheated hearts.

4 **Les Misérables** Writer-director Claude Lelouch's film is less an adaptation of Victor Hugo's epic narrative than a passionate response to it—one overflowing heart heeding the call of another across the years. Resetting the tale mainly in the occupied France of World War II and reimagining many of its incidents, Lelouch remains true to his source's sweep, scale and romantic, entirely unfashionable belief in the conquering power of simple human goodness.

1 **PERSUASION** and **SENSE AND SENSIBILITY** The first of these Jane Austen adaptations is reserved, the second more bustling. But both have heroines (played impeccably by Amanda Root and Emma Thompson) who tend to others' emotional needs while submerging their own, yet find a romantic reward. The enchanted viewer is rewarded too: by subtle ensemble acting, writing that understands the void that tactful conversation fills, direction (by Roger Michell and Ang Lee, respectively) that finds the hidden hungers of the cautious soul. Honorable mention to *Clueless*, the *Emma* of Beverly Hills High.

5 **Apollo 13** Director Ron Howard and protean star Tom Hanks celebrate the virtues of community—ingenuity, patience, humor—with such fidelity and drama that the ill-fated 1970 moon shot becomes a triumph for Hollywood on its best behavior.

6 **Devil in a Blue Dress** The free-lance private eye's lot was never a happy one—ask Philip Marlowe. But he didn't have to fight racism while trying to fight crime. Easy Rawlins (Denzel Washington), a black man, does. And it grants Carl Franklin's cool, crisp adaptation of Walter Mosley's novel (set in classic noir-land, '40s L.A.) the edge, weight and revitalizing relevance long needed by a genre often made limply nostalgic.

7 **Heat** Who will be prince of this soulless city—Robert De Niro's fastidious criminal or Al Pacino's emotionally erratic cop? In the end it doesn't much matter. Their job is to lend familiar dramatic tonalities to Michael Mann's brilliant, jarring, amoral expansion of and meditation on the violent themes running through postmodernist life.

8 **Toy Story** Two generations of kids' playthings—a cloth cowboy and a rocket man—

reach détente in this marvelously inventive buddy film. Yes, the whole thing was animated by computer, but that's not the big news. It's that director John Lasseter is the year's most impressive new comedy visionary.

9 **Get Shorty** A movie-mad mobster (dreamy, incisive John Travolta) reinvents himself as a movie mogul. He's a real shark chewing up Hollywood's rubbery simulacrums while helping some bottom feeders rise to the top in Barry Sonnenfeld's jaunty, well-acted comedy of bad manners.

10 **Babe** The three years that Chris Noonan put into directing real and animatronic dogs, mice and sheep and one adorable pig were well worth the effort. *Babe* is no lumbering effects movie; there's a fairy-tale soul in this machine. ∎

...AND THE WORST

GLUM AND GLUMMER MOVIES Critics often groan about mindlessly optimistic tripe from Hollywood. But in 1995 many of them found moral instruction, even art, in mindlessly *pessimistic* tripe—grotty little films about how rotten life is. If it wasn't the self-destructive singer in *Georgia*, it was a moony, whiny *Priest* or some horny, joyless *Kids*. Cheer up, folks; life ain't that bad. Only movies are.

1 THE O.J. SIMPSON TRIAL: Granted there were moments—days, weeks—of soporific testimony and inscrutable deconstruction. But Simpson's double-murder trial made for irresistible television. It gave us great characters: Kato Kaelin, Rosa Lopez and all those posturing lawyers. It provided a law-school primer on courtroom tactics (and, more often, courtroom theatrics). And with the opening of the envelope that contained the verdict, it delivered the single most suspenseful moment in television history.

2 Murder One pilot (ABC) The story line later grew convoluted and the diversionary subplots tiresome, but the first episode of Steven Bochco's serial drama piqued flawlessly. A murdered teenager; a rich, smarmy suspect; a crafty defense attorney—it paled only next to that other courtroom drama in L.A.

3 The Beatles Anthology (ABC) Remember an age of rock so innocent that young stars actually enjoyed being famous? The grand old geezers—Paul, George, Ringo—recalled the genial hysteria of Beatlemania in a three-night show of rare clips and rockin' good music. Nostalgia nirvana!

4 Dr. Katz: Professional Therapist (Comedy Central) Pay no mind to all those imitation *Friends.* This witty, laconic cartoon comedy, in which a pensive analyst deals with a floundering son and a host of weirdly neurotic patients, is the year's best new sitcom.

5 Band of Gold (HBO) This British mini-series about a group of prostitutes being stalked by a serial killer worked well as a thriller but even more effectively as a grim portrait of life in an impoverished English town. Cathy Tyson (*Mona Lisa*) played a beautiful streetwalker with an affecting, un–*Pretty-Woman*-ish realism.

6 Brian Wilson: I Just Wasn't Made for These Times (Disney) His breezy pop songs were filled with the sort of intriguing musical complexities that made even the Beatles jealous. Using interviews with music scholars and performers, this documentary about the Beach Boys' Brian Wilson conveyed the originality of his compositions in language that was illuminating and never boring.

7 NewsRadio (NBC) At last a sophisticated sitcom about people who actually work rather than sit around all day chatting over coffee. With Phil Hartman as a self-centered radio newscaster, Dave Foley as a straitlaced news director and Andy Dick as a wired producer, the show carries on smartly in the *Mary Tyler Moore* tradition.

8 The Promised Land (Discovery) It was the "greatest peacetime migration in American history"—the movement of blacks from the rural South to the booming cities of the North between 1940 and 1970—and this Discovery Channel documentary series recounted it

in the grave, eloquent words of those who lived through it. Another strong addition (along with PBS' *Eyes on the Prize*, Parts 1 and 2) to TV's ongoing chronicle of the black experience in America.

9 Princess Diana interview (ABC) With a composed fragility, the Princess of Wales yanked the royal family into the age of public confession. Her disclosures—that her marriage was a shambles, that she had suffered from bulimia—weren't shocking. But her doe-eyed candor was. Some found it calculated, but most viewers opened their hearts to the world's most famous victim.

10 Party of Five (Fox) Few series have managed so successfully to overcome such a contrived premise. Focusing on five orphaned siblings who must fend for themselves after their parents are killed in an accident, the show (struggling through its second low-rated season) explores teenage life, romantic commitment and family attachments with a wistfulness and honesty that never seem corny. ■

... AND THE WORST

CROSS-POLLINATION Whiny urbanites are indistinguishable enough on sitcoms; now, maddeningly, they're turning up on one another's shows. On NBC, *Friends'* David Schwimmer visited *The Single Guy;* Matthew Perry made a guest appearance on *Caroline in the City;* and *Caroline's* Lea Thompson returned the favor on *Friends.* Better idea: force them all into group therapy and tape a special.

2 **Alison Krauss** *Now That I've Found You* (Rounder). With this greatest-hits CD, the mass audience found Krauss, a fiddle and viola prodigy with a soprano voice as invigorating as a mountain stream. Her taste ranges from country spirituals to pop standards by the Beatles and the Foundations. No gimmicks, just down-home virtuosity.

3 **Bruce Springsteen** *The Ghost of Tom Joad* (Columbia). Drained of the are-

na-rock testosterone and bourgeois guilt that have marred Springsteen's recent work, this serene album explores the lives of steelworkers, illegal immigrants and migrant farmers. The Boss is gone, and Bruce is back among the proletariat.

4 **The Chieftains** *The Long Black Veil* (RCA). Ireland's favorite sextet comes to call, the pipes and flutes and fiddles and all, with a breakthrough album after only thirtysomething years together. Paddy Moloney's charts for vocalists from Ireland (Van Morrison), England (Sting), Wales (Tom Jones) and Scot-

1 **SMASHING PUMPKINS** *Mellon Collie and the Infinite Sadness* (Virgin). Raucous and sweet, pretentious and populist, this Chicago-based alternative rock group's hubristic double CD soared as high as its lofty ambitions, an Icarus with wings that worked. Bandleader Billy Corgan is adept at turning out swift, radio-ready hits, yet he also excels at creating epic art-pop songs that explore enigmatic ideas and twisting melodic pathways. For listeners looking to take a journey, not just a joyride, this is a trip that shouldn't be missed.

land (Mark Knopfler) do more than revive a splendid set of ancient airs. They are delicious dirges that could wake the dead. Keen music!

5 **Various Artists** *Color and Light: Jazz Sketches on Sondheim* (Sony Classical). High-energy Broadway show music meets low-key cool jazz

on this sleek, satisfying album, as such top performers as bassist Christian McBride and trumpeter Terence Blanchard sensuously redefine and rejuvenate the work of Broadway composer Stephen Sondheim.

6 **Ernesto Lecuona** *The Complete Piano Music, Vol. 1* (Bis). Everyone knows Lecuona's most famous piece, *Malagueña*. But there's much more than that to the prolific Cuban composer, who

died in 1963. Fingers ablaze, pianist Thomas Tirino eloquently makes the case.

7 **Skunk Anansie** *Paranoid & Sunburnt* (Epic/One Little Indian). This British quartet, one of the few hard-rock bands fronted by a black woman, boasts a scaldingly bold sound, mixing chunks of punk, bits of R. and B. and even a dash of gospel in its joyously fierce debut album.

8 **Mariah Carey** *Daydream* (Columbia). Carey is a hitmaking, money-generating corporation; her sometimes over-emoted songs have in the past sounded like a musical interpretation of a bull market. Her new album is different: the vocals are subtler, the melodies more restrained, the lyrics more artful. Carey may be big business, but artistically her stock is on the rise.

9 **Puccini** *La Bohème* (Erato). Conductor Kent Nagano restores the freshness and bloom to Puccini's heart-tugging tale of young love won and lost. Soprano Kiri Te Kanawa as Mimi and tenor Richard Leech as Rodolfo are with him every step.

10 **Jacky Terrasson** *Jacky Terrasson* (Blue Note). Seated at the piano, this 30-year-old Parisian import doesn't just play a song; he seizes it, takes it through his own looking glass and refracts it in audacious new ways that squeeze fresh thrills out of old Rodgers and Hart and Cole Porter jazz standards. Terrasson's debut served notice that here is a star in the making. Like Paris, he's best when he sizzles. ■

... AND THE WORST

PJ HARVEY *To Bring You My Love* (Island). This utterly graceless singer is a favorite of the rock press. But her hopelessly mannered CD—with its distorted vocals and theatrical emotionality—is for musical masochists only. In the world of experimental pop, Björk's whimsically wonderful *Post* and *The Rebirth of Cool: Vol. 3*, featuring Portishead and Tricky, are more daring and eclectic.

1 ARCADIA Tom Stoppard's complex, lucid drama—brought to Broadway under Trevor Nunn's direction after a lengthy London run—shuttles adroitly between the present and the 19th century, the allure of mathematics and the promptings of lust, broad comedy and large-scale tragedy. Stoppard's masterpiece demands comparison not just with other Broadway arrivals this year but also with the best in postwar English and American theater.

2 The Heiress This Broadway revival of Ruth and Augustus Goetz's 1947 melodrama, itself adapted from Henry James' 1880 novel *Washington Square*, speaks with the confident simplicity of all-around excellence: skillful direction by Gerald Gutierrez, inventive sets and lighting, and an icy, crystalline performance by Cherry Jones as the triumphantly loveless spinster.

3 Hamlet Out on the edges, in the supporting cast, one could quibble with this Broadway import from London. But who wanted to carp when Ralph Fiennes stood so commandingly at center stage, embodying a "sweet

prince" of roiling depths and racing intelligence?

4 Mrs. Klein Nicholas Wright's off-Broadway drama apprehends the pioneering child psychologist Melanie Klein at a moment when her life perches above

an abyss. It's an exacting role, and famed acting teacher Uta Hagen, at 76, executes a performance that is instructive at every step, advancing through arrogance, rage, bravado, fear.

5 Twelve Dreams James Lapine's sly, skewed play draws its inspiration from a case study of Carl Jung's in which a young girl's dreams apparently foretold her death. In a Lincoln Center revival,

the haunting logic of dreams, fusing the seemingly arbitrary and the seemingly inevitable, wove an ever tightening web of enchantment.

6 Master Class The role is larger than life: the century's most famous diva, Maria Callas, captured at an age when her voice has left but her ego remains as outsized as ever. The performance is commensurately grand: Zoe Caldwell, by turns imperious and humbled, cruel and sympathetic. Terrence McNally's Broadway play

may have its structural shortcomings, but it is cheering to watch so much talent hurled at so much ambition.

7 The Molière Comedies Hard to imagine a better actor of the great French dramatist's work than Brian Bedford or a better translator than Richard Wilbur. This Broadway revival was a tonic reminder of how compatibly elegance and buffoonery can be married.

8 Seven Guitars August Wilson sets his latest play in the backyard of a ramshackle tenement in 1948 Pittsburgh, where a gifted young blues singer schemes and dreams through his last desperate days. The Pulitzer prizewinner's new work, which has

played in Chicago, Boston and San Francisco, is a rich ragout of melodrama and mysticism that should be cooking by the time it reaches Broadway in 1996.

9 How to Succeed in Business Without Really Trying Winsome Matthew Broderick could have used a little more edge in this tale of maneuvering through the corporate jungle. But bright, innovative sets and a strong supporting cast fashioned a jubilant Broadway revival of Frank Loesser's 1961 musical.

10 Journey to the West Mary Zimmerman's adaptation of a 16th century Chinese novel, in which a man and a monkey spirit embark on a pilgrimage across

Asia, made for an appealingly uncategorizable sortie—part farce, part children's spectacle, part allegory. A keen eye for visual metaphor united the parts and set the stage aglow in a world premiere at Chicago's Goodman Theatre. ■

...AND THE WORST

POMP DUCK AND CIRCUMSTANCE With the squeaky cleanup of 42nd Street, Broadway is about to be Disneyized. But should it be Vegasized? This dinner-theater circus, imported from Berlin, charges $150 (plus the drinks tab) for a lavish if mediocre meal amid four hours of shenanigans—spilled soup, humiliated performers, crude insults—that the most ravenous visitor will find indigestible. The show may be ideal for Las Vegas, where it opens in 1996, but in New York it's the ultimate show-biz debacle.

2 **Sabbath's Theater** *by Philip Roth (Houghton Mifflin)* explores the beginnings of geezerhood (Roth's resolutely obnoxious hero, Mickey Sabbath, is a randy 64) with the comic sexual energy of *Portnoy's Complaint.* Sabbath is an ex-puppeteer whose present occupation is perfecting his scabrous personality. As he searches his disorderly past for meaning, he is an equal-opportunity boor, richly offensive to women and men, Jews and Gentiles. Yet the result is a brilliantly written character, rampaging through a novel about facing death in a lonely old age.

3 **Galatea 2.2** *by Richard Powers (Farrar, Straus & Giroux).* The Galatea in this reworking of the myth is not a statue but an enormously complicated network of computer circuitry that, on

FICTION

1 **AMERICAN TABLOID** *by James Ellroy (Knopf).* This big, brazenly entertaining novel begins in 1958 and ends seconds before the assassination of John F. Kennedy. In between, James Ellroy—a crime-*noir* cult writer making his mainstream debut—propels two rogue FBI agents and a former Los Angeles County deputy sheriff through a fictionalized, nightmarish tour of five tumultuous years in U.S. history that is both horrifying and hilarious.

a bet, is being taught to think. The Pygmalions—there are a couple of them—are an acerbic cyber-scientist and a lovelorn novelist named (hmm?) Richard Powers. A scheme that might seem too clever turns out to be humane, thoughtful and surprisingly moving.

4 **Ladder of Years** *by Anne Tyler (Knopf).* Here's an almost perfect summer-weight, drip-dry, easy-care novel. Delia Grinstead is terminally comfortable in her life as a 40-year-old wife and mother. The trouble is that

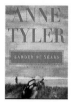

she has become all but invisible, even to herself. So, one day, on the faintest of whims, she wanders away from the family beach house and lights out for the territories. Such fantasies have grabbed all of us now and then, and Tyler writes her runaway's adventures not just as stylish comedy but as intriguing possibility.

5 **Our Game** *by John le Carré (Knopf).* Despite much prophesying to that effect, the end of the cold war did not mean the end of the moral and political murk in which spying and spy thrillers flourish. Le Carré continues to be the master of this shadowy genre, and he is near the top of his form in this outing. ∎

2 **Landscape and Memory** *by Simon Schama (Knopf).* Once upon a time, when early man roamed the African savannas, landscape was where we lived. Columbia University historian Schama's long, richly detailed and fascinating study reveals how our ways of thinking about ourselves and our world, and about national character and destiny, are deeply influenced by landscape. Bearing its scholarship gracefully, the book is a refreshing scenic turnoff from society's hell-bent journey toward clear-cutting our forests and drilling for oil in the Alaskan wilderness.

3 **A Civil Action** *by Jonathan Harr (Random House).* This true story of a gutsy lawyer who takes on a couple of

corporate polluters on behalf of the penniless families of leukemia victims and extracts $8 million from one of the firms

NON-FICTION

1 **DARK SUN: THE MAKING OF THE HYDROGEN BOMB** *by Richard Rhodes (Simon & Schuster)* looks clearly and steadily at the most perilous venture in human history. The only good news: in the struggle in the U.S. between scientists on one side and civilian and military politicians on the other—and, of course, between two such unstable aggregations on either side of the Iron Curtain—we blundered to a fortunate standoff.

should be an inspiring proof that the system works. It's not, and the system doesn't. That's the glum message of reporter Harr's well-researched account. The book's warning to would-be Robin Hoods: Don't even think of trying to fight corporate America—you are bound to lose.

4 **The Nightingale's Song** *by Robert Timberg (Simon & Schuster)* offers five quite different answers to the troubling question, "What is a hero?" His subjects are five decorated Vietnam vets, all Annapolis grads: John McCain, the Republican Senator from Arizona who was once a Navy pilot and then for 5½ years a POW; James Webb, a battlefield hero who became Secretary of the Navy; and three men who smeared themselves with Iran-*contra,* Oliver North, Robert McFarlane and John Poindexter. The author does not decry heroes or the military, but suggests that we look closely at the reputations we buy.

5 **The Liars' Club** *by Mary Karr (Viking).* Poet Karr's memoir of a God-awful childhood in an East Texas oil town is marvelously entertaining, in the manner of a train wreck recalled with guitar accompaniment. Character takes firm hold in this account of fistfights and flood, car crashes and shootings. ∎

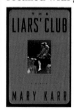

NOBEL PRIZES

Peace
Joseph Rotblat
The British physicist who helped develop the atom bomb but went on to campaign against nuclear weapons

Literature
Seamus Heaney
Irish poet

Medicine
Edward B. Lewis, Eric F. Wieschaus and Christiane Nuesslein-Volhard *For research on the genetics of fruit flies*

Economics
Robert E. Lucas Jr.
Pioneer of the "rational expectations" school of macroeconomics

Physics
Martin L. Perl and Frederick Reines
For discoveries of subatomic particles

Chemistry
F. Sherwood Rowland, Mario Molina and Paul Crutzen
For discoveries about depletion of the ozone layer

TONY AWARDS

Best Play
Love! Valour! Compassion!
Best Musical
Sunset Boulevard
Best Play Revival
The Heiress
Best Musical Revival
Show Boat
Best Actress, Play
Cherry Jones
The Heiress
Best Actor, Play
Ralph Fiennes
Hamlet

Best Actress, Musical
Glenn Close
Sunset Boulevard
Best Actor, Musical
Matthew Broderick
How to Succeed in Business …

BOOKS

Best-selling Fiction
1. *The Celestine Prophecy*, Redfield
2. *The Bridges of Madison County*, Waller
3. *Politically Correct Bedtime Stories*, Garner
4. *The Rainmaker*, Grisham
5. *Beach Music*, Conroy

Nonfiction
1. *Sisters*, Saline
2. *Midnight in the Garden of Good and Evil*, Berendt
3. *The Book of Virtues*, Bennett
4. *The Hot Zone*, Preston
5. *The Death of Common Sense*, Howard
Source:
SIMBA Information, Inc.

ACADEMY AWARDS

Best Picture
Forrest Gump
Best Director
Robert Zemeckis
Forrest Gump
Best Actor
Tom Hanks
Forrest Gump
Best Actress
Jessica Lange
Blue Sky
Best Supporting Actor
Martin Landau
Ed Wood
Best Supporting Actress
Dianne Wiest
Bullets Over Broadway

HOLLYWOOD FILMS

Domestic box-office gross, in millions
1. *Batman Forever*, $184
2. *Apollo 13*, $172
3. *Toy Story*, $150
4. *Pocahontas*, $141
5. *Ace Ventura*, $104
6. *Casper*, $100
7. *Die Hard with a Vengeance*, $100
8. *Goldeneye*, $93
9. *Crimson Tide*, $91
10. *Waterworld*, $88
Source: Baseline II Inc.

TELEVISION

Favorite programs, fall season
1. *E.R.*
2. *Seinfeld*
3. *Friends*
4. *Caroline in the City*
5. *NFL Monday Night Football*
6. *Home Improvement*
7. *Single Guy*
8. *NYPD Blue*
9. *Coach*
10. *60 Minutes*
Source:
Nielson Media Research

SPORTS

Baseball
•World Series
Atlanta Braves over the Cleveland Indians

Basketball
•NBA Championship
Houston Rockets over the Orlando Magic
•NCAA Men
UCLA Bruins over the Arkansas Razorbacks
•NCAA Women
Connecticut Huskies over the Tennessee Volunteers

Football
•Superbowl XXIX
San Francisco 49ers over the San Diego Chargers

•College national champions (consensus)
Nebraska Cornhuskers

Hockey
•Stanley Cup
New Jersey Devils over Detroit Red Wings

Horse Racing
•Kentucky Derby
Thunder Gulch
•Preakness
Timber Country
•Belmont Stakes
Thunder Gulch
•Breeder's Cup Classic
Cigar
•Horse of the Year
Cigar

Golf
•Masters
Ben Crenshaw
•U.S. Open
Corey Pavin
•U.S. Women's Open
Annika Sorenstam
•PGA
Steve Elkington
•LPGA
Kelly Robbins
•British Open
John Daly

Tennis
•Australian Open
Andre Agassi
Mary Pierce
•French Open
Thomas Muster
Steffi Graf
•Wimbledon
Pete Sampras
Steffi Graf
•U.S. Open
Pete Sampras
Steffi Graf

Auto Racing
•Daytona 500
Sterling Marlin
•Indianapolis 500
Jacques Villeneuve
•Formula One
Michael Schumacher

THIS PRINCESS IS A QUEEN OF HEARTS

If Catherine of Aragon had had access to television, the Church of England might never have been created. Even without the media, however, Princess Diana might have been more than a match for old King Henry VIII. In a frank interview shown in late November on the BBC and several days later in the U.S., she delivered as penetrating a kick to the crown jewels as any woman in history.

It's not simply that the estranged wife of a future King appeared poised and articulate; it's not that she failed to come off as the loony blue-blood bimbo she is sometimes made out to be. What was shocking was that she did an interview at all, telling neither her mother-in-law nor her press secretary until it was in the can. Diana was playing by her own rules.

In fact Diana revealed little that was news. But the confirmation of what was rumored was a bit of a bombshell, coming from a member of the royal family. Yes, she knew her husband Charles was making nasty with Camilla Parker Bowles in 1986, thanks to "woman's instinct" and "people who cared about our marriage." Yes, this worsened her bulimia and self-mutilation of her arms and legs. Yes, she had had her own affair, with James Hewitt, her riding instructor. But no, she didn't make all those crank calls to a London art dealer; a "young boy" did it.

In the short term, the score seemed to be Diana 1, Palace 0. Post-show polls indicated that more than 80% of British viewers were favorably impressed, and the Queen said she favored an early divorce. Diana, who admits she probably won't be Queen, may be maneuvering to promote handsome young Prince William—who entered Eton in 1995 (below)—as the next King and ensure her access to him. As for her desire to be "queen of people's hearts," it looked as if she already was. ■

The student Prince, stylin' in his new Eton "penguin suit"

Monica Seles had been absent from the tennis scene since a crazed German fan stabbed her while she was playing in a tournament in Hamburg in 1993. But Seles, 22, thrilled fans by returning in the summer—two years older, an inch taller and a good deal wiser. With the Women's Tennis Association graciously granting her a share of the world's No. 1 ranking, Seles came back in style—signature grunts intact—and won the Canadian Open in August. Then she faced her old rival Steffi Graf in the U.S. Open. Slowed down by tendinitis in her left knee, Seles lost to Graf. But she had already won a larger battle. ■

HOLLYWOOD'S REIGN OF JANE

Who was Hollywood's hottest scriptwriter in 1995? Forget about Michael Crichton. Forget Quentin Tarantino. The toast of Tinseltown, 178 years after her death, was Regency spinster Jane Austen. In the summer there was the surprise hit *Clueless,* which was loosely—O.K., very loosely—based on *Emma.* In the fall came *Persuasion,* a darling with the art-house crowd. But the trend really took off in the winter, led by Emma Thompson's heartwarming version of *Sense and Sensibility.* The U.S. showing of the smash BBC television series based on *Pride and Prejudice* was scheduled for early in 1996. Why the craze for Austen's polite young ladies and their lovers? The New York *Times* had two words for it: manners envy. ∎

Proving his comeback in the 1994 smash *Pulp Fiction* was for real, John Travolta continued white hot in 1995, scoring as Chili Palmer, the gangster who goes Hollywood in *Get Shorty,* a major hit. In Hollywood, fame and salary are one: after earning $150,000 for his *Pulp* role, Travolta reportedly vaulted to $3.5 million for *Get Shorty,* and to $7 million ... then $10 million ... then $16 million for three pictures due in 1996. By the end of the year the ex-disco king was said to be asking $21 million a flick. And to think that three years ago, he was sharing the screen with talking dogs. ∎

The bronze statue in front of Chicago's United Center came to life on March 19, when hardcourt legend Michael Jordan returned from his frustrating detour into baseball to take the floor for the Bulls for the first time in almost two years. The prodigal son was greeted by a welcoming whoop that filled the new arena—and fans everywhere joined in. When the news of the return of Qiao Dan (just say *tshoo dun*) was announced at a game in Beijing, the Chinese fans roared with joy.∎

Young, hip ... and full of (coffee) beans

Buddy check! Let's see, there was Ross, the gawky schlub whose wife left him; Rachel, the waitress with the 'do to die for; Joey, the dim actor; Chandler, the cute data processor; Monica, the gorgeous chef; and Phoebe, the spacy blond folksinger. Or was it Phoebe the waitress? Well, whatever. Names and jobs weren't nearly as important as attitude on *Friends.* NBC's gabfest based on the lives of a set of underemployed and overly chatty Manhattan twentysomethings landed near the top of the year's ratings. *Friends* was in the vanguard of a clutch of kaffeeklatsch sitcoms in which no one did anything except hang out, leaving lots of time for the indolent crew to play Pictionary.

In more serious news, hairdressers everywhere were besieged by requests for the shaggy-on-top, turned-under-at-the-bottom cut of the Rachel character. Actress Jennifer Aniston thus became the face that launched a thousand flips. ∎

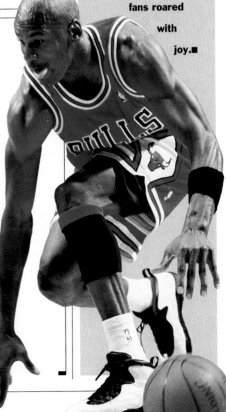

Michael Jackson Comes Down to Earth

Michael Jackson had hoped to revive his faltering career in 1995, but the fancy dancer landed flat on his back instead. A TV interview with wife Lisa Marie Presley went well, as did a flashy opener for the Grammy Awards (with guitarist Slash, above). But despite a $30 million buildup, sales of his CD retrospective *HIStory* sagged.

In December, Jackson collapsed while rehearsing for a highly publicized TV concert in New York City. He was rushed to the hospital, where his doctors diagnosed dehydration, a viral infection and low blood pressure. Jackson improved, thanks in part to the posters of Shirley Temple and Topo Gigio in his room. Meanwhile, the hospital set up a hot line that just might break new ground—by using the word stable to describe Jackson's condition. ■

Calvin and Hobbes Lose Their Jobs

After 10 years, the dreamy boy and the tiger that only he can see called it quits. With his comic strip *Calvin & Hobbes* running in nearly 2,400 newspapers, cartoonist Bill Watterson sensed creative burn-out and opted to explore greener pastures—or snowier expanses. He was never in it for the money, having refused to license his characters for commercial use. When last seen, the two pals were setting off with a sled onto a hill of white as invitingly blank as a sheet of drawing paper. ■

A Divine Encounter —But Hugh Grant Didn't See God

Say it ain't you, Hugh! But it was indeed the British love boat and one-man charm school who was apprehended by police on the seediest section of L.A.'s Sunset Strip while engaging in a sex-for-pay act in a rented car with known sex-for-pay practitioner Divine Brown. "I did something completely insane," the star stammered; few disagreed. The news stunned celebrity watchers, who were baffled as to how Grant could have strayed from a lover with

as many low-cut dresses as Estée Lauder spokeswoman Elizabeth Hurley, above. Later, Grant engaged in today's preferred penitential rite, a round of the TV talk shows to confess his sins. ■

THE AMPERSAND REPORT

HITTING IT OFF IN '95

Brad Pitt & **Gwyneth Paltrow**

Melanie Griffith & **Antonio Banderas**

Nancy Kerrigan & **Jerry Solomon**

Senator Alfonse D'Amato & **Claudia Cohen**

CALLING IT OFF IN '95

Julia Roberts & **Lyle Lovett**

Christie Brinkley & **Rick Taubman**

Cindy Crawford & **Richard Gere**

Emma Thompson & **Kenneth Branagh**

Elizabeth Taylor & **Larry Fortensky**

Camilla & **Andrew Parker Bowles**

A Mogul To Ogle

At the tender age of 19, Alicia Silverstone would seem to have it all—the big eyes, the bee-stung lips, the leading role in the summer hit *Clueless*, the attention of most young (and not-so-young) American males. Satisfied, Alicia? As if! Today's empowered Hollywood teen queen really should have a contract for, say, $10 million to not only star in but also produce a couple of movies. And that's just what she got, thanks to Columbia Pictures. Not bad for an ex–music-video babe and self-proclaimed "klutz and goofball" who just happens to look great in Chanel. ∎

J.F.K. Jr. Says, *Ich Bin ein* Magazine Editor

Buy *George*! Or so said the rookie editor of the new bimonthly he described as a "fan magazine" about politics. John F. Kennedy Jr., a former Manhattan assistant D.A., became the city's most glamorous editor with *George's* fall launch, featuring a cover with supermodel Cindy Crawford masquerading as America's first President. The slick, ad-filled mag was snapped up, but critics were not far behind. Sniffed the *New Republic: "George* sucks."∎

Wheelchair Warrior

Actor Christopher Reeve made a great Superman—but he never soared so high as when fate brought him low. In late May, Reeve, 42, an accomplished equestrian, was competing in Virginia when his horse refused a jump and threw him to the ground, breaking two vertebrae at the base of his skull. Reeve was placed on a respirator, but remained paralyzed below the neck.

Five days later, he recounts, while lying in the hospital, "I looked up and saw a blue scrub hat and yellow gown and heard this Russian accent. There was Robin Williams being some insane Russian doctor." Reeve credited Williams, his close friend since act-ing school days, with helping him laugh—and hope—again. In October an improving Reeve made his first public appearance, at a benefit dinner in New York City. Entering in an electric wheelchair and accompanied by wife Dana, below, he was greeted by a five-minute standing ovation. Eying his transportation, Williams told him, "You're on a roll, bro." ∎

Now—Meet the Threetles!

Nice work, if you can get it. The three remaining Beatles—that's Ringo, Paul and George—collected a cool $100 million in 1995, while releasing only one new song. So estimated *Forbes* magazine, in its annual list of the year's most highly paid entertainers. It was Beatlemania redux as the Fab Three topped the TV listings with ABC's six-hour retrospective of their brilliant career, while a CD anthology ruled the record charts, propelled by the new song *Free as a Bird*. The plaintive ballad was compiled from a demo tape recorded by the late John Lennon in the 1970s, to which the remaining "Threetles" added vocals and instrumentation to create a "ghost" recording. ∎

DEATH OF A M

With courage and dignity, Rose Kennedy played mythmaker to

TO CALL HER A MATRIARCH IS PERHAPS too easy, too simple a description of her place not only in her family but in the nation's history. Her values, by necessity, were a product of her time and place: she was a wife and mother first, protective of her nine children and fiercely ambitious for them. And she withstood her misfortunes with fortitude. But to call her a matriarch and leave it at that shows how much we forget. It was Rose Fitzgerald Kennedy—more than her brash and dashing husband, more than the glamorous daughter-in-law she outlived, even more than her martyred sons—who forged the Kennedy character. It was Rose Kennedy who played mythmaker to America's most mythic clan.

When she died on January 22, 1995, at the remarkable age of 104, she left behind five children, 28 grandchildren—and a motto as legacy to all who mourned her passing: "I know not age, nor weariness, nor defeat." The boast is testament to her ability to craft legend out of the exigencies of real life. Of course, Rose Kennedy knew age and weariness and defeat. Many times over. She outlived four of her children and a husband who loved and humiliated her. She endured haunting gossip and relentless scrutiny. With strictness, with humor, with a sense of style at once down-to-earth and every bit a match for her daughter-in-law Jacqueline Kennedy Onassis, Rose ruled and shaped the clan when sometimes it all must have been too much for her. Jackie once described Rose speaking of her sorrows: "Her voice began to sort of break, and she had to stop. Then she took my hand and squeezed it and said, 'Nobody's ever going to have to feel sorry for me. Nobody's ever going to feel sorry for me,' and she put her chin up. And I thought, God, what a thoroughbred."

Her pedigree, like her father's before her and her children's after, was politics. The oldest child of Josephine Hannon and John Fitzgerald, she was born on July 22, 1890, in Boston. Her father Honey Fitz, who eventually became mayor of Boston in 1906, was the quintessential ward politician, and he kept Rose, his favorite child, close by his side. Though Rose had wanted to attend Wellesley, her parents dispatched her and her sister Agnes to a convent in the Netherlands. At first, she was desperately lonely, but eventually she "was able to find in myself the place that was meant for God," she later said. For the rest of her life, she attended daily Mass for as long as her health permitted.

During a family vacation in Maine, Rose, then 16, met Joseph Patrick Kennedy, 17. Her father did not at first approve of Kennedy, son of another Irish ward boss, but Rose was in love with Joe, and the two married in 1914. The family grew and moved, following Joe Sr. as he became chairman of the Securities and Exchange Commission, then head of the Maritime Commission and, in 1937, the first Irish-Catholic American ambassador to Britain.

"They talk a lot about Dad," said John Kennedy. "But ... Mother deserves more credit than she gets. She is the one who read to us. She took us to Plymouth Rock and the other historic places. She gave me my interest in history." And she helped him and his brothers make history. She took to their campaigns with all the pride and energy she brought to rearing them. "She was a master at knowing how to turn an ordinary event into a special occasion," said a friend. Rose had no false modesty about her powers. "I was giving political speeches before women had the right to vote," she said on the eve of her 90th birthday. "I have always loved politics."

But every victory was matched by a sorrow: her oldest child lost to war and an estranged daughter to a plane crash, a retarded daughter relegated to an institution, an unfaithful husband, two sons assassinated. After her death, her son Ted said, "She sustained us in the saddest times—by her faith in God ... and by the strength of her character, which was a combination of the sweetest gentleness and the most tempered steel." She wrote in her autobiography, "There are the living still to work for, while mourning for the dead." ■

ATRIARCH

America's most mythic family

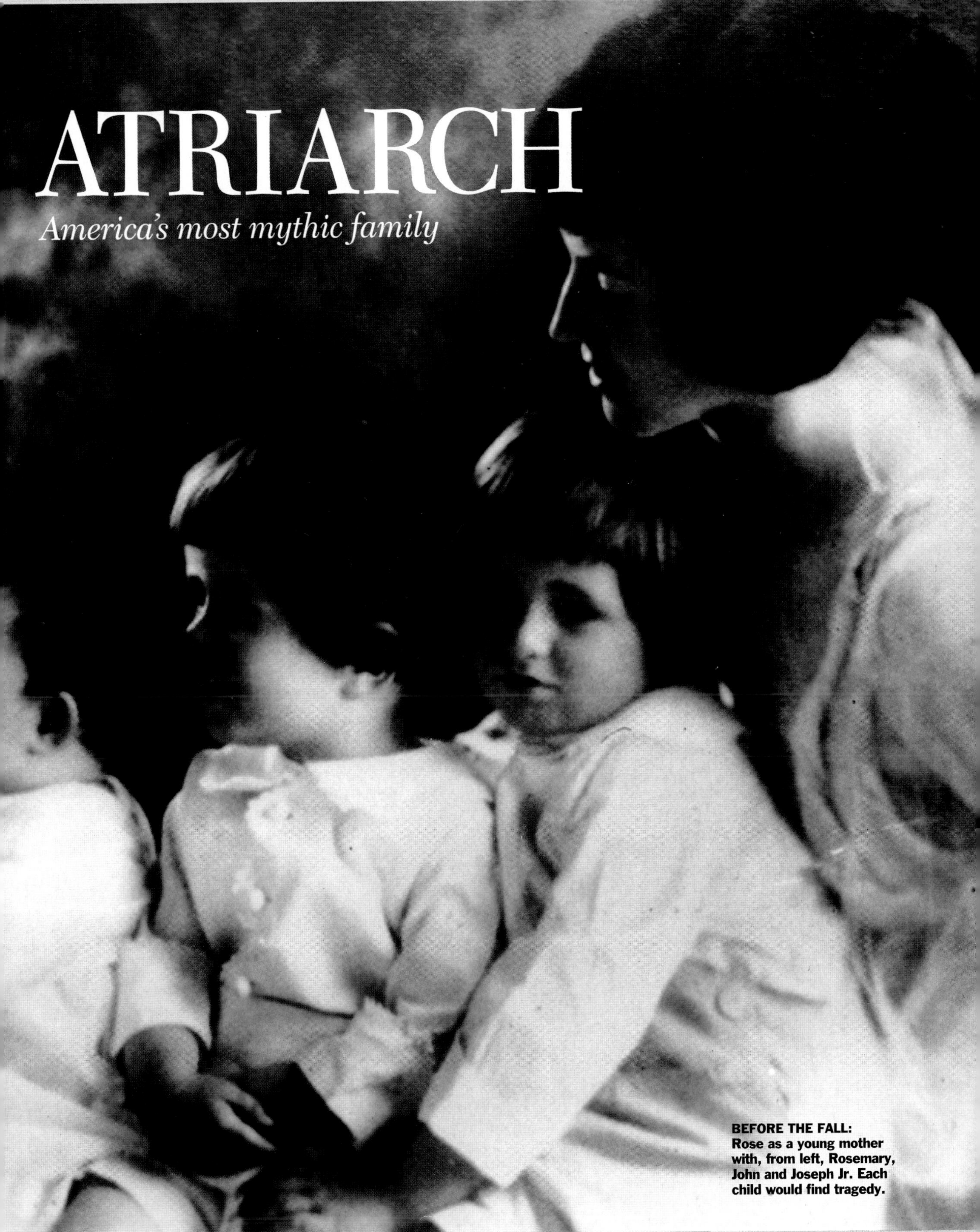

BEFORE THE FALL:
Rose as a young mother
with, from left, Rosemary,
John and Joseph Jr. Each
child would find tragedy.

The End of the Trip

The Pied and Tie-Dyed Piper of the Grateful Dead dies at 53

THE FLAGS FLEW AT HALF-STAFF IN SAN FRANCISCO, and on one a riot of colors replaced the traditional red, white and blue. Hoisting a tie-dyed flag in front of City Hall, the Bay Area was mourning the loss of its Papa Bear, Jerry Garcia. The lead guitarist of the Grateful Dead had died of heart failure at 53 on August 9, after three decades of tunes and trips.

Thousands milled pensively at the corner of Haight and Ashbury streets, in the district where in 1965 the Dead first kicked open the doors of perception with its anthems to the Hippie Nation. The sweet tang of pot smoke drifted from doorways, as Jerry's kids paid the revered pothead a small toke of their esteem. In cities all over the U.S., this gentle elegy was replicated. More than 4,000 people massed in Los Angeles' Griffith Park, creating a huge circle of drum players. In Manhattan's Central Park, 700 Deadheads gathered under the full moon at the shrine of another idol, John Lennon.

Why all this grief for the leader of a group that in 30 years had exactly one Top 10 single? Well, for a few reasons. One is that the Dead were a phenomenon as a live band: they played before more people for more years than any other combo in history. Another is that the band was a time capsule for the élan of the '60s: hopeful and engaged, melodious and raucous. The Dead were also the ragged

JEROME JOHN GARCIA 1942-1995

"The King asked Mozart why he drank so much. Wolfgang said, 'Rock 'n' roll is hot, dry work.'"

champs of the art of improvisation. A single song, in its myriad tonal variations, could go on for the better part of an hour—or the worse part, if inspiration was lacking that night. Deadheads came for that inspiration, and found it in the roly-poly guitarist with a missing middle finger on his strumming hand. Garcia was the soul, the sound—by common consent, the head Dead.

Jerome John Garcia was born in San Francisco to a Spanish immigrant jazz musician and a nurse; they named the boy for songwriter Jerome Kern. When Jerry was nine, Joe Garcia died in a fishing accident. Except for painting, which he loved and worked at until his death, young Jerry found any studies intolerable. He didn't bother finishing high school, enlisting in the Army at 17. Eight AWOLS and two courts-martial later, he was back on the San Francisco streets and hooked up with Robert Hunter, a coffeehouse habitué and soon Garcia's lyricist. He also met Bob Weir and Bill Kreutzmann, who would become the Dead stalwarts on rhythm guitar and drums. They formed a jug band, going electric in 1965, and took the name Grateful Dead from English folktale motifs. When they became the house band for novelist and Merry Prankster leader Ken Kesey's LSD-laced Acid Tests, their rambling jams gave birth to psychedelic music.

At first the Dead were just another San Francisco band. But they could write catchy songs with irony and sidewise angst—jingles for jangled nerves. *Ripple, Friend of the Devil, Uncle John's Band,* lots of others offer sophisticated pleasures in a simple form. Above the Dead's complex polyrhythms floated Garcia's unmistakable lead guitar—lyrical, celestial, enchanting.

Garcia's romance with drugs—including heroin—was his downfall. He was in and out of rehab centers; in 1986 he fell into a coma. Always he vowed to reform, but that was not in his nature. "It's like when the King asked Mozart why he drank so much," said Kesey. "Wolfgang said, 'Rock 'n' roll is hot, dry work.'"

In his drug taking, Garcia was a role model to some, a sacrificial totem to others. Wasn't he killing himself to create more beautiful music? That music *was* wonderful, and as leader of the most fan-friendly band in rock, Garcia was a sort of secular saint of pop culture. But he stuffed himself with seductive toxins—and the myth of the bohemian king—until he burst. His epitaph could be three words: Great. Full. Dead. ■

Superman in Pinstripes

The great Yankee centerfielder inspired generations of baseball fans

WHO WAS MICKEY MANTLE? AS BASEBALL people like to say, "You could look it up." The statistics show the switch-hitting centerfielder played in 2,401 games for the New York Yankees from 1951 until 1968, won the Most Valuable Player award three times, hit a record 18 homers in 12 World Series and entered the Hall of Fame in 1974. Although he was known as No. 7, he wore No. 6 when he first came up to the Yankees as a 19-year-old rookie. In 1953 he slugged the longest home run ever measured, 565 ft., off Chuck Stobbs of the Washington Senators, and in 1956 he won the rare Triple Crown (.353 batting average, 52 homers, 130 runs batted in). He accomplished all this even though he played in constant pain from his injured knees.

But Mantle was more than the sum of his statistics. Left out of the record books were his depression over his father's death at 39 from Hodgkin's disease; his constant and fatalistic drinking; his bumpkinish trust in swindlers; and the indifferent treatment he gave his wife and four sons, one of whom, Billy, died in 1994 at the age of 36, another Hodgkin's disease victim. In later years Mantle tried to atone for his sins, entering the Betty Ford Center, freely admitting his alcoholism and making peace with his sons. Mickey Jr., David and Danny were by his side when Mantle died of a rapidly spreading hepatoma at Baylor University Medical Center in the early morning hours of Sunday, August 13.

What was it about Mickey Mantle that inspired the fierce devotion of four generations of fans? He was handsome, of course, in the way high school heroes were thought to be. There was music in that name; even he said it sounded "made up." He was a country boy in the big city. He came along at a time when the TV set became the centerpiece of the living room. He was Superman in pinstripes.

MICKEY CHARLES MANTLE 1931-1995

"He's got a tough battle. But every time he talks, there's a laugh in his voice."

But there was something more to Mantle, something fans picked up from his most ardent admirers—his teammates. They would watch him come into the clubhouse (sometimes after a late night drinking), tape his legs from buttocks to ankle, then go out and hit tape-measure homers. Unlike the aloof Joe DiMaggio, whom he replaced at center, Mantle was generous and funny and self-effacing. Even in 1961, when he and Roger Maris were chasing Babe Ruth's home-run record, Mantle was supportive of Maris. "I'll always be a Yankee," he once said, and indeed he followed the fortunes of the club religiously.

Though Mantle had been sober for more than a year, 42 years of drinking caught up to him on May 28, when he entered Baylor Medical complaining of stomach pains. On June 8 he received a liver transplant, outraging those who thought, incorrectly, that he got preferential treatment.

Over the years, Mantle may have lost several fortunes, but he never lost his sense of humor. At a press conference a month after the transplant, Mantle spotted noted collector Barry Halper and asked, "Barry, what did you pay for my old liver?" The prognosis for Mantle was hopeful then. But an undetected lung cancer began to spread, and on August 4 he re-entered the hospital for the last time.

The Thursday before his death, some of his old teammates gathered at his bedside: Whitey Ford, Hank Bauer, Moose Skowron, Bobby Richardson, Johnny Blanchard. "He's got a tough battle," said Richardson. "But every time he talks, there's a laugh in his voice." Mantle was said to be especially appreciative of an autographed "Get Well, Mick" ball from the 1995 Yankees. Imagine: baseball's most cherished autographer touched by a ball signed by the current Yanks. But, then, that was Mickey Mantle. ■

KINGSLEY AMIS, 73, author and essayist. Amis had a remarkably prolific career beginning with his academic satire *Lucky Jim* in 1954. He wrote more than 20 additional novels and a comparable number of books of nonfiction and criticism. Though his increasingly conservative and, to some, misogynistic tendencies earned him critics in his later years, he was so prominent, funny and nettlesome for so long—nearly a half century— that the British decades between 1955 and 1995 could in fairness be called the Amis Era.

MAXENE ANDREWS, 79, singer. Reduce World War II to three voices, and the choices are obvious: the rant of Hitler, the rumble of Churchill— and the single, seamless sound blended from the warble of the Andrews Sisters: Maxene, Patti and LaVerne. The trio first flew up the charts with 1937's bilingual *Bei Mir Bist Du Schoen,* a Yiddish ditty infused with the giddy, jivey spirit that followed G.I.s around the globe. Wartime hits included *Boogie Woogie Bugle Boy* (1941) and *Rum and Coca-Cola* (1944). The 1967 death of LaVerne ended the sisters' career, but not Maxene's. She went solo, wrote a memoir and recently helped veterans celebrate the 50th anniversary of a war she and her sisters had made slightly easier for Americans to endure.

LES ASPIN, 56, ex–Clinton Defense Secretary. Aspin's thoughtful manner made for a difficult fit with the snap-to-it Pentagon, where the former chair of the House Armed Services Committee confronted hot-button issues like gays in the military. When it was revealed that he had turned down requests for more tanks and armored vehicles in Somalia prior to the deaths of 18 American soldiers in a Mogadishu fire fight, Aspin resigned, after less than a year at the helm.

HELEN J. BOIARDI, 90, Cleveland restaurant owner whose plates of spaghetti sparked such a demand for doggie bags that the recipes evolved into a line of foods known by the phoneticized name of Chef Boy-ar-dee.

ROBERT BOLT, 70, playwright and screenwriter. The individual's struggle for moral equilibrium in the face of world-shattering historical events runs through much of Bolt's work, from his career-making play, *A Man for All Seasons (1960),* which he fashioned into an Oscar-winning screenplay for the 1966 movie version, to his memorable scripts for the David Lean epics *Lawrence of Arabia* (1962) and *Doctor Zhivago* (1965)—the latter earning Bolt an Academy Award.

W A R R E N   B U R G E R

The somber judicial robes that cloaked the broad shoulders of Warren Earl Burger for 17 years as Chief Justice of the U.S. never really disguised the fact that underneath he was an exuberant prairie yeoman—and proud of it. As a young Minnesota lawyer, he helped his pal Harold E. Stassen in his forays into G.O.P. politics, and ended up being tapped by Dwight Eisenhower for the federal appeals court in Washington. He was somewhat mystified when Richard Nixon chose him to be Chief Justice. Five years later, he wrote the unanimous opinion forcing Nixon to turn over the Watergate tapes to the special prosecutor, the act that doomed his presidency. Burger left the court to head the Bicentennial Commission of the U.S. Constitution; he felt it was time to go. Before his death at 87, he became a white-maned evangelist for the doctrine of simply making the Constitution work the way the Founding Fathers wrote it down.

SELMA BURKE, 94, artist. Burke rose to prominence in the creative cauldron of New York City's "Harlem Renaissance." You may be carrying her best-known work at this very moment: the profile of Franklin Roosevelt that appears on the dime, which is based on a drawing Burke rendered on butcher paper after meeting F.D.R in 1943.

DON CHERRY, 58, jazz musician. In the 1950s, the trumpeter experimented with "free jazz" sound and rhythm opposite the sax of Ornette Coleman. By the '60s, Cherry was a world-music pioneer, exploring influences so diverse—South African, Indonesian, Brazilian, Bulgarian, Middle Eastern—that he was dubbed "the musical Marco Polo."

BERNARD CORNFELD, 67, financier. Cornfeld rose from driving a Brooklyn cab to the helm of a financial empire. But his high-living, high-stakes universe evaporated in 1970 after his mutual-fund company, Investors Overseas Services, Ltd. went public. Ultimately, his empire collapsed, costing Cornfeld and his investors millions and landing the smooth-talking fallen star in prison. He was ultimately acquitted of embezzlement.

DOUGLAS ("WRONG WAY") CORRIGAN, 88, aviator. The high-flying Corrigan broke no records for air speed or distance but set a new standard for sheer gall. In July 1938, when federal officials refused to approve his proposed transatlantic flight, Corrigan took off—supposedly for California—but flew east and landed in Ireland 28 hours later, blaming a faulty compass. His combination of chutzpah and heroism propelled him to international celebrity.

HOWARD COSELL, 82, sportscaster. When, in the 1970's, *TV Guide* asked its readers to name both their favorite and least favorite sportscasters, one man aced both categories: Howard Cosell. For a generation, his nasal drone— abrasive, unmistakable—was the premiere guide to the nation's professional playing fields. Cosell entered sportscasting in 1953 through the unglamorous venue of Little League baseball, but by the '60s he was a fixture at ABC Sports, gaining attention for his support of Muhammad Ali when the boxer was stripped of his title for resisting the Vietnam draft. Cosell reached his peak with the ABC *Monday Night Football* broadcasts of the '70s; his self-promoted willingness to "tell it like it is" brought a refreshing skepticism to the traditionally bland idolatry of "color" commentary.

ROBERTSON DAVIES, 82, author. Davies earned his Merlin-like mien; his novels were steeped in literal and figurative magic, juxtaposing Jungian soul searching and sweeping myth with minutely detailed portraits of Canadian provincialism. Among the best known works of the master magus: the Deptford trilogy and the bestsellers *What's Bred in the Bone* and *The Rebel Angels.*

BESSIE DELANY, 104, co-author with her sister Sadie, 106, of *Having Our Say: The Delany Sisters' First 100 Years.* The wry account of their lives as African Americans in a U.S. moving from Jim Crow to justice was adapted for the stage and became a 1995 Broadway hit.

GERALD DURRELL, 70, British animal lover, conservationist and best-selling writer about the creature kingdom. As a self-described "champion of small uglies," Durrell dedicated his life to the preservation of wildlife. In 1958 he founded the Jersey Zoological Park, where he bred endangered species to return to the wild. Encouraged by his successful novelist brother Lawrence, Durrell (pronounced Durl) began writing about his work, filling bestsellers such as *The Overloaded Ark* (1953) with colorful, witty anecdotes.

J. PRESPER ECKERT, 76, co-inventor of the first fully electronic digital computer. In 1943 Eckert and the late John W. Maulchy created the ENIAC (electronic numerical integrator and computer), a 30-ton leviathan that was 1,000 times as speedy as the standard calculators of its day, making it invaluable for plotting the trajectory of artillery shells—and for designing the first atom bomb.

STANLEY ELKIN, 65, darkly witty, language-obsessed novelist. The author of 17 books, Elkin won the National Book Critics Circle Award in 1983 for *George Mills,* which—in a plot typical of his absurdist bent—follows a thousand-year lineage of losers with the same name, from a misguided medieval crusader to a furniture mover in present-day St. Louis. Elkin

remained a prolific writer despite being stricken with multiple sclerosis.

ISADORE ("FRIZ") FRELENG, 89, animator. In 1930 Freleng joined Warner Bros., where he animated the A-list of cartoondom: Bugs Bunny, Porky Pig, Daffy Duck, Yosemite Sam. Freleng won five Oscars for his blend of frenzied action and idiosyncratic characters.

OTTO FRIEDRICH, 66, writer. Boston-born Friedrich first hit his stride

ALFRED EISENSTAEDT

The 20th century image bank consists in good part—some of the best part, in fact—of what was put there by Alfred Eisenstaedt. When he died at 96, he left behind one of the great lyric troves of modern photography. An incomparable photojournalist, "Eisie" helped make LIFE magazine an indispensable scrapbook of the national memory. Eisenstaedt was born in Dirschau, Prussia, a town now in Poland. A man with a lifelong taste for whatever was close-in, informal and unofficial, he came to photography in the 1920s, at the very moment handheld cameras were making it possible to take pictures in the same unbuckled mood. Seen through Eisenstaedt's Leica, public events became less ceremonious, while ordinary people took on emotional weight. After he fled Hitler, those were the qualities that recommended him to the editors of LIFE, where in 1936 he became one of its four original photographers. His most famous shot: a celebrating sailor and nurse locking lips in Times Square to celebrate V-J Day.

during his 1960s tenure as managing editor of the *Saturday Evening Post.* During his subsequent years in the pages of TIME and in his own nimbly crafted nonfiction, he emerged as an elegant explicator of just about everything: insanity, the pop art of Hollywood, the collapse of German democracy, the demise of a rose garden.

EVA GABOR, 74, actress. Of the notoriously oft-married Gabor sisters, Eva had the least mileage and the most talent. Her career peak: *Green*

Acres, the pastoral sitcom on which she played a socialite unwillingly transplanted by husband Eddie Albert to the surreally corny hamlet of Hooterville.

ALEXANDER GODUNOV, 45, dancer-actor. After 13 years with the Bolshoi ballet, Godunov defected to the West in 1979. For three years his graceful yet powerful dancing was a fixture at the American Ballet Theater. But after falling out with artistic director Mikhail Baryshnikov, he turned to film, playing a farmer in *Witness* (1985) and a terrorist in *Die Hard* (1988).

MALVIN R. GOODE, 87, network television's first black reporter. Hired by ABC News in 1962, Goode refused to be confined to "black stories" and covered the Cuban missile crisis and political conventions as well as the dramatic years of the civil rights movement.

PANCHO GONZALEZ, 67, tennis star with a thermonuclear serve. The crowd-pleasing Gonzalez won U.S. national singles titles in 1948 and 1949. In 1969, at age 41, he was the oldest seeded singles player in Wimbledon history.

CHARLES GORDONE, 70, playwright. Gordone became the first African-American playwright to win the Pulitzer Prize, with the 1969 Broadway bow of *No Place To Be Somebody.*

LAURENCE McKINLEY GOULD, 98, geologist. From 1928 to 1930, Gould trekked across part of Antarctica as second-in-command to Richard Byrd on Byrd's first expedition to the continent. Today maps of Antarctica are replete with Gould's name: Mount Gould, Gould Bay, Gould Glacier, Gould Coast.

J. PETER GRACE, 81, longest-reigning (a half-century) head of a major U.S. company. Grace's death came within weeks of the corporate coup that replaced him as chairman of the chemicals company W.R. Grace & Co, which he had steered from obscurity to become one of America's largest companies. As head of a federal commission during the Reagan presidency, Grace was a highly visible cheerleader for government efficiency and deficit reduction. His free-spending ways with company dollars led to his ouster.

NANCY GRAVES, 54, sculptor. Graves emerged suddenly on the New York art scene in the late '60s with sculptures of a remarkably offbeat subject—camels. Ostensibly realistic, these works were decidedly abstract in their fascination with form. They presaged all that followed from Graves—witty postminimalist pieces with an almost scientific sense of nature and a painterly feel for color.

PAOLO GUCCI, 64, hell-bent-for-leather grandson of the fashion empire founder, whose combative role in the company helped ignite a family feud that ultimately brought about the sad exodus of all the Guccis from the House of Gucci.

ALISON HARGREAVES, 33, Scottish mountaineer. The first woman to scale Everest without using oxygen, Hargreaves died in an avalanche on the world's second-highest peak, K2 in Pakistan.

PHIL HARRIS, 91, singer, bandleader, comic. Harris' hepcat persona was a fixture on radio in the '40s on *The Jack Benny Show* and, for a time, in partnership with his wife Alice Faye. In 1947 he had a hit song with *Smoke! Smoke! Smoke! (That Cigarette).* Today, he's known to the VCR generation as the voice of Baloo the Bear in Disney's animated musical *The Jungle Book.*

JAMES HERRIOT, 78, veterinary surgeon turned best-selling author. The Scottish-born James Alfred Wight did not begin writing until his early 50s, when he took the pen name Herriot and soon made up for lost time. His charming anecdotes of life as an English country vet tapped into the urban reader's apparently bottomless appetite for pastoral simplicity and infirm animals; *All Creatures Great and Small,* published in the U.S. in 1972, made Herriot a literary sensation. His 20 books were eventually translated into as many languages. Meanwhile, British veterinary schools became swamped with applicants, and Herriot's practice in Thirsk (Darrowby in his books) was besieged by tourists attracted by the aggressive marketing of Yorkshire as "Herriot Country."

OVETA CULP HOBBY, 90, public servant and newspaper executive. No job was too big for the "Little Colonel," who in 1941 went from co-managing the Houston *Post* to commanding the Women's Army Corps. She was appointed the nation's first Secretary of Health, Education and Welfare in 1953; her resignation two years later prompted Ike's Treasury Secretary, George Humphrey, to gasp, "What? The best man in the Cabinet?"

RAYMOND W. HOECKER, 82, onetime U.S. agriculture official. In 1968 Hoecker came up with the idea of encoding product information in a scannable symbol. Today the familiar stripes of the Universal Product Code have helped abolish the tedium of waiting for slow cashiers to ring up purchases, replacing it with the more modern tedium of waiting for balky scanners to read the UPC.

LORD HOME OF THE HIRSEL, 92, who, as Sir Alec Douglas-Home, was British Prime Minister from 1963 until the Conservative Party lost the 1964 elections. The Scottish patrician changed party rules to let legislators pick their leader—thus ensuring that he would be the last blue blood to head the Tories. He also served two stints as Britain's Foreign Secretary.

HOWARD W. HUNTER, 87, the 14th president, prophet, seer and revelator of the Church of Jesus Christ of Latter-day Saints. A former corporate lawyer, Clayton was the first Mormon president born in this century; his nine-month term was the shortest in church history.

BURL IVES, 85, goateed crooner and actor. Ives was beloved by generations of children for his mellifluous renditions of *Frosty the Snowman* and *The Blue Tail Fly.* Among the best known of his many stage and screen roles were his starring appearance as Big Daddy in the original Broadway production of Tennessee Williams' *Cat on a Hot Tin Roof* and his narration of the evergreen holiday TV special, *Rudolph the Red-Nosed Reindeer.*

OLGA IVINSKAYA, 83, longtime mistress of Russian novelist Boris Pasternak and inspiration for Lara, the heroine of his epic love story of the Russian revolution, *Doctor Zhivago.*

WILLIAM KUNSTLER, 76, lawyer. His face seemed ready-made for a radical's Mount Rushmore—the broad, furrowed brow, the corona of unkempt hair, the dishabille that left him looking as if he'd been blown around by the furies he provoked with his fierce defenses of civil and criminal rights. In the summer of 1961 he got his first taste of radical politics, springing antisegregationist

WILLIAM FULBRIGHT

The former U.S. Senator from Arkansas was a Rhodes scholar who became president of the University of Arkansas at 34. As a freshman Representative in Washington, he focused on foreign affairs, submitting in 1943 the resolution that led to the creation of the U.N. Independent by nature, in the Senate he cast the lone vote against funding Joseph McCarthy's anticommunist investigation and traded blows on foreign policy with Presidents from Truman to Nixon, though he reserved his greatest criticism for L.B.J. and the Vietnam War. The televised hearings he led as chairman of the Senate Foreign Relations Committee helped turn public opinion against the war. He wasn't always a hero to the left, however, for he voted against the civil rights acts of 1964 and '65. He left the Senate in 1975, and may best be remembered as founder of the international student exchange program now known as the Fulbright fellowships.

Freedom Riders from Southern jails. That experience led to a client list that could serve as an American Dissidents' Hall of Fame: Martin Luther King Jr., Lenny Bruce, Al Sharpton, flag burner Gregory Johnson, Indian activist Leonard Peltier, Attica prison rioters, Malcolm X and—decades later—Malcolm's daughter Qubilah Shabazz. Kunstler's combative defense of the Chicago Seven brought him four years' worth of contempt citations, which Kunstler never served).

VIVECA LINDFORS, 74, actress. Lindfors' neo-Garbo good looks graced a series of forgettable films before the Swede's 1954 breakthrough with a psychologically nuanced performance in the title role of *Anastasia* on Broadway. Lindfors' subsequent career continued to veer between high art onstage (Shakespeare, Brecht) and low on film (1994's *Stargate*).

IDA LUPINO, 77, actress, screenwriter and director. The London-born Lupino starred as the woman from the wrong side of the tracks opposite Golden Age leading men like Humphrey Bogart and John Garfield. When the director of *Not Wanted* (1949) collapsed from a sudden heart attack, co-producer Lupino took the helm, thereby backing into a directing career that peaked with her popular portrait of a murderer, 1953's *The Hitch-Hiker*.

LOUIS MALLE, 63, French film director. Working on both sides of the Atlantic, Malle unflinchingly explored topics like incest (1971's *Le Souffle au Coeur*), France's collaboration with its Nazi occupiers (*Lacombe, Lucien,* 1974) and child prostitution (1978's *Pretty Baby*, his first American film). Yet his high-voltage subject matter contrasted with an often reflective style that reached its apex in his second American film, *Atlantic City* (1981). His second wife was actress Candice Bergen.

DOUG McCLURE, 59, former bronco-buster and star of TV westerns *The Virginian* and *The Overland Trail.*

BUTTERFLY McQUEEN, 84, actress. As Prissy, the comically incompetent slave in *Gone With the Wind,* her panicked "Lawdy, Miz Scarlett, I don't know nothing about birthing babies!" became one of the most quoted lines in film history. When she refused to continue playing servants, her screen career collapsed.

JAMES MERRILL, 69, poet. Merrill was a novelist, essayist and a playwright, but it's as a poet—the author of 11 volumes of verse, with a 12th

DEAN MARTIN

Did anyone ever care less about being in show business than Dean Martin? Singer, actor, host of a TV program, headliner in Las Vegas—these were just things people paid Dino to do when he wasn't on the links. Born Dino Paul Crocetti in Steubenville, Ohio, he left school in the 10th grade, boxed a while, dealt cards at the local gaming houses, sang a little. His progress was slow until he met Jerry Lewis, then just 20. Martin was the first sexpot straight man, a perfect complement to Jerry's goony girly-boy. Teaming up in 1946, the two clicked immediately. For a decade they dominated nightclubs, concert stages, films and TV, while Dean's records went gold. After they split, Martin rebounded as a solo film star. He had more hit tunes, anchored a nine-year TV franchise, appeared in casinos with Frank Sinatra, Sammy Davis Jr. and other Rat Pack pals. After that, Dino coasted. He became a Southerner on record and a Westerner onscreen—he loved to ride to his chosen destination, nowhere. His last years were lonely, but when the silky-voiced crooner died at 78 lights on the Las Vegas strip were dimmed in his memory.

awaiting publication at his death—that he made his ineradicable mark. The son of a founding partner of Merrill Lynch, he was an unlikely poet, but he combined ferocious industry, inexhaustible radiance and unorthodox verse forms to create a glittering shelf of books.

ELIZABETH MONTGOMERY, 62, actress. Montgomery developed an enduring following with her '60s series *Bewitched.* She played Samantha Stephens, a perky suburban

helpmate who happened to be a witch. Post-*Bewitched*, Montgomery appeared in grim but well-received TV movies such as *A Case of Rape* (1974) and *The Legend of Lizzie Borden* (1975).

U NU, 87, former Prime Minister of Burma (now Myanmar). U Nu was named the country's first P.M. in 1947, a year before independence. A popular politician, he promoted non-alignment abroad and democracy at home—but discord within his government led General Ne Win to seize power in 1962.When pro-democracy activity swept aside Ne Win in 1988, U Nu proclaimed himself Prime Minister of a "parallel government," but the military quickly placed him under house arrest. Released in 1992, he spent his last years in seclusion.

FRANK PERRY, 65, director of such diverse films as *David and Lisa* (1962), a portrait of disturbed adolescents; *Diary of a Mad Housewife* (1970), a scorched-earth satire of mores and marriage; *Mommie Dearest* (1981), a high-camp Hollywood biopic; and *On the Bridge* (1992), a documentary of his own battle with cancer.

ORVILLE REDENBACHER, 88, popcorn potentate. His persona on TV spots made him an icon of, well, pure corn: the crisp bow tie, the Alfalfa-style hair, the good-natured Midwestern geekiness. But beneath this hayseed hucksterism, Orville Redenbacher was the Luther Burbank of popcorn. The decades he devoted to the staple food of double features produced a gourmet hybrid that exploded to twice the size and twice the sales of its competitors.

JAMES RESTON, 86, journalist. Originally a sports reporter, Reston had a grasp of global gamesmanship that led him to the New York *Times*. His first job: correspondent during the London blitz. He went on to win a Pulitzer chronicling the birth of the United Nations. In 1953 he became the paper's Washington bureau chief. As a thrice-weekly columnist, "Scotty" gained fame for his deft prose, solid reporting and enviable access. Later he helped nurture the paper's op-ed page into a valuable national forum.

CHARLIE RICH, 62, easy-going country singer whose proto-Kenny Rogers ballads like *The Most Beautiful Girl* and *Behind Closed Doors* fused Nashville with Las Vegas in the '70s.

BOBBY RIGGS, 77, tennis star. In 1939 Wimbledon-winning Riggs was the greatest tennis player on the planet. But his enduring legacy is surely the antics of his later life—most notoriously the 1973 "Battle of the Sexes" against legendary women's tennis star Billie Jean King. King cleaned the court with the 55-year-old Riggs, who raised sexist posturing to self-parody—and inadvertently fueled the nation's growing interest in women's tennis.

GINGER ROGERS, 83, movie star. She was a young but scrappy veteran of more than 20 films and shorts, he a neophyte with one movie and a screen test behind him when they first danced together in 1933's *Flying Down to Rio.* Before the decade was over, Ginger Rogers and Fred Astaire had become the most famous pair of dancers that would ever cut their way across a high-gloss floor or up a spiral staircase. In the memorable words of Katharine Hepburn, the pairing gave him sex and her class—yet Rogers' own singular combination of pathos and spunk would make itself evident in non-Astaire efforts like 1937's *Stage Door.* In the years following the screen couple's parting of the ways in 1939, she also scored such triumphs as her Oscar-winning work in the tearjerker *Kitty Foyle* (1940). A Christian Scientist, Rogers believed in avoiding tobacco and alcohol. She also believed in marriage: she did it five times; all ended in divorce.

GEORGE ROMNEY, 88, three-term G.O.P. Governor of Michigan and, earlier, the man who spearheaded the revival of Detroit's American Motors. Romney's 1968 presidential bid died before the first primary, haunted by his remark that his earlier support of the Vietnam War had been due to "brainwashing" by the U.S. military.

HENRY ROTH, 89, author of the acclaimed 1934 novel *Call It Sleep,* about a Jewish immigrant boy in a Manhattan slum. Despite this over-whelming early success, Roth did not publish again for 60 years, finally producing a new novel in 1994.

LANA TURNER

Turner first strode across the screen in a form-following sweater in her big-screen debut in 1937. The film's title: *They Won't Forget.* They didn't. The "sweater girl," who, legend had it, was discovered sipping a soda in a Hollywood drug store, simmered through three decades of movies, mostly for MGM, which was the ideal studio for her high-wattage, big-screen glamour. Aglow in white shorts, white top, white turban and acres of bare flesh for *The Postman Always Rings Twice* (1946), she bedazzled John Garfield into murder; in *Johnny Eager* (1942), she helped Robert Taylor live up to his character's name. Her turn in 1957's *Peyton Place* won Turner an Oscar nomination. She followed it with a role in the real-life melodrama that erupted in 1958 when her daughter fatally knifed an abusive boyfriend of Turner's. Things went a bit better for her seven husbands; they merely got divorced.

JONAS SALK, 80, physician and medical researcher. If it is hard now to recall the sheer terror connected with the word polio in the mid-1950s, it is largely thanks to the work of Dr. Salk. On April 12, 1955, a colleague announced that Salk's new polio vaccine had proved "safe, effective and potent." As a result of the nationwide effort of mass inoculation that followed, new cases in the U.S. dropped to fewer than 1,000 by 1962. The son of a New York City garment worker became a celebrated man, and in 1963 he opened the Salk Institute for Biological Studies at a magnificent compound designed by Louis Kahn in La Jolla, California. In 1970, two years after divorcing his first wife, Salk married Françoise Gilot, the onetime companion and muse of Pablo Picasso.

MAY SARTON, 83, author and poet. Sarton's seven decades of poems, fiction and personal journals were championed by feminists and college students. The same personal honesty that spurred her to reveal her lesbianism in 1965 informed her clear-eyed explorations of the human condition.

SELENA, 23, Tex-Mex singer. Before she turned nine years old, a pretty Texas girl named Selena Quintanilla Perez was singing at roadhouse dance halls and weddings, purveying a bright, up-tempo version of traditional Mexican-American border music. A little more than a decade later, she was the Grammy-winning queen of the booming "Tejano" music market, playing to crowds of 60,000 and selling more than 1.5 million records. Two weeks shy of her 24th birthday she was shot to death in a motel in Corpus Christi. In November a jury found Yolanda Saldivar, 32, who once headed Selena's fan club and later ran a boutique owned by the singer, guilty of her murder. For her devoted fans, Selena was the embodiment of smart, hip, Mexican-American youth; her death, just as she was reaching out to vast crossover audiences, was particularly cruel.

MOHAMED SIAD BARRE, 84, former Somali dictator. Siad Barre seized power in a 1969 coup. For the next 21 years he ruled his country with a blend of Marxism, Islam and Somali traditions he dubbed "scientific socialism"—though the philosophy bore an uncanny resemblance to brute force. Siad Barre skillfully rode the waves of cold war politics, initially drawing support from the former Soviet Union and later from the U.S., which overlooked his human-rights abuses. At home he manipulated tribal tensions to his advantage. As a result, after his 1991 ouster and flight to Nigeria, Somalia predictably disintegrated into chaos.

MARGARET CHASE SMITH, 97, former G.O.P. Senator from Maine. Smith was the first woman to win election to both houses of Congress and the first to be put forward as a presidential candidate at a national political convention (in 1964, when she was swept aside by the Goldwater rush). Her prickly independence often put her at odds with more doctrinaire members of her party. She backed F.D.R.'s New Deal legislation, opposed two of Richard Nixon's Supreme Court nominees and was a withering early critic of her red-hunting colleague Joseph McCarthy.

TERRY SOUTHERN, 71, novelist (*Candy*) and screenwriter. Southern's film work helped define the '60s sensibility. His script for 1964's *Dr. Strangelove*, co-written with director Stanley Kubrick, showed an unerring ear for atomic-age Orwellianisms ("You can't fight here," cries President Muffley. "This is the War Room!"). The script won Southern an Oscar nomination, as did his work on another definitive film, *Easy Rider* (1969).

STEPHEN SPENDER, 86, British essayist and poet. Along with his friends W.H. Auden and Christopher Isherwood, Spender retained rigorous standards of literary craft while rejecting the introspection of predecessors like T.S. Eliot in favor of a more worldly and socially aware art. Spender's brief membership in the Communist Party in the '30s would result in a lifetime of determined anticommunism, climaxed by his 15 years with *Encounter* magazine, which Spender left in the '60s after its links to the CIA were revealed. In later years, Spender concentrated on prose.

JOHN STENNIS, 93, U.S. Senator. During his 41-year run in the upper chamber, Stennis, a Democrat from Mississippi, was known as "the conscience of the Senate" thanks to his respect for its traditions as well as his tutelage of younger members. In the outside world, he was often more admired for his personal tenacity—he survived a 1973 mugging and 1984 cancer surgery—than for his segregationist voting record.

JOHN CAMERON SWAYZE, 89, newscaster turned pitchman. Swayze found fame in 1949 "hopscotching the world for headlines" on *Camel News Caravan*, a network-news prototype. The Kansan later attained pop icondom hawking Timex watches, the ones that would "take a licking and keep on ticking."

KRISSY TAYLOR, 17, model. The younger sister of supermodel Niki Taylor, Krissy seemed destined for superness herself. But Niki discovered her sister's body on the living-room floor of their parents' home. The cause of death: asthma.

PETER TOWNSEND, 80, British war hero and tragic romantic figure. A decorated fighter pilot, Townsend downed 11 enemy planes during World War II. But he lost his postwar battle with the royal family and Queen Elizabeth, who disapproved of her sister Princess Margaret's romance with the dashing but divorced royal attendant. "She could have married me," Townsend wrote in his 1978 autobiography, "only if she had been prepared to give up everything." She wasn't. Townsend went into tasteful Continental exile in 1955, forging careers as a disk jockey, wine buyer and U.N. adviser.

MATT URBAN, 75, World War II hero. Lieut. Colonel Urban's World War II exploits across the European theater ultimately earned him more combat decorations than any other soldier in American history, including the Medal of Honor and seven Purple Hearts for wounds received in combat, like the bullet that tore out a vocal cord and left him raspy-voiced to the end of his days. He led a milder civilian life as a recreation director.

JUNIOR WALKER, 53, saxophonist. As the front man for the Motown hit-makers, Junior Walker and the All Stars, Walker wielded a sax drenched in the blues in such hits as *Shotgun.*

HAROLD WILSON, 79, former British Prime Minister. Wilson came to power in 1964, occupying 10 Downing Street for seven years, longer than any other 20th century peacetime premier except Margaret Thatcher. The silver-haired Labour Party leader was known for his pipe, raincoat and Yorkshire accent. Among his legacies: the 1967 devaluation of the pound to rescue a declin-

ing economy, the 1975 referendum that committed Britain to E.C. membership, and his recommendation of the Beatles for knighthood.

WOLFMAN JACK (ROBERT SMITH), 57, disk jockey. Armed with a voice that sounded as if he gargled with iron filings, Jack was the Elvis of rock radio—a white phenom who found success emulating the black deejays he admired (and always credited). Broadcasting from a clear-channel station based in Mexico, he developed a national following, serving North America a flavorsome stew of R. and B., jazz, rockabilly, rock 'n' roll, sporadic wolf howls and interjections of black slang. His 1973 appearance in the movie *American Graffiti* finally gave his fans a face to go along with the famous *nom de air*.

EVELYN WOOD, 86, educator. In a nation where faster is synonymous with better, the Evelyn Wood Reading Dynamics Institute, with its promise to boost reading speed from a dilatory 250 words per minute to a galloping 1,500—or more—made its diminutive founder an unlikely star when the institute opened in Washington in 1959.

ROGER ZELAZNY, 58, author. Armed with pyrotechnic prose and a stylish command of mythic themes, Zelazny broke new ground in science fiction as part of the 1960s "New Wave." The movement presented socially and psychologically complex views of the future, at sharp odds with the genre's traditionally upbeat portrayals of tomorrow. The winner of every major award in the field, Zelazny saw his grim vision of a postapocalyptic America, *Damnation Alley*, made into an uncompelling 1977 film.

JEROME ZIPKIN, 80, social moth. Loyal and insulting—often to the same people—Jerry Zipkin served for a half-century as full-time party guest, escort and confidant of socially prominent, financially comfortable women (Betsy Bloomingdale, Pat Buckley). In the 1930's, his friend Somerset Maugham had modeled the snobbish Elliot Templeton of *The Razor's Edge* on Zipkin, a real estate heir. But Zipkin's greatest coup was his friendship with First Lady Nancy Reagan, who dished and danced with him so regularly that he became known as "the other man in her life." ■

Clockwise from top left, except as noted.

iv Charles H. Porter IV—Sygma, Christopher Morris—Black Star for TIME, Barthelemy—SIPA **v** Remi Benali—Gamma Liaison, Des Moines Art Center, Mark Seliger—Outline

The Year in Review 1 Ralf-Finn Hestoft—Saba, Reuters/Bettmann, Lionel Cherrualt—SIPA, Judy Griesdieck for TIME **2-3** Charles H. Porter IV—Sygma, Steve Liss for TIME **4-5** David Rubinger, Barbara Kinney—The White House **6-7** P. F. Bentley for TIME, Chien-Chi Chang—Magnum **8-9** Kaku Kurita—Gamma Liaison, Patrick Robert—Sygma **10-11** Steve Lehman—Saba, Sam Marcovich—Reuters, Archive Photos—pool **12-13** Tony Suau for TIME, Christopher Morris—Black Star for TIME **14-15** Jeff Hester and Paul Scowen—Arizona State University/NASA, Kirk Borne—STSCI/NASA **16-17** (left to right) Anita Kunz, S. B. Whitehead, Eric White, Gary Kelly, Lauren Uram, Tim O'Brien, Alan B. Cober, C. F. Payne, Warren Linn, Tim O'Brien, James Bennet, Michael Dougan (digital color by A.P. Voss), Ray Bartkus, Johanna Goodman, Moira Hahn, Joseph Salina, John S. Dykes, C. F. Payne **18-19** Art Zamur—Gamma Liaison for TIME, Smith—Sygma, Chris Taylor—Retna, Jeffrey Markowitz—Sygma **20** Joe Ciardiello (art)

Nation 21 AP (2), Brooks Kraft—Sygma **22-23** Gregory Heisler for TIME **25** Dennis Paquin—AP **26** University Archives—Tulane University **27** no credit, courtesy of Gingrich family, Calvin Cruce/Atlanta Journal Constitution **28** P. F. Bentley for TIME **29** P. F. Bentley for TIME **30-31** P. F. Bentley for TIME **32-33** Karen Kuehn—Matrix for TIME, Frank Trippett—SIPA for TIME **34-35** Dirck Halstead for TIME **36** Dirck Halstead for TIME **37** Ira Wyman—Sygma **38-39** Steve Liss for TIME (3), Martin Simon—Saba **40-41** Lester Bob Larue—Sygma **42-43** Dawson-Coy—SIPA, Steve Gooch/The Daily Oklahoman—Saba, Owen LRH—Black Star **44** Ralf-Finn Hestoft—Saba, Orlin Wagner—AP, Mike Harmon, AP—CNN, Laura Rauch/Wichita Eagle—Sygma **45** David Model—Katz—Saba **46-47** AP, Eric Drotter—AP, Mark Peterson—Saba **48-49** Myung J. Chun—pool **50** Myung J. Chun pool **51** Hal Garb—pool **52** Myung J. Chun—pool, Steve Starr—pool, Dan Groshong—pool, SIPA **53** Todd Bigelow—pool, Myung J. Chun—pool, Janet Gough—Celebrity Photos, Todd Bigelow—Black Star, Cindy Yamanako—Orange County Register/Saba, Steve Starr—Saba **54** Tracy Wilcox—Panama City News Herald—AP **55** Doug Mills—AP, Novovitch—Reuters/Archive **56** Luciano Mellace—Reuters/Archive Photos, Terry Ashe for TIME, Ted Thai for TIME, AP **57** Porter Gifford—Gamma Liaison, Robert Trippett—SIPA, Kim Kulish—SIPA

World 58-59 Christopher Morris—Black Star for TIME **60** Win McNamee—Reuters/Archive Photos **61** Jose Pablo

Bijman—AP **62-63** AP **64** map by Steve Hart—TIME **65** Laski/East News—SIPA **66-67** AP pool, Sergei Guneyev **68** China News Service—Reuters/Archive **69** Jimenez—SIPA, Chesnot—SIPA, Piotr Malecki—Gamma Liaison **70** Flor Marin—SIPA, Albert Facelly—SIPA, ETHIO TV—Sygma, (inset Barry Iverson), John Martel—SIPA

Anniversaries 71 Carl Mydans—LIFE, O.W.I./National Archives, Hubert Van Es—UPI/Bettmann **72** Keystone **74-75** W. Eugene Smith—LIFE, Keystone **77** A.F.I.P. **78-79** Corps of Engineers/National Archives, Bernard Hoffman—LIFE, Hajime Miyatake for Asahi Graph Tokyo **80-81** Vietnam National Archive **82** Vietnam National Archive **83** Lois Raimondo/AP

Business 84-85 Edel Rodriguez (art) **86** Edel Rodriguez (art), Scott Goldsmith—FORTUNE, Alan Tannenbaum—Sygma **87** Edel Rodriguez (art), Alan Tannenbaum—Sygma (2) **88** Edel Rodriguez (art), Rick Maiman, Sygma, Bob Strong—SIPA **89** Joe Ciardiello (art) **90** Mike Urban—Sygma **91** AFP, AP **92-93** no credit **94** Hiroyuki Matsumoto—Black Star **95** John Blackford (art), Chris Corsmeier, AP

Society 96-97 N. Ascencios (art) **98** David Graham **99** Fritz Hoffman—JB Pictures, Kathrin Miller **100-101** Terry Ashe for TIME, Ron Haviv—Impact Visuals, Rick Maiman—Sygma **102** Christopher Little—Outline, F. Scott Schafer—ONYX, Sygma **103** Mark Peterson—Saba **104** Donna Bender—Impact Visuals **105** Kathy Willens/ AP **106** Rick Rickman—Matrix **107** Stanley Tretick—Sygma, Gerardo Somoza—Outline **108** Gerardo Somoza—Outline, Frederic Stevens—SIPA, Barthelemy—SIPA (2) **109** Mark Peterson—Saba **110** Ted Thai for TIME, Ron Hawes—pool/SIPA, Peggy Peattie—The State

Cyberspace 111-15 Mark Marek (art) **116-17** Mark Marek (art), Steve Liss for TIME **118-19** Matt Mahurin (art), Mark Marek (art) **120-21** M. Bishofs (art), Mark Marek (art), **122-23** Mark Marek (art), Chriss Wade

Science 125-26 Anita Kunz (art) **128** Remi Benali—Gamma Liaison **129** N'geyen Tien—Gamma Liaison, Sinclair Stammers—SPL-Photo Researchers, Roberto Brosan, Mark Richards—Contact **130-31** Jason Lee (map), Jean Marie Chauvet/Jean Clottes—Sygma **132** Jean Clottes—Ministre de la Culture—Sygma, Jean Marie Chauvet (3)—Sygma **133** David Levenson—Black Star, Discover Reconstructions ©1995 (chart) **134** Bruce H. Robinson (4) **135** Bruce H. Robinson (3), Woods Hole Oceanographic Institute **136-37** Charles Nickin—Images Unlimited, Bruce H. Robinson, Marty Snyderman for TIME, Robert Ballard—WHOI, Rod Catanach—

WHOI, PH2 Agust Sigur—U.S. Navy, Koji Nakamura for TIME, U.S. Navy, Koji Nakamura for TIME, Bruce H. Robinson, Norbert Wu—NSF Oasis Project, Flip Nicklin—Minden Pictures **138** computer imagery by Alexander Tsiaras—Photo Researchers **139** Washington University School of Medicine **140-41** Steve Hart (charts), Manfred Kage/Peter Arnold **142-43** J. P. Harrington and K. J. Borkowski—NASA, Joe Lertola (chart) **144** Joe Lertola (charts) **145** NASA, Ames Research Center, NASA, Bob Campbell—Sygma, AFP

The Arts & Media 146-47 Grant Peterson for TIME, White—ABC, Don Cadette, Everett Collection, Bob D'Amico—ABC **148** Photofest, Everett Collection, Bob D'Amico—ABC **149** David Rose—NBC, Memory Shop, Don Cadette **150** Steen Sunland—Visage, Jeffrey Newbury—Outline, John Paschal—Celebrity Photo **151** Miranda Shen—Celebrity Photo, Dorothy Low—Outline, Jeffrey Thurner—Outline **152-53** Frank Micelotta—Outline, Redferns—Retna, Frank Micelotta—Outline, Jeff Slocomb—Outline **154-55** Columbus Museum of Art, Whitney Museum of Art, Des Moines Art Center **156** Museum of Contemporary Art, Chicago, Haags Gemeente Museum, the Hague, Ted Thai for TIME **157** Frederick Charles **158-59** Jerry Wachter—SPORTS ILLUSTRATED, Gregory Heisler—Outline for TIME **160** Tony Festa, John Chiasson—Gamma Liaison, Paul Kolnik—New York City Ballet, Carol Rosegg/Joan Marcus, Rickerby—SIPA, Carol Rosegg, Joan Marcus

The Best of 1995 161 Exit, Joseph Pluchino—Retna, Clive Coote, no credit **162** Bob Armstrong, Clive Coote—Columbia, The Walt Disney Company, Townley—Universal, Batzdorff—Universal, Sony Pictures Classics **163** Alex Koster—JB Pictures, BBC Panorama—AP, David Moir, the Library of Congress, no credit, J. Fitzgerald **164** Neal Preston—Retna, Mark Hauser—Outline, Jo Ann Toy, Caroline Greyshock, Joseph Pluchina—Retna **165** Joan Marcus, Eric Y. Exit (2), Ivan Kyncl, Carol Rosegg **166** Ted Thai for TIME, Department of Defense

People 168 Villard—SIPA, Lionel Cherrault—SIPA, Paul J. Sutton—Duomo **169** Granger Collection, Brent Smith—SIPA, Jeffrey Thurner—Outline, Michael Tighe—Outline **170** Frank Micelotta—Outline, ©Watterson—Universal Press Syndicate, F. Trapper—Sygma, no credit **171** Lillo—SIPA, AP/PA, Mark Lennihan—AP, Alan Tannebaum—Sygma

Milestones 172-73 Julian Wasser—Pix Inc., AP **174** Mark Seliger—Outline **175** Ralph Morse—LIFE **176** Neil Leifer for TIME **177** Carl Mydans—LIFE, Alfred Eisenstaedt—LIFE **178** Walter Bennett for TIME **179** Alan Grant—LIFE **180** The Lou Valentino Collection